Chinese Overseas
Comparative Cultural Issues

MW01046028

Hong Kong University Press thanks Xu Bing for writing the Press's name in his Square Word Calligraphy for the covers of its books. For further information, see p. iv.

Chinese Overseas
Comparative Cultural Issues

Tan Chee-Beng

香港大學出版社
HONG KONG UNIVERSITY PRESS

Hong Kong University Press
14/F Hing Wai Centre
7 Tin Wan Praya Road
Aberdeen
Hong Kong

ISBN 962 209 661 1 (Hardback)
ISBN 962 209 662 X (Paperback)

Secure On-line Ordering
http://www.hkupress.org

British Library Cataloguing-in-Publication Data
A catalogue record for this book is available from the British Library.

Printed and bound by United League Graphic & Printing Co. Ltd., Hong Kong, China

Hong Kong University Press is honoured that Xu Bing, whose art explores the complex themes of language across cultures, has written the Press's name in his Square Word Calligraphy. This signals our commitment to cross-cultural thinking and the distinctive nature of our English-language books published in China.

"At first glance, Square Word Calligraphy appears to be nothing more unusual than Chinese characters, but in fact it is a new way of rendering English words in the format of a square so they resemble Chinese characters. Chinese viewers expect to be able to read Square Word Calligraphy but cannot. Western viewers, however are surprised to find they can read it. Delight erupts when meaning is unexpectedly revealed."

— Britta Erickson, *The Art of Xu Bing*

Contents

Acknowledgements

This book offers a way of understanding and studying Chinese overseas. It shows that the study of Chinese overseas can contribute to our understanding of theories on ethnicity and identity as well as ethnic relations. This book is based on papers written at different times. The first three chapters are papers that have not been published in English. Chapter 1 on the Chinese ethnological field is based on a revision of a paper presented at a conference in Taipei in April 2001. The main ideas of the paper were first developed for presentation in Chinese at the Sixth Modernization and Chinese Culture conference in Wujiang, Suzhou, China. This Chinese paper has been published (Tan 2001). The idea of the Chinese ethnological field has guided my writing of various papers selected in this volume.

Chapter 2, 'Acculturation, Ethnicity and Ethnic Chinese', is a revision of a paper presented at a conference in Hawaii in 1988 and is the earliest written paper in this book. It has since been translated into Chinese and published (Tan 2002c). The issues discussed are still original and relevant, and I have made considerable revision for publication in this book. Chapter 3 is based on a talk delivered at Keio University in Tokyo in December 1999. The original paper has been translated into Japanese and published in Tan (2002b). The other chapters in this book have been published in various venues in Southeast Asia. Their publication in this book should make the chapters more accessible to interested readers. However, the overall intention of coming out with this book is to provide a comparative perspective to the study of ethnicity and identities of Chinese overseas and to illustrate the idea of the Chinese ethnological field.

Although I have updated the papers, there is a limit to this effort without completely rewriting them. Thus the revision involves only integrating the chapters, reducing repetition and incorporating new references that are relevant to the issues discussed. I am grateful to Ms Viki Li and Ms Carmen Chow, research assistants of the Cultural Relations and Identities in East Asia Program of the Hong Kong Institute of Asia-Pacific Studies at The Chinese University of Hong Kong for clerical assistance. I wish to thank the two anonymous reviewers for reading the manuscript carefully and providing very good suggestions for revisions. I remain responsible for any defect in this book.

SOURCES

Chapter 1: Revised from 'Chinese Ethnological Field: Anthropological Studies of Chinese Communities,' presented at the Fourth International Chinese Overseas Conference, organized by the International Society for the Studies of Chinese Overseas, and ISSP Sun Yat-Sen Institute for Social Sciences and Philosophy, Academia Sinica, Taipei, 26–28 April 2001. The preliminary Chinese version is published in *Ershiyi shiji de zhongguo shehuixue yu renleixue* (Anthropology and sociology of China in the Twenty-first century), edited by Qiao Jian, Li Peiliang and Ma Rong, Gaoxiong (Taiwan): Li Wenhua Shiye Gufen Youxian Gongsi, 2001.

Chapter 2: Revised from the paper presented at the Lucky Come Hawaii conference, organized by the Institute of Culture and Communication, East-West Center, Honolulu, 18–21 July 1988. I thank Profs. David Y. H. Wu and Harry Lamley for their comments.

Chapter 3: Revised from the paper delivered to the project, The Chinese Immigrants and the Creation of Culture, Keio University, Tokyo, 4

December 1999. The original paper has been translated into Japanese by Kawaguchi Mitsuo and published in *Expansion of Chinese World, and the Creation of Cultures: Basic Trends in Asia and Pacific*, edited by Yoshihara Kazuo and Suzuki Masataka, pp. 344–76 (Tokyo: Kobundo, 2002). I thank Prof. Yoshihara Kazuo and Prof. Leo Suryadinata for their comments.

Chapter 4: 'Chinese Identities in Malaysia', *Southeast Asian Journal of Social Science*, 25(2) 1997: 103–16. Reprinted with minor amendments.

Chapter 5: 'People of Chinese Descent: Language, Nationality and Identity', *The Chinese Diaspora: Selected Essays*, volume 1, edited by Wang Ling-chi and Wang Gungwu (Singapore: Times Academic Press, 1998), pp. 29–48. Reprinted with corrections.

Chapter 6: Reprinted with revisons from 'The People of Chinese Descent and Ethnic Relations With Special Reference to Some Economic Explanations', *Dimensions of Tradition and Development in Malaysia*, edited by Rokiah Talib and Tan Chee-Beng (Petaling Jaya, Malaysia: Pelanduk Publications, 1995), pp. 383–420. The earlier Chinese version was published in *Bulletin of the Institute of Ethnology, Academia Sinica*, 69 (Spring) 1990: 1–26.

Chapter 7: Reprinted with revison from 'Culture, Ethnicity and Economic Activities: The Case of the People of Chinese Descent with Special reference to Southeast Asia', *The Ethnic Chinese: Proceedings of the International Conference on Changing Identities and Relations in Southeast Asia*, edited by Teresita Ang See and Go Bon Juan (Manila: Kaisa Para Sa Kaunlaran, Inc., 1994), pp. 27–59.

Note on Transcription

Mandarin transcription follows the *pinyin* system. In the case of Hokkien (Minnan) words, o̲ is pronounced /ɔ/.

Introduction

This book offers a comparative perspective on the anthropological study of Chinese overseas. There are numerous works on Chinese of specific countries and a few works that compare Chinese of two or three countries. However, insufficient attention has been paid to using ethnographic knowledge of the Chinese of specific communities for discussion in a wider context, which I call the Chinese ethnological field. This book provides a comparative perspective of studying Chinese worldwide. Anthropologists study particular localities or regions, but their discussion can be related to similar studies elsewhere. There are ethnic Chinese all over the world, and a study of the Chinese in a particular locality can be described in a global context of Chinese in diaspora. In this book, I use my experience of long-term research among the Malay-speaking Chinese in Malaysia, called Baba, as well as my field experiences among other Chinese communities in Malaysia to understand the complex issues of localization and Chinese identity and relate them to the study of Chinese elsewhere in Southeast Asia and in other parts of the world. Thus, the Baba ethnography provides a base for discussion in most chapters.

In this book, the non-China citizens of different nationalities are referred to as 'ethnic Chinese' and 'Chinese overseas' rather than the commonly used 'Overseas Chinese', which today refers more accurately to *huaqiao*, citizens of China residing overseas. Southeast Asian scholars writing in English generally prefer the label 'ethnic Chinese' as equivalent of *huaren*, the label used by the Chinese themselves when writing in Chinese. Among the earliest to use this label in a book title is Yong (1981). Wang Gungwu (1977) is the earliest to discuss comprehensively the origin of the term *huaqiao*, which literally means 'Chinese sojourners'. It has been a dilemma for scholars writing in English to find a general term for *huaren* without using 'overseas Chinese'. Historically, especially before the Second World War, most Chinese in diaspora did consider themselves *huaqiao* or Overseas Chinese, but today they are mostly citizens of different nationalities. Some scholars, like Wang Gungwu (1991b), have used 'Chinese overseas', no doubt a translation of the Chinese term *haiwai huaren*, used by scholars from China. However, the term 'Chinese overseas' can be rather clumsy in certain English contexts when referring to the Chinese worldwide. Most scholars from the West generally continue to use the term 'Overseas Chinese' or the increasingly popular term in disaporic discourse, 'Chinese in diaspora'. I prefer 'ethnic Chinese', but I also use the term 'Chinese in diaspora' where necessary. In doing so, I do not assume that the Chinese overseas still look to China as their homeland. In addition, I have occasionally used the term 'people of Chinese descent' to refer to Chinese overseas more generally. Strictly, ethnic Chinese are people of Chinese descent who still regard themselves as 'Chinese' in one way or another. I have discussed the politics of these labels in Tan (1997b).

The peopling of Chinese in different parts of the world provides an exciting opportunity for the cultural study of social adaptation and cultural reproduction as well as ethnicity and identity. Chinese communities worldwide may be studied in an ethnological field that can be called the Chinese ethnological field. This is discussed in Chapter 1. As long as the Chinese migrants and their descendants see themselves as Chinese, albeit differently, there is basis for comparison on issues relating to cultural reproduction, ethnicity and identity. The reproduction of different aspects of Chinese culture as well as local transformation and invention can be seen in better perspective in this larger ethnological field. Chapter 1 explains the idea of the ethnological field. The continuity and transformation of Chinese culture as reproduced by Chinese overseas is best illustrated in Chinese beliefs and practices. This chapter uses the examples of ancestor worship and the celebration of the 'hungry ghost festival' in Southeast Asia and in China, to show the similarity and diversity in Chinese cultural reproduction. Related to this is the issue of localization, how Chinese become localized in different localities and national societies. Chapter 1 seeks to show how cultural issues related to localization can be studied in the wider context of the Chinese ethnological field. The concepts of localization, acculturation and assimilation as well as the distinction between ethnic identity and cultural identity are explained in this chapter.

Indeed, the book is very much about localization and its effects on cultural and ethnic identities. An obvious cultural issue is how the Chinese have changed culturally and ethnically as they adapt to living in different national societies and specific localities. Chapter 2 on acculturation and ethnicity examines this issue. Acculturation — cultural change as a result of direct interethnic contact — affects cultural identity. It is my study of the Baba that led me to pay attention to the localization of ethnic Chinese, but in the context of localization I see continuity, too. In Chapter 2, I begin with a description of the acculturation of the Baba and compare them to other 'creolized' Chinese communities as well as ethnic Chinese elsewhere in the world. Acculturation and ethnicity must be studied from the perspective of socio-cultural adjustment to a larger society. In this process of adjustment, a combination of factors account for the rate and nature of acculturation. It is therefore necessary to analyze the context of inter-ethnic social interaction as well as the cultural, social and political factors involved.

Acculturation results in different models of Chineseness not only across nations but also within a country. Different such categories of Chinese have different emphases of cultural identity. The issue of Chineseness arises from such diversity when one category of Chinese is compared to another, such as between Chinese-speaking Chinese and non-Chinese-speaking Chinese. This often leads to prejudice of those Chinese who consider themselves 'pure' against those Chinese who cannot speak Chinese. Yet Chineseness cannot be defined by any particular standard. There are different ways to be Chinese, as shown by the Malay-speaking Baba of Melaka in Malaysia. One can be ethnically Chinese, but there are different kinds of cultural expression of that identification. As a result of localization, ethnic Chinese everywhere can always construct and re-construct their Chineseness, leaving much room for identity politics. The discussion in Chapter 2 illustrates the distinction between ethnic identity and cultural identity. People identify ethnically as Chinese, and following that identification are different ways of expressing that identity culturally, depending on individuals' socialization and experience of localization.

In order to examine the issue of localization in greater detail, Chapter 3 uses the case of the Baba to discuss localization and the production of a local Chinese culture. It is not sufficient to pay attention to the political and economic environments of the larger society to study localization of ethnic Chinese, as provided in Chapter 2. Chinese individuals themselves are active agents in localization. They have been active in reproducing and reinventing culture by their innovative use of both Chinese and local non-Chinese cultural principles as well as local resources. Chapter 3 draws attention to the roles of individuals in localization and construction of their local culture. In other words, ethnic Chinese are not passively acculturated by the local majority people; it is they themselves who bring about their own localization through their interaction and participation in the local society. In this chapter, I use the metaphor of food to illustrate the production of culture. As a result of localization, descendants of Chinese immigrants acquire the knowledge of local ingredients and local non-Chinese culinary principles, while they also have knowledge of Chinese culinary principles. Individuals are able to put this combination of knowledge into practical use, cooking up a localized version of Baba food that is both hybridized and local. The food metaphor expresses both Baba ethnicity and Baba culture. The example of the Baba illustrates the production of ethnic Chinese culture in different parts of the world.

The degree of localization influences the expression of cultural identities between Chinese communities.

In Chapter 4, I use the example of Chinese in a national society — Malaysia — to examine ethnic Chinese identities. Chinese Malaysians do not just have one Chinese identity. There are various types of Chinese identity influenced by localization, education and other factors. Localization affects cultural expression, and individuals are socialized into particular kinds of ethnic identity. By focusing on analysis in a national context and in comparison with Chinese of other countries, one can see more clearly that the Chinese identity really has two dimensions: the bounded national and local dimensions and the unbounded dimension as Chinese of whatever nationality or cultural expression. Chinese Malaysians are both ethnic Chinese and Malaysian. Ethnic identification in Malaysia is very distinct in that everyone is expected to have a distinct ethnic identity, and a Chinese cannot become Malay unless he or she converts to Islam and joins the Malay community. Elsewhere, one may not need to exhibit oneself as a member of an ethnic community when interacting in the larger society. Still, racial features place a person of Chinese origin in a minority community.

In Chapter 5, I further discuss the issues of language and nationality in relation to identity. Since language is such a fascinating aspect of Chinese ethnicity, it is useful to discuss this in the context of the Chinese ethnological field. As in other chapters, the discussion is built up from knowledge on Malaysia. The paper shows that the persistence of an ethnic identification does not depend on the persistence of a particular language, but linguistic change does affect the perception and cultural expression of an identity. The Baba, for example, are not just Chinese but a particular kind of localized Chinese. The paper distinguishes ethnic identity, cultural identity and national identity. Identification of ethnic Chinese with a national society involves development in local consciousness, and more or less expression of Chinese cultural identity does not mean that Chinese are less or more integrated into a national society. One can identify strongly as an ethnic Chinese and at the same time proudly identify as a Malaysian.

The Chinese ethnological field is most useful for cultural comparison between Chinese communities and for understanding Han Chinese cultures in a global perspective. What of other topics like ethnic relations and economic activities? It is still relevant for locating a study in a wider perspective and seeing how Chinese cultures and Chinese ethnicity influence ethnic Chinese socio-economic life. After all, ethnic Chinese generally live as minorities in national societies that may be friendly or hostile. Even the Chinese in Singapore live in the larger Malay world in Southeast Asia. Many of those in Southeast Asia are engaged in commerce. Indeed, Chinese overseas live in different countries and encounter different social relations. As such, their experiences are useful for studying ethnic relations. This is discussed in Chapter 6. Chinese-Malay relations in Malaysia are used to discuss the major factors affecting the relations between ethnic Chinese and the majority people. The nature of ethnic relations is explained by the nature and intensity of socio-economic competition between Chinese and non-Chinese. State policy and such ideology as nationalism also affect the nature of ethnic relations. These, together with the economic and geographical visibility of the Chinese in Southeast, make them easy scapegoats for economic problems within a country, as has often happened in Indonesia. Ethnic Chinese are generally politically insecure because of their minority status, and so they further seek security in economic success or professional achievement. In fact, political insecurity affects their sense of social and economic security. Ethnic Chinese are very conscious of being treated as somewhat alien in a land that they see as home.

Chapter 7 discusses culture, ethnicity and economic activities. Originally published in 1994, when it was popular to relate Chinese culture (in particular the Confucian part) to Chinese economic success, this chapter seeks to provide a more balanced discussion of the extent to which culture and ethnicity is relevant to Chinese economic activities. Comparison between ethnic Chinese communities provides a clearer picture. Chinese immigrant experiences and cultural attitudes in relation to economic achievement can be better understood in a comparative perspective. It can enlighten us not only about Chinese overseas but also about China. The comparison gives us a clear picture of the significance of the larger economy to Chinese commercial activities. Chinese success in commerce in Southeast Asia is related to the nature of migration (Chinese traders have a long history of doing trade in Southeast Asia) as well as to the opportunities offered by the colonial economy, which was not dominated by the indigenous people. In North America, white dominance in economy restricted the Chinese opportunities to laundry and restaurant businesses in Chinatowns. Even in Sri Lanka, the rather small minority of ethnic Chinese do not have 'material and human resources' to compete with the indigenous Sri Lankans (Rodrigo 1998, 236). This shows the fallacy of the myth in Southeast Asia that Chinese are good entrepreneurs, or that Confucianism helps the Chinese succeed in business. Many criticisms have been made on the cultural determinist approach with regards to Chinese business (cf. Gomez and Hsiao 2001). This chapter, however, shows how cultural aspects can be relevant to Chinese economic performance, while giving attention to the larger political economy.

In studying ethnic Chinese, ethnic relations and Chinese economic involvement are closely interrelated. The Chinese are seen as dominating the economy in Southeast Asia, and indigenous elites see Chinese economic achievement as a threat. The Chinese have become the scapegoat for economic hardship in Indonesia; and the cultural liberalization of ethnic Chinese after 1998, as I learned from my interview with some leaders of Chinese associations in Surabaya in December 2002, has not convinced Chinese Indonesians that they will not become the target of future riots. In North America, the success of ethnic Chinese in education and in professional occupations has led them to be labeled a 'model minority'. But as discussed in Chapter 6, this compliment carries negative implications on ethnic relations.

Overall, the book deals with culture, ethnicity and economic activities of Chinese overseas. The focus on localization of ethnic Chinese discussed in the larger Chinese ethnological field provides a way to study and understand ethnic Chinese. The chapters show that there are many ways to be Chinese, and no one essentialized Chinese identity can be considered as standard for judging others. Localization produces different models of being Chinese, and identity politics is linked to an essentialized view of Chineseness. It is up to the localized Chinese to reject rather than accept such an essentialized view and to realize that one can be not so Chinese — in an essentialized sense — to be Chinese. In an ethnicity-free society, one need not be ethnic in any way, but most Chinese as minorities are often reminded of their ethnic status even if they choose to ignore it.

1

Chinese Ethnological Field: Anthropological Studies of Chinese Communities Worldwide

INTRODUCTION

Anthropological studies of Chinese communities began in China. The beginning of anthropological and ethnological studies there can be traced to the 1920s, developing considerably in the 1930s and 1940s (cf. Guldin 1994; Wang Jianmin 1997). After 1949, for well-known reasons, these studies came to be defined narrowly as the study of minorities and were restricted by the dominant Marxist ideology. The development of anthropology in China became rather hindered, as the discipline was deprived of the chance of catching up with development outside mainland China. Foreign anthropologists had no access to fieldwork in China. They thus turned to studying Chinese cultures and societies in Taiwan and Hong Kong as well as ethnic Chinese overseas, especially in Southeast Asia.

There are now significant numbers of studies on Chinese in diaspora. As is obvious in the survey by Wang Gungwu (1998) and Wickberg (2000), these are useful for comparative study. I propose that studies on the Chinese in diaspora and in China can be more comprehensively compared and studied in an ethnological field that may be called the Chinese ethnological field. This is particularly useful for the anthropological study of such issues as cultural persistence, cultural transformation, Chinese symbolism, Chinese religion, culture and economic activities, as well as cultural and ethnic identities and so on.

The logic behind the Chinese ethnological field is that the ancestors of the Chinese in diaspora migrated from China, and ethnic Chinese generally have some interest in the larger Chinese civilization. Most descendants of these ancestors still see themselves as Chinese in one way or another. What strikes observers most about the Chinese overseas is their diversity, not just of ancestral origin in China (which is understood) but the diversity resulting from localization and cultural change in general that has made the Chinese appear different from their counterparts in China and from Chinese in other countries. There are even Chinese who do not speak any Chinese language. Nevertheless, Chinese immigrants carried with them aspects of Han Chinese culture, which have become an important part of ethnic Chinese cultural life in interaction with non-Chinese cultures. Thus in the Chinese ethnological field, we can find interesting aspects of cultural continuity and transformation, which are part and parcel of the localization experience of ethnic Chinese. Cultural continuity here means continuity in transformation, as localization transforms the nature of continuity in cultural expression as well as incorporates new cultural elements.

The ethnological field calls attention to comparison and the need for multi-site research. Multi-site research within the Chinese ethnological field gives us a more comprehensive perspective of the dynamics of cultural change and socio-cultural adaptation. The end of the Cold War has made it convenient for academic exchange between scholars of various nationalities, as well as research in countries of different political ideologies. Of equal significance is the opening up of China since the end of the 1970s, which allows scholars to carry out on-site research. At the same time, an increasing number of students and scholars from mainland China are now also able to go overseas to study and do research. The limited number of mainland researchers doing research outside China is mainly due to a lack of funding.

One kind of comparative study and multi-site research in the Chinese ethnological field is the study of two or more Chinese societies outside China. This would include such research as that on the Chinese associations in the Philippines and Canada studied by Wickberg (1988) and the assimilation of the Chinese in New York City and Lima, Peru studied by Wong (1978). There is also the comparative study of Chinese in diaspora and Chinese in China. Of course, multi-site research involving China is only possible since the opening up of China in the late 1970s. The comparative study of emigrant villages in China and related Chinese communities overseas is of particular interest, as this will allow us to see the dynamics of Chinese cultures and identities as well as transnational practices.

Over the years, I have been interested in relating my study in Malaysia to similar studies in other regions, as reflected in the papers selected for publication here. As the idea of the Chinese ethnological field has influenced my writing, in this chapter I discuss the relevance of the ethnological field as well as some of the themes studied.

CHINESE FIELD OF ETHNOLOGICAL STUDY

Most anthropological studies have focussed on regions or countries as geographical units of study. The area studies in the West, such as Southeast Asian Studies, Latin America Studies, Middle Eastern Studies and so on, have also divided the studies in various parts of the world by geographical region. The field of ethnological study as an ethnological rather than merely geographical area of study was first proposed by the Dutch anthropologist, J.P.B. de Josselin de Jong (hereafter J.P.B.) in 1935. He proposed the idea of 'fields of ethnological study'. By this he means 'certain areas of the earth's surface with a population whose culture appears to be sufficiently homogeneous and unique to form a separate object of ethnological study, and which at the same time apparently reveals sufficient local shades of differences to make internal comparative research worth while' (J.P.B. de Josselin de Jong 1983, 167–8).

J.P.B. used this idea to study the Malay Archipelago as a field of ethnological study. According to him, although differences exist between peoples in different parts of present-day Indonesia, they have structural similarities, making up the structural core of this field of ethnological study, such as the double descent system and socio-cosmic dualism (cf. P.E. de Josselin de Jong 1984a, 2). J.P.B.'s approach influences structural anthropology in the Netherlands, and many anthropologists writing on Indonesia have adopted his idea of fields of ethnological study (cf. P.E. de Josselin de Jong 1984b). In this chapter, we are interested in the concept of the field of ethnological study, not his structural analysis of cultures in the Malay Archipelago.

It is relevant and useful to study Chinese people worldwide within a field of ethnological study, the Chinese ethnological field of study. A particular country or geography does not determine this, nor is China treated as the center of this study. Different political systems and geographical factors may influence Chinese people all over the world, but they do have certain similar cultural symbols that originated in China. Of course, culture is ever changing, and ethnic Chinese have also developed distinct cultural expressions. Nevertheless, they share some similarities in Chinese 'culture'. The idea of a Chinese ethnological field facilitates our comparison of cultural expressions in different countries, as well as those between Chinese overseas and Chinese in China. Similarities and diversities exist in Chinese cultural continuity and cultural transformation, as well as in expression of cultural identities.

The Chinese ethnological field is not just useful for comparing cultural continuity in the context of change. It is also useful for comparing variations. For example, one can compare the factors that have brought about acculturation and the diverse expressions of cultural identities. The Malay-speaking Baba of Malaysia (Tan 1988a), who identify themselves as Chinese, can be compared to the 'creolized' Chinese communities elsewhere (cf. Skinner 1996; Hall 1998). One can compare the loss of Chinese language and the implication on Chinese cultural identity. The local development of Chinese food in different parts of the world is another exciting field of study.

Within China, Chinese cultural expressions are also constantly changing, as the state, market forces, local politics and so on, are influencing them. Some cultural features, having developed from a similar Chinese civilization, continue to be comparable to those of

Chinese overseas; thus, anthropological studies of cultural life in China remain relevant to the study of Chinese cultures overseas and vice versa. For example, Fei Xiaotong's *Peasant Life in China* (1939) describes peasant life in Kaixiangong in Wujiang of Jiangsu. However, the work is also relevant to the study of the cultural life of the Chinese in Southeast Asia, even though their ancestors mostly originated in Fujian and Guangdong. The 'pseudo-adoption' (87–9) and 'financial aid society' (267–74) described by Fei can also be found among the Chinese in Southeast Asia. Wu (1974), in his study on the Chinese in Papua New Guinea, for example, has also described the rotating credit society, i.e., Fei's 'financial aid society'. Thus Fei's work is relevant for the larger Chinese ethnological field, not just for the study of China.

Another example is Yan's (1966a, 1966b) analysis of *guanxi*. The analysis of *guanxi* has been an important theme in the study of China and Chinese social relations. The nature of *guanxi* in Xiajia Village in Heilongjiang Province is very similar to what I have seen of the Yongchun people in my village in Batu Pahat, Johor, Malaysia. According to Yan (1966a, 7), 'Xiajia villagers perceive *guanxi* to be a social space divided into several zones by the various degrees of reliability of personal relations that are embodied in everyday gift-giving activities'. The ancestors of the Yongchun people in Malaysia came from Fujian in south China, whereas Yan's study is in northeast China. Nevertheless, the observation of *guanxi* in the two villages is not just specific rural Chinese culture but a type of Chinese culture that has persisted explicitly in various regions, both within and outside China. There is much for us to reflect on in the core underlying principles of Chinese culture.[1]

Here we are dealing with the persistence and spread of Han Chinese cultures. Defining Han cultures is controversial, for the so-called Han cultures are constantly being reproduced through the long-term interaction between Han and non-Han cultures. There is no static pattern or model of Han people or cultures. In this dynamic process of cultural reproduction, certain aspects of Han cultures have become the mainstream Chinese cultural expressions, which influence Han and non-Han Chinese in different provinces, as well as cultural expressions of

Chinese overseas. The dynamic process of the reproduction of dominant Han cultures is closely linked to several issues. These include the political process of the state, the use and spread of language and literature, the promotion and reinterpretation of scholars and ruling élite, the interaction between different groups of people in China, and the daily practices of ordinary people. Aspects of Han cultures thus reproduced are not merely Confucian but also cultural principles found in social organization (such as surname patrilineality), popular religious practices, economic activities, and other cultural practices (such as the use of chopsticks and the classification of hot and cold food). Many ethnic Chinese also observe these main cultural principles.

How do the Chinese in diaspora maintain and perpetuate Chinese cultures? We can discern dual aspects of Chinese cultural traditions - the ancestral tradition and the localized tradition. The ancestral tradition is closely linked to the original cultural tradition in China. In fact, some of the cultural practices that are lost in China can still be found among ethnic Chinese outside China. An example is the old-fashioned wedding ceremony of the Babas in Malaysia. Despite the loss of Chinese language, the Babas continue to observe what they see as traditional Chinese religious practices, and at weddings some still put on the wedding attire that is otherwise nowadays only seen in Chinese operas. The localized Chinese tradition is the Chinese tradition that has become localized, or that is locally created. It incorporates much transformation and reinterpretation of the local Chinese, but its underlying Chinese origin may still be discernible. In fact, most cultural expressions of ethnic Chinese contain these two aspects, the ancestral and the localized, and it is often difficult to distinguish between the two.

When we compare Chinese cultures in China to Chinese cultures overseas, we do not see this as a relationship of the center to the periphery. In the Chinese ethnological field, each Chinese 'society' is its own cultural center. The cultural practices in China are also changing, and in each locality, there are also localized traditions, which at the same time reflect common Han cultural principles. In fact, global cultural forces, including Chinese cultures from overseas, also influence local cultures in mainland China. The emigrant communities have long received some cultural influences in Southeast Asia. When I first began my research in Fujian in 1998, I was careful to exclude Southeast Asian elements in my Minnan dialect (known as Hokkien in Southeast Asia). However, I soon found that many older Chinese in Yongchun and Quanzhou do use or are familiar with some Malay loanwords. A common Malay loanword used is *tahan* which means 'bearing a difficulty' or 'tolerating', and *boe ta-han* means 'cannot bear it any longer' or 'cannot tolerate any more', just as it is said by the Hokkien in Malaysia and Singapore. In our conceptualization of the Chinese ethnological field, there is no hegemonic Chinese culture versus a marginalized Chinese culture. In fact, the study of Chinese overseas is a study in its own right, not merely for understanding China-centered Chinese culture, as was the aim during the Cold War period. Studying in a broader Chinese ethnological field helps to understand Chinese cultural practices in a locality in the context of a broader comparative perspective, to understand how similar phenomena are practiced in the Chinese diaspora and in China.

CHINESE RELIGION AND THE CHINESE ETHNOLOGICAL FIELD

Scholars influenced by postmodernism emphasize discontinuity and de-territorialization and tend to dismiss discussion of cultural continuity and tradition as essentialist. This is often misleading. In the study of Chinese cultures globally, I wish to emphasize that there is cultural continuity in transformation. We need to examine both change and continuity in order to understand changing cultural life. This is most obvious in the religious expressions of ethnic Chinese. I use ancestral worship and *pudu* worship (Hungry Ghost Festival) to illustrate the continuity and change in the Chinese ethnological field. The discussion is based on the data from my own research in Malaysia and in China.

Chinese religion here refers to Chinese popular religion. There is continuity in Chinese religious practices among the Chinese in China and outside China. From this perspective, the usefulness of analysis in the larger context of a Chinese ethnological field is evident. Most deities worshipped by the Chinese overseas originated in China. In the Chinese ethnological field, Chinese worshippers have certain common deities (such as Guanyin or the Goddess of Mercy, Guangong, Mazu, Tudi or Earth God, and so on) and common birthdays of deities as well as festivals (such as the Chinese New Year, Qing Ming, Duanwu or Fifth Moon Festival, Zhongyuan or the Hungry Ghost Festival, Zhongqiu or Mid Autumn Festival, and so on). Chinese in different localities also have certain common concepts of deities, ancestors and ghosts as well as major rites, which are features of cultural persistence from the cultural heritage in China. This shows that Chinese of different localities and nationalities do share certain common features of cultural identity. At the same time, when we compare Chinese religious practices in different localities, there are diverse localized traditions.

Ancestor Worship

Most anthropologists who study China or Chinese overseas continue to focus on a particular locality. If we place our study in the larger context of the Chinese ethnological field, then we can see better the expressions of Chinese cultures that are common or variant. In the study of Chinese religion, for example, scholars outside China can better understand its historical context and development by relating to studies in China, whereas scholars in China can also note the related studies outside China. In addition, comparisons of cultural phenomena in different Chinese communities in diaspora provide us with a fuller picture of cultural practices. Thus, comparative studies within the Chinese ethnological field can help to widen one's scope and erase some limitations in theoretical discussion. For example, the study of lineage in China has long been influenced by the functional model of Maurice Freedman (1958a, 1966), which emphasizes common property and land ownership as the basis of the formation and development of lineage. Emily Ahern (1973), in her study of ancestor worship in Taiwan, even points out that ancestor worship is linked to inheritance of property. 'Anyone who hands down land receives a tablet' (246). However, for Chinese overseas, who generally do not have the kind of lineage communities or lineage property found in China, their ancestor worship has little to do with ancestral property or land. It is mostly a matter of cultural heritage. Chen (1985) has criticized Maurice Freedman's and Emily Ahern's functional views of lineage and ancestor worship, and he emphasizes the Chinese patrilineal culture.

From my study of the Chinese in Melaka and elsewhere in Malaysia since 1977, I find that those Chinese who worship Chinese deities generally also worship ancestors in one form or another. Those who do not worship ancestors at home have reasons, such as not owning a house or having to move house frequently or discontinuing the worship at home as the older people think that their sons and daughters-in-law are unlikely to continue the practice after their death. Nevertheless, these people generally do install tablets for their deceased parents in the ancestral hall of a temple, a clan hall, or other Chinese religious organizations (such as Dejiao Hui, a syncretic Chinese religious organization). They visit these places during certain festivals (such as Chinese New Year and Qing Ming) to worship their loved ones. Of course, this kind of ancestor worship is very different from that of the lineage communities in south China. In homes that have set up ancestral altars, tablets, photographs of the deceased, or a red sheet of paper bearing the ancestors' names represent the ancestors. The altars of the ancestors are usually on the stage right of the deities' altar, and these are placed against the wall facing the front entrance in the living room. In principle, one has to offer joss sticks every morning and evening, certainly on the first and fifteenth days of the lunar month, when candles are lit, too. Sacrifices are offered on festival days and anniversaries.

Where an ancestral altar is set up at home, the Hokkien in Malaysia call such a worship *hok-sai*. Another common type of ancestor worship at home is the *chhià* or 'invitation' system. In this case there is no altar, nor are ancestors worshipped regularly at home. An *ad hoc* altar is set up only on the day of worship, whereby a table in the living room or an inner room is used to place the *ad hoc* joss-stick holder and offerings. A worshipper lights some joss sticks and goes to the front of the house (facing the direction of the graveyard if possible) to invite the ancestors to return for the worship. Then he or she goes to the *ad hoc* altar in the house to place the joss sticks into the holder, which can be a glass filled with raw rice. Tea is offered. Offerings are then laid out for the ancestors. At the end of the rite, a pair of divining blocks is used to determine if the meal is over. If the blocks turn out to be one facing up and the other facing down, it is a positive answer, and joss papers are burned outside the house. The offerings are then taken away and the temporary altar dismantled.

The above discussion shows that Chinese ancestor worship undergoes different transformations and manifestations in different places and contexts. In the wider context of the Chinese ethnological field, we can think about the meaning of ancestor worship in Chinese culture and note that it is not necessarily linked to lineage organization or lineage property. We can compare the ancestor worship of the lineage communities in China and the ancestor worship without lineage organization outside China. Where lineage organizations exist outside China, these, too, can be compared with lineage communities in China. Recent studies by Faure (1989), Siu (1990), and Liu (1997) show that the lineage-focussed ancestor worship in the Pearl River Delta was a kind of cultural construction that emerged mainly in the Ming Dynasty. The nature of ancestor worship of the Chinese overseas, by contrast, developed outside the influence of the Chinese state. Yet the developments outside China, such as the transformation of lineage to clan association, the simplification of rituals, and the divorce of ancestor worship from lineage organization, perhaps show a trend of ancestor worship and lineage organization in China.

Pudu Worship in Malaysia and China

Pudu Worship in Malaysia

Besides Chinese New Year, a major Chinese festival in Malaysia is *zhongyuan*, popularly known in English as the Hungry Ghost Festival.

Two major rites are performed. The first is what the Minnan people (of south Fujian origin, known as Hokkien in Southeast Asia) call *choe chhit-goeh poã*, literally doing the mid-seventh moon rite, as it falls on the fifteenth day of the seventh lunar month. On this day of the month, offerings are made in the house for the ancestors and outside for the wandering ghosts. This is a domestic affair. In addition, there is a communal celebration, which the Hokkien call *choe po-to*, celebrating *po-to* or *pudu* in Mandarin. For this celebration, each local Chinese community or section of an urban Chinese community, especially the business sector, organizes the communal worship of *Pudugong* and the ghosts under his jurisdiction, offering sacrifices. The date of this communal worship differs from locality to locality. It is said that the ghosts are released from purgatory during the month, and worship is offered to pacify the ghosts and to expel evil, as well as to ritually ensure the community peace, success and prosperity. Chinese people in Southeast Asia generally avoid holding weddings during this month.

A *pudu* celebration in Malaysia is held in a public arena (such as in a temple compound or at an available space in an urban quarter) and usually lasts two or three days, during which Chinese operas may be staged. In addition to the Daoist (Taoist) rites and communal worship as well as a communal feast, which I do not describe, many items are sold by auction during the communal *pudu* celebration. The most prestigious item is a piece of nicely wrapped charcoal, symbolically called *o-kim* in Hokkien (*wujin* in Mandarin) or 'black gold'. Depending on communities, the final bid for this usually runs into hundreds or thousands of Malaysian dollars. In addition, a small ceramic tub of raw rice, if made available, is also considered a prestigious item. This is called *mitong* in Mandarin, that is, 'rice tub'. The bidding of these two items is the climax of the whole auction. The successful bidder is allowed to bring the 'black gold' home to keep, symbolizing that this will bring prosperity and peace to the family. The rice brought home can be kept or cooked. The auction is one way for a ritual community to collect funds. In addition to financing the *pudu* worship, the money collected can be used for other religious and charitable purposes. For example, the Chinese in the state of Penang have a *zhongyuan* organization that coordinates *zhongyuan* activities statewide. The money collected was even used to contribute towards building a private hospital (Tan Sooi Beng 1988).

Bid items can differ from community to community. In a rural Yongchun community that I observed in Batu Pahat, Johor, Malaysia on 17 August 2000, farm products such as pineapples, coconuts, jack fruit and whole bunches of bananas were also included. Then the 'black gold' reached RM$3188 and the rice fetched RM$3000. The contest was between a local businessman and the leader of a Chinese political party. The latter won both, to the cheers of the villagers.

Bidders for the charcoal and the tub of rice are generally business people and the local rich. Why do they bother to bid such a high price for a piece of charcoal or a small tub of rice? This ceremony is in a way comparable to the potlatch of the Kwakiutl Indians in North America, whereby the greatest prestige was conferred on individuals who gave away the greatest quantity of valuable goods (Mauss 1967, 31–7). In the *zhongyuan* auction here, the successful bidder gains prestige, and his status as a person of some wealth or good credit rating is reconfirmed. It is a public display of his wealth and success. It gives symbolic capital (Bourdieu 1977, 179) to business people, local leaders or individuals aspiring to be in such positions. The bid has to be paid before the next ceremony the following year. If, however, by the following year one cannot pay the bid, then one loses face. Here, the study of a religious festival helps us to understand the social structure and business culture of a local Chinese community.

Pudu Worship in China

Under communist rule, *pudu* celebration is seen as superstitious. Thus we do not see the kind of large-scale communal celebration in China. In the historic port city of Quanzhou, Fujian, the local people still practice their unique way of observing the festival, locally referred to as *po-si* or *pusi* in Mandarin. *Pusi* should not be confused with the 'mid-seventh month' worship; the latter, as we have seen in Malaysia, involves worshipping ancestors, not *Pudugong*. *Pusi* in Quanzhou is celebrated from the sixth to the eighth lunar month. The long period of celebration is a result of the practice of the *chongpu* system, that is, multiple *pusi* worship.

Historic Quanzhou City in southern Fujian is divided into 36 *pu* or wards (cf. Wang Mingming 1999), each with its own communal temple. During the months of *pusi*, each ward takes its turn to observe the *pusi* worship. Unlike the communal worship in Malaysia, each family in the ward worships *Pudugong* on the same day and around the same time. On the day of worship, each household carries out its worship between 4:00 p.m. and 6:00 p.m. Offerings are laid out on a table in front of the house, prayers offered and joss papers burnt. After the worship, the offerings are cooked, and close relatives and friends are invited to the family feast. This practice is different from that in Malaysia, where the worship and feast is communally held at a public place. However, the idea of celebration and worshipping *Pudugong* is similar, and there is the similar function of *pudu* for local communal identity.

The *Pusi* celebration in Quanzhou begins in the sixth lunar month with a small-scale worship called *kia-ki* in Minnan, or *shuqi* in Mandarin. The *pusi* proper is held in the seventh month. A small-scale *pusi* in the eighth month concludes the long celebration. This final *pusi* is called *jiewei yuan*, the final rite.

In rural Minnan, such as in Yongchun District, communal *pusi* worship takes place, but the scale is smaller than observed in Malaysia. In the Half Moon Hill section of Beautiful Jade Village, where I have conducted fieldwork among villagers surnamed Chen, the *pusi* celebration is fixed on the twentieth of the seventh lunar month. I observed the *pusi* worship in 1999. The rite was quite simple. At around 4:00 p.m., a representative from each household in Half Moon Hill carried some dishes of offering to the front yard of the ancestral hall of this branch lineage. The offerings were laid out on the ground. After all the representatives had arrived with their offerings, a senior man burnt joss sticks and invited the *Pudugong* and the wandering ghosts of the area to enjoy the feast. He threw a pair of divining blocks to ascertain that his invitation had been accepted. Having obtained a positive answer, the women and children burned the joss papers that the representative of each household had brought. Letting off firecrackers followed. After a while, the senior person prayed and threw the divining blocks again to ascertain whether the meal had been taken. After receiving a positive answer, the worshippers carried their respective offerings home to cook them for dinner.

By comparing the *zhongyuan* celebration in various sites in and outside of China, one can have a better picture of the *pudu* culture. One can see similar and diverse expressions of the Chinese cultural principle of observing *pudu*. Here I treat both the Minnan people in Malaysia and the Minnan (in south Fujian) in China as belonging to the Chinese ethnological field, which renders a wider perspective of comparison and understanding of 'Chinese culture' as expressed in the celebration of *pudu*. One can see not only cultural continuity and transformation but also the significance of *pudu* for local communal identity. In Quanzhou, the *pudu* celebration expresses *pu* or ward identity, and in the village in Yongchun it expresses the identity of a section of a lineage community. In Malaysia, it expresses the identity of a ritual community, which can be a village, an urban quarter or a business community. In China, the celebration is constrained by the state ideology, and there is no large-scale celebration as seen in Malaysia. Nevertheless, the family-based ward celebration, which developed long before the communist rule, turned out to be very adaptive. Even during the Cultural Revolution, my informants told me that the *pudu* worship was observed, excited children standing on guard at each end of the street to inform of the coming of government inspectors. As the local officials also belonged to the *pudu* culture, some of them would even inform the people of their coming inspection, so that the celebration could be suspended during that time. The celebration in Malaysia also shows us the link between religion and business as well as local leadership. The role of religion is not only symbolic but also social, and this includes a charitable contribution to the community.

In the above examples, we see that it is useful to study Chinese religion in the larger context of a Chinese ethnological field that is not limited by national boundaries. It also highlights the significance of multi-site research. The comparison enables us to have a better perspective of issues, such as the link between religion and business. The active involvement of the Chinese in Southeast Asia, Taiwan, Hong Kong and Macao in religious practices does not hinder business success. In fact, one can argue that such involvement gives psychological support and encouragement to business people. This is good for reflection in mainland China, where religion is officially regarded as 'superstition'. Labeling a religion superstition prevents one from seeing the symbolic and social significance of religion, including its important contribution to charity, as we have seen in the celebration of the Hungry Ghost Festival in Malaysia. Overall, studying Chinese religion in the larger Chinese ethnological field enables us to compare and see the dynamics of religion, the effects of state policy, the role of business people, the dynamics of local politics, the significance of identity and so on. All this cannot be fully grasped if we do not compare a study to relevant practices elsewhere in the ethnological field.

LOCALIZATION OF ETHNIC CHINESE

Having understood the nature of cultural continuity, it is easier for us to have a more comprehensive understanding of change, which is a major focus in this book. The cultural change that ethnic Chinese have experienced may be described by the term 'localization'. My usage here differs from that of globalization theorists, who posit localization as a local process versus globalization. By localization I mean 'the process of becoming local, which involves cultural adjustment to a local geographical and social environment, and identifying with the locality. The cultural adaptation involved is not merely a passive process of being influenced by local forces but also one of active participation and innovation' (Tan 1997c, 103). There is the cultural dimension of localization, which may be referred to as cultural localization, and there is localization of consciousness, of becoming part of the local and identifying with it.

Most people live in a particular locality, although they may have wide transnational networks. Local-born Chinese, especially if they are more than one generation in settlement, generally identify with a particular locality as 'home'. In fact, it is increasingly common for people who live transnationally to identify with more than one home, such as a home where one regularly resides and one where one originally migrated from and where one's immediate family members still live. In astronaut families, this often involves the men working in Hong Kong, for instance, while their wives and children live in another country such as in Australia (cf. Pe-Pua et al. 1998). Flexible citizenship (Ong 1993, 1999) may allow individuals to live in different countries without having to embrace a regular identity; actually, such Chinese are still in the minority. In works that emphasize the diaspora-ness, ethnic Chinese are often described as de-territorialized, but such popular views are actually expressed by a small group of, in the words of Chun (2000, 10), 'diasporic intellectuals in the ivory tower'. Most ethnic Chinese live locally and identify to different degrees with the local, often as Chinese Americans, Chinese Malaysians, etc., or just merely Chinese if they live transnationally and do not wish to emphasize any particular 'home' as more important. Citizenship should not be measured by loyalty or strong identification to a state. In the globalizing world, more and more people are free from the ideology of state loyalty, and citizenship is more a matter of belonging, to claiming rights and performing obligations in return. In this sense, ethnic Chinese are like other citizens in a state, and they are not unique in using flexible citizenship.

The transnational experience and previous localization experience, including not speaking Chinese, allow transnational migrants much room for negotiating identities. Nevertheless, wherever they locate their children, they will be localized in their residential national context. People are generally localized in national states, where the majority people and state policies including national education have a strong influence on children. Thus it is common to hear of Chinese being Canadianized, Americanized, Australianized, and so on. Localization occurs in nation-states, but it should not be confused with state identification, which is a separate matter. Whatever it is, cultural localization is relevant to identity negotiation.

Cultural localization greatly affects ethnic Chinese cultural life, so much that even after they have migrated from a locality they may retain their original localized experience. Chinese Indonesians who speak Indonesian continue to speak the language and attach to certain aspects of Indonesian Chinese cultural life after they have migrated to Europe or elsewhere. In Hong Kong, there is a population of Indonesian Chinese re-migrants. Godley and Coppell (1990a), and my students who interviewed some of the older ones, report that some of them still speak Indonesian at home. Similarly, Chinese-Thai transmigrants in the US still exhibit their Thai-ness (cf. Bao 1999, 107). We also find this phenomenon in Chinese Malaysian migrants in Australia. We can find Chinese-Malaysian restaurants in Melbourne, for instance, and the popular Ipoh *hor-fun* (Malaysian-style fried flat noodles associated with the Malaysian city Ipoh) is available.

Anthropologists and sociologists have long discussed the issue of acculturation and assimilation. A major part of localization is actually acculturation, although scholars nowadays seldom use this term. By acculturation, I mean 'the kind of cultural change of one ethnic group or certain population of an ethnic group (A) in relation to another ethnic group (B) such that certain cultural features of A become similar or bear some resemblance to those of B' (Tan 1988a, 2). This kind of cultural change is a result of the process of direct contact between members of the two ethnic groups. It can be a two-way process, although it usually involves greater socio-cultural adjustment on the part of the minority to that of the majority group. In any event, the ethnic identities of both groups are not lost.

Many sociologists, journalists and laypeople use the term 'assimilation' to refer to both acculturation and socio-cultural change accompanied by the loss of the original ethnic identity. I distinguish acculturation from assimilation, which involves a change in reference group and out-group acceptance (Teske and Nelson 1974, 365). In other words, assimilation involves not only socio-cultural change but also ethnic change such that when we say members of group A are assimilated into group B, we mean that they have been ethnically merged into group B and thus have lost their original ethnic identity. If we take note of the agency theory and do not assume that individuals are passively being changed, then the concept of acculturation is still a convenient concept to use. As shown in Chapter 3, acculturation occurs when individuals select and incorporate non-indigenous cultural principles rather than passively being changed as a result of interethnic contact.

Assimilation does not mean that individuals become exactly the same as the majority people. Our distinction of acculturation and assimilation is that in assimilation there is a change in ethnic membership. Here it is relevant to make a distinction between cultural identity and ethnic identity. Ethnic identity refers to ethnic identification with a particular ethnic category; cultural identity refers to cultural expression. Individuals identifying with the same ethnic category may emphasize different cultural traits in expressing their ethnic identity. An approach to the study of ethnicity is to see how individuals identify themselves ethnically and then study how they express that ethnic identity culturally; in other words, how people use cultural features to express ethnic identity. Acculturation allows Chinese to use not only traditional Chinese cultural features that they still have but also their localized cultural features, to express their Chiness-ness, so to speak. Even not speaking Chinese becomes an important feature of identity negotiation, as Ang (2001) has shown so well in her work.

This book deals a lot with localization and identity. The issue of national identity is also discussed. Identification with national identity differs from country to country and from individual to individual. In some countries in Southeast Asia, the Chinese are often treated as somewhat alien; they tend to emphasize their local roots, and their state-bound identities are generally strong. In the West, where there is a more open view of citizenship and less rhetoric on nation-building, individuals often can take their ethnic and state-bound identity for granted. However, after they have interacted with Chinese in other countries, they may reflect on their own identity, especially after they have been confronted about their 'Chineseness'. In *Cultural Curiosity*, Khu (2001) compiles the experiences of a number of ethnic Chinese after visiting China for the first time. One of them, Lily Wu, a Chinese American, writes, 'Before my trip to China, being "Chinese" meant almost nothing to me, and even being "American" was something that I had simply taken for granted. Ironically, both levels of awareness sharpened at the same time' (Wu 2001, 223–4). Interaction between ethnic Chinese and Chinese of China generally makes the former realize their distinct localized Chinese identity and even helps the more localized ones to accept their 'hybridity', or in the words of Chan (2001, 126), to 'become at ease with my hybridity'. Generally, interaction between Chinese of different nationalities makes them more conscious of their diversity, and speaking different languages, including English of different nations (such as Singapore English and Filipino English), is one marker of diversity.

CONCLUSION

From our discussion above, it is obvious that the idea of the Chinese field of ethnological study is useful for studying Chinese cultures worldwide. It gives a broader perspective to the comparative study of Chinese cultural persistence and transformation, allowing us to understand Chinese cultures in wider spatial and temporal contexts. Other than the examples described, Chinese cultural expressions, such as the lion dance and the practice of *qigong* (a breathing exercise), are popular elements of Chinese culture that are increasingly emphasized by ethnic Chinese. Scholars can study these in specific Chinese localities, but if we place them in the context of a Chinese ethnological field, we will then see the nature of their persistence and transformation in different localities as well as their significance to cultural identities. We can also see their roles in the cultural politics of the Chinese in different localities.

The study of China and the study of Chinese overseas have been rather separated, each going its own way. Most scholars on China do not feel the need to pay attention to works on Chinese overseas and vice versa. Although country-specific studies are still important and many issues need to be studied in this context, it is also useful and important, as this chapter has shown, to relate the study in China to the study of Chinese overseas. The Chinese ethnological field will help to promote this, not just the linkage between the study of China and Chinese overseas but also between Chinese societies in different countries.

In this increasingly globalized world, many issues are relevant to study in the Chinese ethnological field. For example, the effect of mass media on cultures is an important phenomenon, and the effect of Chinese mass media on different Chinese communities is an important issue. Yang (1997) has analyzed the effect of mass media in Shanghai. In the globalized world, especially with the use of the Internet and other modern technology, people are not limited by national boundaries. The Chinese in one locality are exposed to the influence of Chinese mass media elsewhere and increasingly they share 'common sets of programs', allowing them to construct 'transnational Chinese imaginary' (Yang 1997, 300, 309). For example, the Chinese in Malaysia are exposed to the influence of mass media from Taiwan and Hong Kong. Many Chinese Malaysians learn Cantonese from watching Cantonese serials made in Hong Kong. Similarly, in recent years, mass media (especially in the form of videos) from Hong Kong and Taiwan have influenced audiences in mainland China. At the same time, mass media and publications from mainland China, especially documentary programs on Chinese arts and civilization as well as famous sites in China, are popular overseas. It is relevant to study the effects of Chinese mass media on ethnic Chinese cultural identities in different parts of the world.

Since most of the papers selected for this book were written, a number of works on ethnic Chinese since the 1990s have adopted various kinds of transnational and globalized network theoretical analyses (e.g., McKeown 2001; Ong and Nonini 1997). The papers selected for publication here were not originally written in that theoretical framework, which is no doubt an important mode of analysis. As explained, they were written in the ethnological field framework, which emphasizes comparison of ethnic Chinese between societies. The Chinese ethnological field is not itself a transnational theoretical model, but it can incorporate a transnationalism perspective, even though it emphasizes culture rather than networks. The study of ethnic Chinese can benefit from different kinds of approach and theoretical analysis. The current transnationalism theoretical framework is important, but it cannot replace the comparative study of ethnic Chinese in different localities. I trust the papers selected here contribute in a small way to the understanding of Chinese communities and Chinese cultures.

2

Acculturation, Ethnicity and Ethnic Chinese

INTRODUCTION

As a result of migration overseas, especially during the last two centuries, Chinese now reside all over the world. Chinese have acquired many nationalities, although some overseas emigrants and their descendants have remained virtually 'stateless'. They have all been generally referred to as 'Overseas Chinese', in contrast to the Chinese population in China. Although historically correct, the label 'Overseas Chinese' is now outdated, inaccurate and, in fact, rather offensive to most of the people so labeled who do not take China as a point of reference anymore and have themselves become citizens of the country of their birth. Most Chinese in Southeast Asia prefer to call themselves *Huaren* (or Hua people) rather than *Zhongguoren*, which has the literal meaning of 'people of China', although both labels mean 'Chinese'. [1] *Zhongguoren* is of course both an ethnic label and a label of nationality. Such abbreviations as *Feihua* (Chinese of the Philippines), *Mahua* (Chinese of Malaysia), and *Yinhua* (Chinese of Indonesia) have also been used. These people are all *Huayi*, that is, descendants of Chinese migrants. These may also be described by their nationality as *Huayi Meiguoren* (Americans of Chinese descent, i.e., Chinese Americans), *Huayi Malaixiyaren* (Chinese Malaysians), and so on.

I propose that the term 'overseas' be dropped when geographical location is specified. Thus we speak of the Chinese in Hawaii instead of the overseas Chinese in Hawaii. Similarly, when referring to the Chinese in Southeast Asia, the term 'overseas' should be dropped; even the qualifying term 'ethnic' is unnecessary. Some stateless Chinese identify with either mainland China or Taiwan, and some identify with the country where they were born but are classified as 'stateless' or are not recognized as full citizens, because of legal problems or discrimination.

Ethnic Chinese, except those in Singapore and to some extent Malaysia, constitute small minorities in their respective countries. Throughout their history of settlement, they have had to make cultural and social adjustments. While they have exhibited varying degrees of cultural persistence, they have also experienced many socio-cultural changes. Some of them have even been assimilated by the indigenous people. Thus it is most interesting to study the cultural localization of ethnic Chinese in the wider Chinese ethnological field.

Of particular relevance to this study is the dominant majority cultural argument. In his study of ethnicity in Indonesia, Bruner (1974, 255) mentions that the concept of a dominant culture may be divided into 'three separate components of the larger system that are sociologically relevant to ethnic expression in any multi-ethnic group situation', that is, the population ratio or social demography, the established local culture, and the locus of power. He compares the expression of ethnicity in two Indonesian towns, Medan and Bandung. Medan, a city of minorities, lacks a dominant culture, whereas the Sudanese form the dominant cultural group in Bandung. Thus most migrants in Bandung tend to be acculturated by the Sudanese, since they have to orient their behavior to suit the Sudanese. For example, the Toba Batak in Bandung retain their Toba Batak identity but speak mostly Sundanese and Indonesian and 'practice a culture that is at least partly Sudanese' (269). As a result of acculturation, these Toba Batak have assumed a special kind of Batak identity, 'Bandung Batak'. Here lies a close relationship between acculturation and the expression of ethnicity.

For the dominant culture argument to be fully relevant to the study of acculturation and ethnicity, one must note the extent of social interaction between ethnic groups. Studies have shown that many

Chinese emigrants in Britain speak very little English even after years in Britain. According to Watson (1975, 127), the Chinese restaurant niche allows the Chinese emigrants 'to live, work, and prosper without coming into significant contact with the British public and without acculturating to the patterns of the life in a Western metropolis'. The restaurants form 'isolated pockets where the emigrants can interact with the alien outside world on their own terms'. In other words, the restaurant niche forms a social world, which shields the emigrants from the dominant British socio-cultural environment.

Similarly, the Hakka Chinese in Pulai (cf. Carstens 1980), a Chinese village in inland Kelantan, Malaysia, remain very little acculturated by the Malays in a state which is overwhelmingly Malay, compared to the highly localized rural Chinese in northeast Kelantan where the Chinese live in the dominant Malay cultural environment. In social demography, the established local culture and the locus of power, the Malays are clearly dominant in northeast Kelantan. Furthermore, the Chinese live close to the Malays and interaction is inevitable. In Pulai, however, the villagers live in their own community, which until recently has been rather isolated from the larger society. They come out of their village to meet the Malays only when necessary, and they interact with them on their own terms. Thus their village community forms an ethnic niche that shields the Hakka farmers from the dominant Malay environment.

I will discuss the acculturation experiences of the Chinese Peranakan (Malay-speaking Chinese) in Indonesia, Malaysia and Singapore and compare them to the Chinese Mestizo in the Philippines. I will then use relevant literature to survey the acculturation of ethnic Chinese in different parts of the world, in order to have a better idea of the factors that account for acculturation. The chapter discusses the implication of cultural localization to identities.

CHINESE PERANAKAN

In the study of the acculturation of people of Chinese descent, the Chinese Peranakan in Southeast Asia deserves special attention. They are very much the product of acculturation. Although ethnically Chinese, they have assumed various cultural traits under the influence of the indigenous cultures in the Malay Archipelago. The most noted acculturated features are the adoption of Malay as a home language, the Malay cooking and eating habits and, for women, the Malay-style dress called *sarong* and *kebaya*. Because of their higher degree of acculturation than other local Chinese, they have become a distinct category known by themselves and the Malays as *Peranakan Cina* (Chinese Peranakan) in Malaysia, or as *Peranakan Tionghua* (Chinese Peranakan) in Indonesia (often abbreviated to Peranakan).

The term *peranakan* means 'local-born' or 'native'. To Chinese who are not Peranakan, the acculturated Chinese are 'Baba' and are regarded as not fully Chinese or as 'half Malay', because of their lack of certain Chinese cultural traits. Although the Chinese Peranakan in Indonesia prefer to identify with the label 'Peranakan', those in Malaysia (Melaka) and Singapore have a self-identity as both 'Baba' and 'Peranakan'. Historically, the labels were used to contrast the local-born Chinese in the Malay Archipelago from the *Sinkeh* or new immigrants from China. Today these labels distinguish the acculturated Chinese from the 'pure' Chinese (the less acculturated Chinese) who are called 'Totok Chinese' (literally, 'pure Chinese') in Indonesia. The contrast between the Peranakan and the 'pure' Chinese is much more distinct in Malaysia than in Indonesia, for in Indonesia it is normal for the Chinese to speak Malay among themselves; in Malaysia, it is still not a norm for the Chinese to do so, except for the Chinese Peranakan.

The history of the formation of Chinese Peranakan society and identity is rather complex, but it is obviously associated with a small minority adjusting to the dominant indigenous culture. The early Chinese immigrants had to learn Malay in order to trade and interact with the indigenous people. Lack of Chinese women made it necessary for the more successful Chinese settlers to marry local women. Once married to a Chinese man, these native women acted as agents of acculturation. This resulted in the local-born offspring speaking Malay and losing or partially losing the language of their Chinese ancestors. The Chinese

Peranakan women also adopted Malay dress and various types of Malay cuisine. However, despite the dominant Malay environment, there was strong will on the part of male Chinese immigrants to retain their Chinese identity. They married Malay women but did not want their daughters to marry the indigenous Malay.[2]

In Malaysia, the center of Baba culture was Melaka. When Singapore was opened up as a commercial center by the British in 1819, many Melaka-born Chinese moved there. Hence the Baba in Melaka and Singapore were culturally similar. Today the small minority of Babas in Melaka continue to speak Malay, and the urban ones also speak English. Most of them adhere strongly to traditional Chinese religion. The small group of Babas in Singapore speaks mainly English, and some families still speak Malay at home. Unlike those in Melaka, many Babas in Singapore are Christians.

During the period of British colonization, the local-born Chinese in the settlements of Penang, Melaka and Singapore were called 'Straits-born Chinese' or 'Straits Chinese'. Most of these in Melaka and Singapore were Baba. The 'Straits Chinese' in Penang were also called Baba. However, they spoke the Penang version of the Hokkien language at home rather than Malay. Although the cuisine and the older women's dress of the 'Penang Baba' are locally created and adopted, they should be distinguished from the Malay-speaking Chinese Peranakan.

In northeast Kelantan and Terengganu of Malaysia, there are Chinese (especially rural ones) who have been highly acculturated by the Malays and the Thai of the region. They speak the regional Malay (Kelantan Malay and Terengganu Malay) among themselves in addition to the highly creolized Hokkien language. However, they do not identify themselves as Baba, although the 'pure' Chinese regard them as such. They may be regarded as Peranakan-type Chinese.[3]

In Indonesia, the Chinese Peranakan are mostly in Java, where the capital Jakarta was the center of Chinese Peranakan culture. The Chinese Peranakan are not a homogeneous group of people, as they have adapted to different cultural environments. The linguistic situation, for instance, is quite complicated. They speak the Malay dialect, which has been described as 'Chinese Malay' by some writers, although in East Java, Oetomo (1984, 167) thinks that it should be termed East Java Malay. In the Sukabumi area of West Java, however, the Chinese Peranakan speak both Malay and 'low-style Sudanese' at home. In some families, Sudanese prevails and in others Malay (Tan, Mely G. 1963, 15). In East Java, many Totok and lower-class Peranakan also speak *ngoko* (low-level) Javanese in the family (Oetomo 1984, 453).

It is useful to compare the experience of the Chinese Peranakan to the Chinese mestizo in the Philippines. The latter were originally the descendants of Chinese-Indio parents. According to Wickberg (1964, 62), Chinese mestizo were neither Chinese nor natives; they formed a separate group and were legally recognized as such by the Spanish colonial government. The Spanish authorities differentiated the Chinese mestizo from the Chinese and the Indio, the latter being Filipino natives. The Indio and the Chinese mestizo had to supply free labor to the government, but Chinese were exempted. The Indio, who were mostly engaged in agriculture, paid the least tribute, whereas the Chinese, who were largely engaged in commerce, paid the most. The Chinese mestizo, who were engaged in both commerce and agriculture, paid an amount in between, twice the amount paid by the Indio. The Indio and the Chinese mestizo enjoyed more or less the same rights but the Chinese did not. The Chinese were restricted in geographical mobility, whereas both the Indio and the Chinese mestizo were free to go about. Chinese could not participate in local government but Chinese mestizo and Indio could (Wickberg 1964, 64-5). This legal recognition of the Chinese mestizo as different from both the natives and the Chinese was an important factor for making the Chinese mestizo a distinct category.

One important factor that led to the gradual loss of a separate Chinese mestizo identity was the abolition of the legal distinction of Indio and mestizo by the Spanish government in the late 19th century (Wickberg 1964, 95). There were then only Spaniards, Filipinos and Chinese. Most Chinese mestizo chose to be Filipino, a label that replaced the term Indio after 1898. This was not surprising, since culturally the Chinese mestizo were closer to the Indio than to the Chinese. They were, like the Indio, almost all Roman Catholic. The Spanish government prohibited Chinese from marrying Indio unless these Chinese converted to Christianity. This policy brought the Chinese mestizo culture close to that of the Indio. Furthermore, in the Philippines, it was not simply a matter of the Chinese mestizo adapting themselves to a 'pure Indio culture', for both the Indio and the Chinese mestizo were developing towards some kind of Hispanicized Philippine culture (Wickberg 1965, 18).

Both the Chinese Peranakan and the Chinese mestizo originated from small Chinese communities adjusting to dominant indigenous cultures. However, the mestizo eventually merged with the indigenous people, whereas the Peranakan have remained Chinese. We have seen that both Hispanicism and the absence of religious barriers led to the Chinese mestizo identifying with the Indio. The situation is like that in Thailand, where the acculturated Chinese and the offspring of intermarriage can identify as either Chinese or Thai, depending on which immediate cultural environment (family and neighborhood) the children are more exposed to. Those who grow up in a strong Thai milieu rather than in Chinese neighborhoods will naturally identify with the Thai (cf. Skinner 1957, 132). However, the laws of the Spanish colonial government prevented the offspring of the union of Chinese men and native women from becoming either Chinese or Indio: they were classified as Chinese mestizo and so were their male descendants. A mestiza (female mestizo) and her children remained mestizo only if she married a Chinese or a mestizo. She became an Indio by marrying an Indio (Wickberg 1964, 65). Thus, unlike the Peranakan identity, the separate Chinese mestizo social group was legally created. Once the legal classification was dropped, natural social forces operated and moved the Chinese mestizo in the direction of the Indio.

The identification of the Chinese mestizo with the indigenous people was inevitable with the growth of nationalism. Unlike that in Indonesia and Malaysia, Filipino nationalism was not just a movement of the indigenous people. It was a movement of both the indigenous people and the Chinese mestizo and was very much shaped by the latter. Thanks to Hispanicism, both the Chinese mestizo and the indigenous people were not only Roman Catholic, but those who could afford schooling were educated in Spanish, the common language. The opposition to Spanish colonization and oppression served to unite the Chinese mestizo and the natives. The struggle brought forth Filipino consciousness and Filipino identity. Being generally wealthier, the Chinese mestizo were better educated and formed an important middle class (Antonio S. Tan 1985). The nationalistic writings of Chinese mestizo like Pedro Paterno, Gregorio Sancianco and Jose Rizal, as well as their struggle for reforms and freedom, contributed much to the growth of nationalism and the formation of the Filipino nation. The Chinese mestizo eventually found an identity in common with the natives, the Filipino identity.

Yet another unique factor accounts for the 'assimilation' of the Chinese mestizo. For the Chinese Peranakan, Chinese-native marriage was significant only in the period before large numbers of Chinese migrated to Southeast Asia during the 19th century. In the Philippines, the concept 'Chinese mestizo' has always been linked to intermarriage. The term was derived from the Spanish, who called people of mixed parentage 'mestizo'. The label was continuously applied to individuals 'no matter how obscure the image of their ancestors may be in their memory when the peculiar physical characteristics as well as manners are still traceable' (Jesus Merino 1969, 46). Despite the label, present-day Chinese mestizo do not form a separate social group. They are merely Filipinos who can trace their descent to a Chinese ancestor. Often an individual is not known to be a mestizo until he or she becomes prominent. Then his or her family becomes a matter of interest. As Jesus Merino (1969, 51) points out,

> Only when incidentally a member of the family won prominence in the community did that family and its mestizo origin and articulation came (*sic*) to be known. The mestizo condition of the families of Rizal and Paterno would have never been historically remembered had not Rizal and Paterno become what they did.

A relevant example is, of course, President Corazon Cojuangco Aquino whose great-grandfather José Cojuangco was Chinese. In her visit to China and amidst much publicity, the president visited the birthplace of her great-grandfather in Hongjian village in Fujian Province on 14 April 1988. The very fact that Mrs Aquino was willing to publicize her ancestry illustrates that being mestizo is not considered being inferior and is acceptable to the Filipino. In a sense, her visit was a public display of a prestigious Filipino status; it was not a declaration of being Chinese.

The description of Chinese mestizos identifying as Filipinos and ceasing to consider themselves Chinese is, in fact, a generalization (cf. Chu 2002). To this day, the term 'mestizo' refers to offspring of unions between Filipino natives and non-Filipinos. There must be circumstances that enable some individuals to identify as both Filipino and Chinese, and not Filipino only. This is so, if they have received considerable Chinese cultural influence (such as Chinese socialization, Chinese education, etc.) A friend of mine in Manila is a mestiza who identifies as both Chinese and Filipino. She was much influenced by her Chinese father and received Chinese education. However, Chinese mestizo/mestiza like her who identify as ethnic Chinese are exceptions rather than the norm.

The cases of Chinese Peranakan in Indonesia, the Baba (who also call themselves Peranakan) in Malaysia and Singapore, and the Chinese mestizo in the Philippines, have been analyzed by Skinner (1996), who describes them as the three intermediate creolized societies during the colonial era. The first step in the 'historical formation of these inter-mediate social systems' was intermarriage of Chinese immigrants with local women, and he notes that these societies were formed 'only after establishment of European outposts' (53). As discussed above, under the colonial administration, they occupied a higher social status than the indigenous peoples, whereas the Chinese Peranakan and the Chinese mestizos rather than the China-born immigrants dominated the Chinese share of the local economy. This must be an important factor that caused the Chinese Peranakan and the Chinese mestizo to distinguish themselves not only from the indigenous peoples but also from China-born immigrants. In fact, in Kelantan and Terengganu, where the localized Chinese were mostly not of the commercial class, and unlike the Babas of the British Straits settlements (Melaka, Penang and Singapore), they did not identify themselves with a separate category of Chinese. To this day, they identify themselves as 'Teng-lang', the Hokkien label for 'Chinese', although the other Chinese may refer to them as 'Baba' because of their acculturated cultural features (cf. Tan 1982, 2002).

With the end of colonialization, Chinese mestizo becoming Filipino is not surprising, given the process of its creation by the colonial regime. The Chinese mestizos were becoming Filipinos, as discussed by Wickberg (1965), rather than a separate category of Chinese as the Babas were. Roman Catholicism is not as exclusive as other forms of Christianity, as I have also observed in Sarawak, Malaysia, where Ibans who have become Catholics are still able to observe many of their traditional beliefs and practices. Thus there is no significant cultural barrier for Chinese to become Filipinos, as long as they speak Filipino and see themselves as Filipinos. Furthermore, the Chinese mestizos were already Roman Catholic.

A significant contribution of Skinner (1960, 94) is his argument that there is an institutional channel in Thailand for Chinese to become Thai, unlike in Java, where Islam is a considerable barrier to intermarriage and for Chinese to become indigenous. Chan and Tong (1998, 19) disagree. They criticize Skinner by arguing that, 'To say that because both Thai and Chinese practice Buddhism and, therefore, religion is no barrier to assimilation is like saying that since both Protestants and Catholics are Christians, they should get along very well'. This is a misrepresentation of Skinner on two counts. First, Skinner analyzes the Thai case in relation to the Javanese case. As he has done long-term fieldwork in Thailand, it is unfair to assume that he is not aware of the differences between Thai Theravada Buddhism and Chinese religious practices. Second, Skinner is not discussing ethnic relations, and the cited criticism is unfair. In fact, most married couples quarrel rather often, to put the argument another way. Although Chan and Tong's (1998) critique of Skinner is obvious today, one should note that, as was usual for scholars of his time, he did not make a clear distinction between acculturation and assimilation. Often when he talks about assimilation, he is describing what anthropologists call acculturation, or the localization that makes aspects of Chinese cultural life similar to those of the Thai. In this respect, the term 'acculturation' is still useful. Indeed, some senior anthropologists continue to use the term assimilation to also cover acculturation, *see* for example, Serrie and Hsu (1998, 7) and Bernard Wong (1978; 1998, 170).

Indeed, the term assimilation is still the popular term for academicians and non-academicians, since 'acculturation' meaning cultural assimilation but not ethnic assimilation is generally used by anthropologists only. There is a need to understand the meaning of assimilation instead of treating it as a red herring for argument. Supang (1997, 256), for instance, writes about the Chinese in Thailand becoming 'more assimilated because of Thai schooling and generational factors'. At the same time, he tells us that today the Chinese in Thailand can be called 'Chinese Thais because they keep their national identity and only identify themselves as Chinese in terms of descent'. We can take the writings about Chinese assimilation in Thailand to mean that the Chinese are becoming more acculturated or culturally assimilated; some have become Thai and ceased to be Chinese, whereas others, although becoming Thai, still identify themselves as ethnic Chinese. There is a legal channel for Chinese to become Thai. Chinese who have acquired Thai nationality, and their children, become 'Thai with Thai nationality and Chinese common origin' (*khonthai sanchat thai, chuachat chin*). By the third generation, these Chinese are legally classified as Thai (Bao 1999, 98). Thus in Thailand by taking Thai nationality one can also be an ethnic Thai. There is no clear boundary between the two, making it easy for a Chinese Thai to negotiate his or her identity as both Thai and Chinese. In Malaysia, Malaysian is always a national identity; it is not at the same time the ethnic identity of the majority population, Malays.

Another debate about Chinese assimilation in Thailand is whether Chinese can really be totally assimilated. The distinction between cultural identity and ethnic identity, as discussed in Chapter 1, is relevant here. The larger society that absorbs members from minorities inevitably becomes culturally more diverse. Thus, whether Chinese can truly be assimilated into Thai society becomes irrelevant if we do not assume that ethnic identification is the same as cultural identity. Burusratanaphand (2001) points out that Thai population derived from Mon, Lao, Khmer and Chinese (in the context of her paper) are not all 'totally assimilated into Thai social norm'. In fact, if the people have identified as Thai and are accepted, it does not matter if they follow the Thai culture in every detail. Basham (2001, 132) mentions that Chinese who are acculturated and become Thais retain some Chinese cultural features. Thus assimilation can occur, but it does not make the assimilated people totally homogeneous with the majority people. In fact, it makes the majority population more diverse and status differences may exist between internal categories within the larger population.

Skinner's cultural channel of assimilation is useful for the comparative study of Chinese in Thailand and Chinese in Indonesia and Malaysia. There was no easy cultural channel to socialize the localized Chinese to become indigenous people. At the same time, the higher social status in the colonial hierarchy did not encourage the Chinese Peranakan to identify with the indigenous people; Skinner is correct here. Today in Malaysia, the population of Babas is dwindling, as more and more of the younger generation are merging with the mainstream Chinese. The Babas do not have any special status in post-independence Malaysia and Singapore, nor do they dominate Chinese commerce. But the small Baba communities remain in both countries. Depending on socialization, there are individuals from Baba families who continue to be socialized to be Baba.

In Indonesia, the assimilation policy of the Suharto regime (Suryadinata 1976; 1998, 93–116) has had much effect on the Chinese. The younger generation of Chinese Indonesians are so localized that many speak Bahasa Indonesian and Javanese instead of Chinese, and most have Indonesian names. The distinction of Peranakan versus Totok (Pure Chinese who can speak Chinese) is becoming irrelevant. However,

I learned from my 2002 visit to Surabaya that the older Chinese still speak their Chinese mother tongue (generally Hokkien) and many still speak Mandarin. My informants from Chinese associations describe the situation thus: generally those below the age of 40 do not speak Chinese, although many know a few words of Hokkien. Nevertheless, the situation is changing in the more liberal post-Suharto era. The economic significance of China is encouraging many people to learn Chinese, and it is likely that many of the future younger Chinese Indonesians may be able to speak Chinese again, this time probably more Mandarin than Hokkien. In fact, the growing economic power of China is encouraging more people in the world, Chinese and non-Chinese, to study Chinese, and this must have implications for the changing nature of ethnic Chinese cultural life and identities.

COMPARISONS AND DISCUSSION

The experiences of the Chinese Peranakan, the Chinese mestizo and the Chinese in Thailand reflect intensive patterns of localization experienced by the Chinese abroad. Such intensive localization was possible in the early phase of migration when the immigrants were few in number and there was a lack or shortage of Chinese women.

In late 19th-century Trinidad, for instance, the Chinese were reported to have been 'assimilated into the local communities'. As Howard Johnson (1987, 89) states, 'many Chinese immigrants had become creolized in certain important aspects'. He reports of Chinese intermarrying with Creole women, since the immigrants were predominantly male. Johnson also mentions that Creole women acted as agents of creolization. Many Chinese adopted Christianity or at least Christian names and surnames used by the Creoles. This encouraged further acculturation and even assimilation into the dominant Creole society. In fact, in 1871, Chinese numbered only 1,400 in a population of 109,638; in 1891, their number decreased to 1,006 in a population of 200,028 (Johnson 1987, 90). Without a great increase in Chinese immigration, the Chinese were easily acculturated and assimilated. As reported in the *San Fernando Gazette* of 1878: 'Socially, no one doubts the ease with which the Chinese have assimilated their habits to those of the country of their adoption, neither can any one look at them without noticing the astonishing effects of such assimilation' (Quoted in Johnson 1987, 90).

Even in Taiwan, Han Chinese settlers living in the dominant cultural environment of indigenous minorities are reported to have become highly acculturated. Ruan Chang Rui has studied the Chinese who migrated from Guangdong to Takangk'ou (Dagangkou) on the east coast of Taiwan and reported on those who have remained living alongside the Makutaai, a large group of coastal Ami. At the time of his study, Ruan (1971, 52) observed 25 households containing 109 male and 81 female acculturated Chinese in Takangk'ou. Because of their isolation from other Han Chinese, these Chinese adopted the Ami language while keeping some Chinese loanwords to express terms not found in Ami. Their food and dress reflect Ami cultural influences. Their marriage and kinship systems have also been influenced by the Ami. The Chinese traditionally observe the patrilineal descent system and marriage is normally patrilocal, whereas the Ami system is matrilineal descent and marriage is matrilocal. According to Ruan, among 40 Takangk'ou couples, 26 practiced matrilocal marriage and only 14 followed the Chinese way.

There has been much intermarriage between the Takangk'ou Chinese and the Ami. In fact, Ruan thinks that intermarriage is the main cause of the intensive acculturation of the Takangk'ou Chinese. As with Chinese immigrants in Southeast Asia, the men married the native women and tried to keep their own women within the group. However, the Takangk'ou Chinese not only married Ami women, but the matrilocal system of the Ami enabled Ami men to marry into the Chinese community as well. Both the married-in Ami men and women served as agents of further acculturation of the Chinese who in time became predominantly 'mixed blood'.

Despite this intensive acculturation, the Chinese have retained their traditional Chinese religion, although it has incorporated some Ami religious beliefs and practices. Regarding identity, some consider themselves Chinese, whereas others consider themselves Ami. Generally, the richer ones regard themselves as Chinese and the poorer ones regard themselves as Ami (Ruan 1971, 58), reflecting the relationship between class and ethnicity. However, these 'mixed bloods' are despised by the other Chinese and the Ami who do not regard them as real Chinese or real Ami.

The experience of the Takangk'ou Chinese is similar to that of the Chinese Peranakan, except that the former have not acquired a separate sub-ethnic identity. This further illustrates that the Peranakan identity has been fostered by the presence of strong religious definition of ethnicity on the part of the indigenous people. In other words, if there are no strong institutional barriers to ethnic membership, acculturated Chinese can identify with either the Chinese minority or the indigenous majority, as has happened in Thailand, Cambodia,[4] the Philippines, and many other places.

The intensive localization experienced by early Chinese immigrant offspring and their descendants in different parts of the world is due to their need to adjust to a dominant indigenous socio-cultural environment. A combination of factors tends to ensure the high rate of acculturation: the relatively small number of immigrant offspring and descendants, an uneven sex ratio (because of the lack or shortage of Chinese women), continuous intermarriage with local women, and the need to adjust to the economic and political systems of the larger society. The most fundamental adjustment is the learning of the local lingua franca. Intermarriage is also crucial in intensifying acculturation, especially in respect to the adoption of the local language, for the married-in natives serve as agents of intensive acculturation even though they in turn receive Chinese cultural influences. In the past, the socialization of children was largely left to the women, so offspring of Sino-native marriages always learned the native language. Furthermore, the Chinese husband had to speak the native language to his native wife. This has been the common experience of the Chinese in different parts of the world, not just the Chinese Peranakan. Fong (1959, 125), writing about Chinese marrying local women in New Zealand, mentions that the non-Chinese mother, whether European or Maori, teaches her children her own native language. This indicates that linguistic acculturation or assimilation in regard to offspring of Chinese-native unions was a rather natural process.

The necessity of intermarriage on the part of the Chinese is obvious. Generally, those who married were those who had made sufficient fortunes to be able to afford a family, in particular, successful Chinese traders. The indigenous people, who were mostly subsistence peasants, were not well off and their women were willing to marry the more-established Chinese immigrants.[5] This class factor is important. It explains why there was less intermarriage between the Chinese and the Whites who occupied higher social status, although racial feeling was involved as well. For example, studies have shown that English women married to Chinese immigrants were mostly from the working class (Ng 1968, 76; Watson 1975, 126). Similarly, Ban Seng Hoe, who has studied the Chinese in Canada, reports that the incidence of intermarriage between Chinese and Whites was low and, where such intermarriages occurred in Canada, it usually involved Chinese and White girls from lower socio-economic levels, 'especially those who worked in Chinese restaurants' (Ban 1976, 279). Of course today, with better education and upward mobility, Chinese men and women can intermarry more easily with middle- and upper-class Whites (cf. Ling 1998, 172–7).

The lack of strong religious barriers makes intermarriage easier. Traditional Chinese religion is tolerant as far as marriage is concerned. A Chinese can marry a person of any faith unless the religion of this other person does not permit the marriage. The syncretic nature of traditional Chinese religion makes it easier for the Chinese to adjust to local popular beliefs. In Malaysia and Indonesia, it was possible in the past for Chinese to marry Malay women and bring them into the Chinese community. Alternatively, the Chinese could become nominal Muslims in order to marry local women before bringing them to the Chinese side. Such an arrangement is not possible today in Malaysia, due to both the more effective control of the state over the Islamic population and an Islamic resurgence. In Indonesia, nominal conversion for intermarriage was practiced, too, whereas in the past, Islam attracted Chinese converts (The 1993). Under the assimilation policy of the Suharto government, becoming Muslim was a choice among a section of Chinese Indonesians, and there is now a community of Chinese Muslims (Mely Tan 2000).

Where there was missionary activity,[6] or when Christianity was firmly established, the early Chinese immigrants might be converted. This expedited intermarriage, as we have seen in the case of the Chinese in the Philippines and Trinidad. Of course, the class factor remains important in respect to intermarriage.

The early Chinese settlers obviously were conscious of the need to maintain their Chinese identity. This explains why they married local women but did not want to give away their daughters as wives for the indigenous people. This was so with the Chinese Peranakan and the Takangk'ou Chinese. In fact it was the general pattern everywhere.[7] In Peru, for example, Kwong (1958, 47) writes, 'Today as yesterday, the pattern of intermarriage sanctions the mating of pure Chinese men with pure or part-Peruvian women; rarely, if at all, does there occur a marriage between pure Chinese women and pure or part-Peruvian men'.[8]

Although language is an important marker of an ethnic identity, the case of the highly acculturated Chinese shows that it is easily changed or even replaced. The reason is that language is crucial for social interaction, and ethnic Chinese everywhere have to learn the lingua franca. In Papua New Guinea, for instance, Wu (1977, 91) reports that many Chinese cannot speak any Chinese language, and Chinese children's first language is 'predominantly Melanesian, Pidgin or both'. We have seen that certain unique circumstances of cultural adjustment have even resulted in the Chinese minority losing their own Chinese language and adopting the language of the indigenous people.

In contrast, religion is most resistant to acculturation. The reason is that it is least subject to the forces of adaptation, except where there is missionary activity. There is no need to adopt the religion of the indigenous people in order to interact with them, but it is necessary to learn their language. Furthermore, the syncretic nature of the Chinese folk religion allows easy incorporation of certain local beliefs and practices. There is no need to drop the Chinese religion in favor of that of the indigenous people. This is not so with the more 'exclusive' religions like Islam and Christianity. One cannot worship Chinese ancestors and deities and be a Christian or a Muslim at the same time. Moreover, religion involves the symbolic world, the meaning of life and death, and so it cannot be changed or dropped as easily as language (as a medium of communication) or other material aspects of culture. Between language and religion, there is a wide range of cultural features, which may be acculturated. For example, ethnic Chinese everywhere have, to some extent at least, incorporated some cuisine of the dominant society into their own cuisine.

We can therefore make two conclusions about the dynamics of acculturation. Firstly, the instrumental aspect of a culture, as represented by language as a medium of communication, is easier to be acculturated and even replaced, whereas the symbolic aspect of a culture, as represented by a religious or worldview is more resistant to change. The symbolic world is of course less exposed to the forces of socio-cultural adjustment. However, where religion is subject to the forces of acculturation, as in the case of a Chinese minority living in dominant Christian environment where there is missionary activity, the Chinese may be converted. For example, the Chinese in British Guiana not only speak English, they are almost entirely Christians (Fried 1958, 55; Shaw 1985, 165; Hall 1998, 105).

Secondly, when a cultural component of ethnic group A has to adjust to that of the dominant group B, its natural propensity is to incorporate some elements of the cultural component of B rather than to drop its own component in favor of B. This is very much so in culinary acculturation. The cuisine of the Baba, for example, is not Malay but comprises both Chinese and Malay cuisine: it is Baba. It happens in religion, as we have seen. This happened to the Chinese in Thailand, Takangk'ou in Taiwan, and other places. Even in Peru 'there is rural syncretism and overlapping of Catholic and Chinese beliefs and practices'

(Kwong 1958, 45). This mixing of Chinese and Roman Catholic beliefs and practices is also common in the Philippines (See and Go 1990). However, where the contrasting cultural components are in direct competition with that of the dominant culture that exerts the pressure of assimilation, the cultural component of the minority may be replaced, as we have seen in the case of language. This may happen even in respect to Chinese folk religion in a dominant Christian environment, which puts pressure on the minority to convert. Even in the US, where there is religious freedom, more Chinese are becoming Christians. Citing Fenggang Yang, a researcher on Chinese Christianity, Ly (2003) reports that 'nearly a third of Chinese Americans now attend Church', and there are now more than 1000 Chinese churches in the United States. Nevertheless, as long as people perceive themselves to be Chinese, certain Chinese cultural symbols will continue to remain meaningful.

Before the large influx of Chinese immigrants in Southeast Asia and elsewhere from the mid-19th century onwards, the acculturation of the 'local-born' Chinese was a natural and easy process. In Malaysia, the Hokkien (*Minnanren*) have a saying that after three generations, one becomes a Baba (*sā-tai seng ba*). This saying may be regarded as a summary of the localization experience of ethnic Chinese in Malaysia. As we have seen in the case of the Baba, when a Chinese immigrant married a local woman, his offspring were bound to speak Malay although they might still have some knowledge of the Chinese language of their father. By the third generation, the descendants were even more acculturated and perhaps lost the Chinese language altogether. It is therefore not surprising that the term 'Baba' has become the metaphor for acculturation. Ruan (1971, 60) also mentions that after three generations, the Han Chinese in Takangk'ou became totally mixed with the coastal Ami through intermarriage and were highly acculturated as well. Even where there is little intermarriage, the third generation still represents a generation of 'full' acculturation or even assimilation for individuals of a minority living and interacting in a dominant environment of the majority people. It is at the third generation that acculturation becomes most significant and stabilized, for the first generation represents the beginning, and the second, the transition. In her description of the third-generation Chinese (not a large group in New Zealand), Fong (1959, 49) writes, 'unless there is a return to the racial intolerance of former years, these third-generation New Zealanders of Chinese origin will be Europeans in every way but their physical appearance'. This is of course localization, not necessarily assimilation in the sense of ceasing to be Chinese. As Ip (1996, 144) points out, the people of Chinese descent are constantly reassessing their identity, and many 'Chinese New Zealanders came to value their cultural heritage and ethnicity as never before'.

The increase in the Chinese immigrant population reduced the rate of acculturation, for the sex ratio became more balanced and the local Chinese could interact more among themselves. A larger Chinese community makes it possible to have an ethnic neighborhood. It allows more scope for community power. Many socio-economic services can be internally organized, and Chinese leaders can represent the interest of the Chinese more effectively. A sizable community also allows for the formation of voluntary associations, which help to promote the social, cultural and political interests of the Chinese.

Ban (1979, 252) is of the opinion that the greater the community power, the lesser 'assimilation' and vice-versa. In general, this is true. Community power depends on a number of factors like the size of the population and the socio-economic and political influence of the community. In a sizable community, Chinese social organizations are able to exert considerable influence over inter-community affairs and inter-community relations. This is especially so if the Chinese yield considerable economic power in a country. Thus the Chinese in colonial Southeast Asia had more community power than those in the United States of America or Europe. This is due to the relatively larger size of the Chinese groups that established influential urban communities: their presence was visible throughout most big and small towns. Sizable groups were able to build Chinese-medium schools and in some places even hospitals. They established their own newspapers. Above all, they created a wide network of associations. After independence, the 'new' states in Southeast Asia have adopted various policies to curb the economic and political power of the Chinese. These policies have been more oppressive in some countries than in others. Nevertheless, even in Indonesia and the Philippines, where 'economic nationalism' against the Chinese has been severe, the Chinese as a community continue to remain influential in the urban commercial sector.

Malaysia is the place, other than Singapore, where the Chinese have developed the strongest community power. They have attained a certain degree of influence due to factors relating to social demography, their own established culture, and the loci of power vis-à-vis Malays, the majority people. Forming about 32% of the total population of 13.7 million in 1980 and 26% of the total Malaysian population of 21.9 million in 2000, the Chinese maintain a presence that can be seen throughout the country. Their dominant role in commerce is evident in most towns, as shown by their signboards. In most urban centers they have been able to form their own established social order in which Chinese individuals can socialize without dealing much with the Malays outside of the context of work or games, if they so choose. They have many associations, some of which are quite influential in national politics, which is organized along ethnic lines. Indeed, Chinese community politics remains an important aspect of the Malaysian scene. There are also Chinese and Chinese-based political parties, and the Chinese are represented in the government and the bureaucracy. Ho (2002, 154) summarizes the nature of Chinese Malaysians' political participation as exhibiting 'bureaucratic involvement at the top government hierarchy' and 'mobilized opposition at the grass roots'. However, as aptly described by Strauch (1981, 164), Chinese Malaysian politics has become more and more encapsulated in the dominant Malay political culture.

Today, Chinese Malaysians still have Chinese vernacular primary schools run by the government. At the secondary level, most Chinese students enroll in the Malay-medium government schools (some of which teach Chinese as a subject), and many others still attend Chinese-medium private schools (cf. Tan Liok Ee 1997). There are local Chinese newspapers, and the Chinese-educated have access to both local and most overseas Chinese publications. As expected, the Chinese-educated are the least acculturated of the Chinese Malaysians. Skinner, in his study of the Chinese in Thailand, has already pointed out the relationship between Chinese education and acculturation: a Chinese education retards, whereas a Thai education accelerates assimilation, and an absence of formal education is intermediate in its effect on assimilation (Skinner 1964a, 86).

Thanks to their number, economic influence and community power in general, the Chinese in Malaysia, although experiencing economic and political constraints, do not have to suffer from a policy of forced assimilation, as did the Chinese in Indonesia under the Suharto regime. Yet their community power may have given some leaders of the Chinese-educated the false hope of resisting all forms of acculturation. Some form of acculturation is unavoidable and may even be necessary. For example, the adoption of Malay as the common language in education is inevitable in this multi-ethnic state.

Singapore is an interesting example. The Chinese account for 77% of the total population (Singapore Department of Statistics 2001, viii). Yet former Prime Minister Lee Kuan Yew has turned it into the most 'Westernized' Asian state, and English is the most important language for commerce and official purposes. The younger generation of Chinese Singaporeans is English-speaking, although most of them also speak a Chinese language. The choice of English for planned acculturation is not just related to its usefulness for Singapore as an international commercial and financial center. It is a choice of identity in the Malay Archipelago. Obviously, Singapore does not want to be perceived as a Chinese state — this would be disadvantageous for a land whose history and geography are in the Malay world and its present existence still closely linked to that world. In fact, Malay is the national language of Singapore, albeit in practice rather nominally. Nevertheless, the education policy was reviewed in the 1970s, presumably to check moral deficiency and unhealthy westernization associated with drug abuse, consumerism, political liberalization, etc. (Chua 1995, 113). Since then, bilingualism and moral education have been emphasized in schools. The students have to learn their mother tongue (Mandarin, for Chinese students) in addition to English. The promotion of the Chinese language coincides with the emergence of China as a major economic power in Asia.

In Indonesia, the Chinese number only about three per cent of the total population and are totally at the mercy of the state's power. Although they have been quite prominent in the commercial sectors, their community power was curbed by the government's assimilation policies during the Suharto era, some of which were very oppressive. In fact, the events following the 1965 coup resulted in the Chinese being deprived of their cultural and political rights (cf. Suryadinata 1976; 1998, 93–116). It was after the fall of Suharto in 1998 that Chinese Indonesians were able to express their Chinese cultural life more openly and freely.

The oppressive cultural policies aimed at the Chinese in Indonesia were rather unnecessary, as the overwhelming dominant Indonesian political and socio-cultural environment of the post-independent state had already ensured the eventual acculturation of the Chinese. For example, unlike in Malaysia, Chinese Indonesians speak fluent Indonesian among themselves. Even the Totok Chinese are moving in the direction of the Peranakan. This is not simply a result of the policy of assimilation. The dominant Indonesian cultural environment has already ensured that the younger generation of the Totok Chinese will be more acculturated.

In the West, the Chinese do not have strong community power *vis-à-vis* the larger society. However, they are compensated by the established democratic system of the wider society. Despite the anti-Chinese campaigns in the past, the Constitution of the US protects the civil rights of Americans. As long as Chinese Americans observe the laws and are willing to adjust to the dominant White culture, they can compete with other Americans. Moreover, they have done well in education, an important means of upward mobility. In the Third World, however, democracy as indicated by the tolerance of dissent and of minorities is not well developed. Chinese stand to lose from strong executive governance or even dictatorial rule. This is especially so in countries where ethnicity is not just a principle of mobilization but may be a principle of legitimization as well. In such a situation, oppressive policies and political action against the Chinese may be acceptable and even welcome by the indigenous people. Chinese may be made the scapegoat for economic failure or even political instability. However, institutional discrimination persists in the West. The experience of Lee Wen Ho, a Chinese American scientist who was falsely accused of being a spy, is a good example of this (Lee and Zia 2001).

Whatever the political system, education has become an important means of acculturation. In a modern state, access to the national language becomes a crucial factor for access to socio-economic resources and for upward mobility. Even where Chinese immigrants are able to avoid acculturation by living largely within their own ethnic niche, as we have noted in Chinatowns in the West, the need to send their children to national schools exposes the children more directly to the larger society. In attending government schools, Chinese children are inevitably acculturated in one way or another by the dominant culture. They interact with the children of the larger society and so acquire certain values and behavior of the majority people, some of which contradict the traditional values of their Chinese parents and ancestors. These children in turn bring the influence of the larger society to their families. As pointed out by Glick (1980, 344), the Hawaiian-born Chinese 'brought home the pressures they felt at school and at work to conform to patterns prevailing in the Westernized community'.

Thus when we compare acculturation experienced by the early Chinese settlers to the situation in the modern state, we may say that the acculturation of the early settlers was largely informal, whereas the present-day acculturation is both informal and formal (mainly through education). As in the past, the generation factor is also important. The younger generations of the Chinese who attend local schools are more acculturated than are their parents. In the West, for example, they adopt more Western forms of life. If they grow up in the United States of

America or Canada, for instance, they adopt English as their own or one of their own languages. This is confirmed by a number of studies. Peter Li (1998, 107), for example, points out that the first-generation immigrants account for the higher level of ancestral language retention among the Chinese in Canada, whereas the 'second and subsequent generations of Chinese-Canadians are highly susceptible to the loss of Chinese as a mother-tongue or home language'. A similar trend is reported by Crissman, Beattie and Selby (1998, 104) about the Chinese in Brisbane, Australia.

As the younger generation of Chinese advance up the social ladder, as professionals or civil servants for instance, they identify more with the larger society unless they find themselves discriminated against or not accepted. The next generation will be brought up in a more acculturated home environment, thus enhancing the process of acculturation. Some of them may even intermarry, say with Whites, and the offspring may remain Chinese or be assimilated. There is in fact a tendency for the acculturated and the offspring of mixed marriages to further intermarry (cf. Choi 1975, 103). Crissman, Beattie and Selby (1998, 105) report that '60 per cent of the male Australian-born Chinese had married non-Chinese'.

Our discussion shows that acculturation arises from socio-cultural adjustment to a dominant cultural environment. Many factors account for the rate and nature of acculturation. The main factors may be summarized as follows.

1. *Social demography.* We have seen that the size of the population and sex-ratio influence acculturation.
2. *Family and kinship.* Acculturation has a lot to do with how individuals are socialized. In general, Chinese who grow up in 'traditional' Chinese families and interact frequently with Chinese relatives are able to preserve more 'Chinese' culture.
3. *Marriage.* Whether an individual marries a member of the same ethnic group or of a different ethnic group affects the acculturation or the lack of acculturation of the offspring.
4. *Geographical ethnic concentration.* Those who live in a

predominantly Chinese neighborhood acculturate less than those who live scattered among the majority people. Chinatowns, for example, provide an ethnic niche, which makes it possible for some immigrants not to participate much in the larger society. Other studies have also shown the importance of ethnic neighborhoods in preserving 'traditional' culture and identity. In his study of Mexican Americans, Amado M. Padilla (1980, 77) concludes that 'the more acculturated individuals resided in the low ethnic dense neighborhoods than in the high ethnic dense barrios...'. Regional differences in the density of geographical ethnic concentration also account for the regional differences in the level of acculturation. In many countries (e.g., in Southeast Asia) Chinese who live in small numbers in the rural areas where the indigenous people predominate are more acculturated than those in the cities and towns where most of the 'pure' Chinese live.

5. *Extent of interaction with the established local culture or the dominant culture.* Where Chinese can remain fairly independent of the larger society economically and socially, there is less acculturation. The more the need to interact with the dominant culture, the more the chance for acculturation.

6. *The political and economic power of the community versus that of the larger society.* This is not just a question of interaction. With more economic and/or political power, the Chinese can organize their community more effectively and cope with the political pressure of the larger society. If, for example, Chinese can run their own schools, Chinese newspapers, and other internal affairs, the rate of acculturation will be low.

7. *The state policies bearing on minorities.* This is of course related to the question of democracy and the liberal or conservative policies of the larger society.

8. *The presence or absence of ethnic discrimination and the nature of that discrimination.* Equal opportunity for a minority to have access to socioeconomic opportunities encourages acculturation.

Wong (1979), for instance, has argued that their lack of greater participation in the economic system of the larger American society forces the Chinese to keep to traditional ethnic business pursuits in Chinatowns and prevents their greater participation in American life. Wong's later study shows that as economic opportunities widen, the Chinese take up middle-class American careers and move into White neighborhoods (Wong 1998, 70). Sung (1967, 271) also argues that opportunities for economic advancement are necessary for their greater participation in the larger society and 'being fused with the "dominant culture".'

9. *Social Mobility.* Since upward mobility means moving in the direction of the dominant culture, it is associated with greater acculturation. Skinner (1957, 300; 1960, 90) has illustrated this very clearly in Thailand. Other studies also confirm this. Spiro (1955, 124), for example, points out that 'ethnics with high social status tend to be most acculturated'.

10. *Education.* Acculturation through formal education has become important in modern states. Furthermore, education in the national system is an important means of upward mobility. Where Chinese continue to have access to Chinese-medium education, there is less acculturation.

11. *History of settlement.* Generally, the older the generation of settlement, the higher the level of acculturation.

12. *Level of acculturation.* Those who have experienced some acculturation tend more easily to be further acculturated.

The result of acculturation is actually brought about by the interplay of a number of factors. For example, low population and the shortage of women, combined with intermarriage and the need to participate widely in the larger society, inevitably lead to high acculturation. We should also consider, as pointed out by Bruner (1974), the relative strength of the dominant culture by considering the social demography as well as the socio-economic and political power of the ethnic majority.

Depending on the nature of acculturation, certain cultural

components are more easily adopted than others. Overall, we can conclude that linguistic change is the most fundamental aspect of acculturation. Adoption of the dominant local language was necessary in the past, and it is still the most basic aspect of cultural localization today.

ACCULTURATION AND ETHNICITY

What is the effect of acculturation on ethnicity in respect to people of Chinese descent? The acculturation process gives rise to different models of Chinese culture all over the world. It creates a consciousness of the diversity of Chinese identities. At the transnational level, for example, it contributes to the perception of Chinese Americans versus Chinese Malaysians. Within a country, where there is a marked diversity between the most acculturated and the least acculturated, the most acculturated Chinese may acquire a distinct sub-ethnic identity, as the Baba have. For the people themselves, acculturation has psychological effects in that it affects how they perceive themselves and how others perceive them.

The least acculturated people of Chinese descent tend to consider themselves 'pure Chinese' and look down on the highly acculturated ones. They ignore the fact that compared to the Chinese in Guangzhou or Taipei, they themselves (e.g., Chinese Malaysians) are in fact quite localized, too. This does not mean that the more acculturated Chinese always feel inferior about their identity. The Baba can be quite proud of their Baba identity, too. Being Baba also justifies their not speaking Chinese. Emphasizing the local content of the Chinese identity is a way for the people of Chinese descent to reconcile the fact of acculturation and avoid an inferiority complex or even identity crisis. When the English-speaking Chinese Americans are compared to the Chinese from Taiwan, they may be culturally inferior from the Taiwanese point of view. The Chinese Americans, however, can ignore this attitude by emphasizing their local identity, of being American, that is, Chinese

American. In so identifying themselves, they want to be judged in the context of their Chinese identity. In this way, they define their own identity *vis-à-vis* the Chinese of other countries. At the same time, the more acculturated ones can claim to be more American and therefore superior to the new immigrants and the less acculturated.

The emphasis on being local in their ethnic identification on the part of ethnic Chinese is quite universal. In Malaysia, for example, the Chinese have various unflattering versions of 'Chinaman' to describe Chinese whose values or behavior are deemed too traditional and not local enough. The Hokkien, for example, use the label *Teng-suã A-peh* (Uncle from China) derogatorily to describe these types. The Baba still use the term *Cina-gɔ* (probably meaning 'China guests') to refer derogatorily to 'pure' Chinese individuals. Historically, the label 'Baba' was used by the Straits-born Chinese to emphasize the local Chinese identity in contrast to the *Sinkeh* or the new immigrants. The Peranakan-type Chinese in Kelantan, when they want to refer derogatorily to the less acculturated Chinese, call them *Tok Pek*. No Chinese in Kelantan, including the 'pure Chinese' like to be described as *Tok Pek*.[9] In the Philippines, the term *Intsik* referring to the Chinese is now seen as pejorative, even though the word was probably derived from the Hokkien term *chek* or *inchek* for 'uncle'. The reason is that the term has come to be associated with the negative image of Chinaman. In Thailand, *chek* is also a derogatory term to refer to the Chinese (Bao 1999, 98). In Indonesia, the label used for Chinese Indonesians is *Tionghoa*, and the local Chinese feel insulted when they are called *Cina*, which is also 'Chinese'. *Tionghoa* is the Hokkien pronunciation for *Zhonghua* in Mandarin and, like the word *Cina*, refers to China or the Chinese. The latter term, however, does not convey the idea of local identity as does the term *Tionghoa*, as perceived in Indonesia.[10] In other words, once acculturation takes place, it is accepted by the people themselves and plays a meaningful role in establishing their identity. Acculturation also has a strong bearing on the formation of proper or at least acceptable local identities as well as on acquired perceptions that make the *A-Peh* (Uncle) type of identification unacceptable.

Acculturation, especially for the offspring of intermarriage and the highly acculturated Chinese who have access to both the Chinese and the dominant ethnic identity of the larger society, allows for situational ethnicity. That is, such people of Chinese descent may choose either identity, according to the situation in which they are interacting. Often, class or economic considerations became the basis of choice of identity to be assumed or even adopted totally. According to Barton (1983, 62), who did his research among the Chinese merchants in South Vietnam prior to the Communist takeover in 1975, the 'merchants at higher levels in the marketing system stressed their Chinese identity in order to maintain their credit ratings', whereas at the lower levels, 'it was more important to stress Vietnamese characteristics in dealing with customers than it was to stress a "Chinese" identity when dealing with suppliers'. For the Takangk'ou Chinese, we have noted that the richer ones tend to stress their wealthier status by identifying with the Chinese rather than the indigenous people who are generally less well off. We have seen that the Malay-speaking Chinese Peranakans have no easy access to the indigenous identity. Therefore, they remain Chinese, but a special kind of Chinese, unless they learn to speak Chinese and choose to merge fully with the wider Chinese identity. In this case, situational ethnicity is an inter-group phenomenon among Chinese groupings that invokes sub-ethnic identities rather than interethnic identity.

Thus, a high degree of acculturation paves the way for access to more than one ethnic identity. This is especially so in intermarriage. Ng (1959, 105) reports that in North Island in New Zealand, where more Chinese of mixed blood live, the people of mixed descent can remain Chinese if they so choose. But because of their high degree of acculturation, the European-Chinese tend to associate more with Europeans, whereas the Maori-Chinese associate with the Maori (*see also* Ip 1996, 150).

Our study shows that acculturation does not necessarily lead to assimilation, as illustrated in the case of the Baba. Nevertheless, a high degree of acculturation does provide the means for individuals to be assimilated into the larger society. In Thailand, the highly acculturated Chinese are generally assimilated into the Thai society, especially through intermarriage. Although some individuals are assimilated, others remain ethnically and even culturally Chinese, hence the persistence of the Chinese identity. I have shown that later generations of people of Chinese descent overseas tend to be more acculturated than earlier ones. Nevertheless, one should note that at all times even the most acculturated could remain ethnic Chinese as long as there is a Chinese community to identify with. Indeed, in most places, there are two categories of ethnic Chinese, the 'pure' Chinese (actually, the least acculturated ones) and the acculturated Chinese, or to use the Indonesian labels, the Totok Chinese and the Peranakan Chinese.

In countries like Indonesia and Burma, the 'pure' Chinese are mainly the older generations, for their offspring are becoming the Peranakan type or even becoming assimilated. In other places like Malaysia and dense Chinese settlements in different parts of the world, the 'pure' Chinese continue to cling to a more traditional or ethnocentric Chinese identity. In the more developed countries where immigration is still possible, the migration of Chinese from the 'Chinese land', along with Chinese from the Third World, continues to add to the population of the 'pure' Chinese, but their descendants are moving in the direction of the Peranakan-type, being more localized.

CONCLUSION

In a way, the history of Chinese migration, as well as the acculturation and assimilation of Chinese around the world, is an ongoing history, except that now Chinese migrants are not just traders and laborers. Instead, they range from refugees to professionals and rich business people. Moreover, they are not just migrants from the 'Chinese land' but include Totok Chinese and Peranakan-types from different parts of the world.[11] As most of the latter are middle- and upper-class Chinese and can speak English, they (whether Totok or Peranakan types) can adjust to the English-speaking countries fairly easily.

Therefore, nowadays, the ethnic Chinese in any one country actually constitute quite a heterogeneous group as far as their self-identity is concerned. Historically, ethnic Chinese have acquired different kinds of identity, from China-centered to local national identity, for instance, as Wang (1988) has shown. In this chapter, we have seen how Chinese identities, culturally and ethnically, have changed as a result of settlement and localization. Ethnic Chinese live in state societies and are influenced by the cultural processes therein. Most of them identify as a particular national type of Chinese, or are culturally identifiable as particular national type, such as Chinese Americans or Chinese Malaysians. Among themselves in a country, they are very heterogeneous. There are Chinese who have a long history of settlement and there are new immigrants. There are foreign-born Chinese and there are local-born Chinese, and there are those who are highly localized and those who see themselves as 'pure' Chinese, being the least acculturated. There are different attitudes among them, those who claim to be 'pure' despising those who have lost their Chinese mother tongue. Sometimes, the prejudice one receives from within the Chinese community can be very serious. Thus Sharon Lee (1992, 95) points out, the Hong Kong Chinese in Vancouver 'were prejudiced against Canadian-born — even more so than whites'. However, as we have seen, the locals also look down on the new immigrants who are not local enough.

Lest one should confuse acculturation with assimilation, it should be pointed out that whereas the 'pure' Chinese generally stress their communal identity, the Peranakan-type do not necessarily identify fully with the larger society. The latter can be very Chinese in identification although highly acculturated. In Malaysia, the Babas do not feel less Chinese ethnically than the 'pure' Chinese. In fact, both the 'pure' Chinese and the Peranakan-type Chinese (including the actual Peranakan) have retained a communal level of identification although they may have developed different perceptions and outlooks as a result of acculturation and integration. Acculturation, of course, does affect the means of displaying identity. Because of the loss of the Chinese language, the Baba emphasize certain Chinese traditions to express their Chinese cultural identity. To this day, many Babas in Melaka are proud of the old-fashioned Chinese wedding (dating to the 19th century), and some of the well-off ones still try to marry in this manner. Although they may not read Chinese, many Babas still display Chinese characters in their house, such as in the form of Chinese couplets at the main entrance. The 'pure' Chinese, in contrast, emphasize literacy in the Chinese language and even Chinese education.

If we take the case of the Chinese in the United States, as far as identification is concerned, there are Chinese Americans who choose to be more ethnic Chinese than American. There are also those who seek to be more American than Chinese. There are even some who try not to be Chinese at all. Whether individuals perceive themselves as more ethnic or more 'national', or else lose their Chinese identity through assimilation, depends on many factors that also affect acculturation. For example, individuals who grow up in dense ethnic neighborhoods are more likely to retain their ethnic identity. Under such conditions, as I have shown elsewhere, the network of interaction among Baba relatives helps to maintain the Baba identity in the presence of a dominant 'pure' Chinese culture in Melaka (Tan 1984). Moreover, minority individuals who experience discrimination may reject identification with the dominant group, and even highly acculturated types who have been discriminated against may be led to adhere more closely to their communal identity. In contrast, easy upward mobility within the larger society not only encourages acculturation of minority individuals but also encourages assimilation where possible. This is especially so if intermarriage can take place easily. Many other factors are involved, but in the ultimate analysis, acceptance by the dominant group is crucial for assimilation.

The analysis here shows that it is unnecessary and in fact impractical (and even immoral) to force the minority to acculturate or assimilate. Ideally, acculturation should be left to the natural process of people adjusting to the dominant culture without state intervention, except where it is necessary to have a common language and to promote it through education, as in Malaysia. Even when people are highly acculturated, the assimilation of the Chinese ethnic groups cannot be achieved unless there is full acceptance on the part of the majority people and the Chinese are not discriminated against in any respect.

Just as acculturation does not necessarily end with assimilation, acculturation alone cannot bring about integration, that is, the harmonious adjustment among different ethnic groups fully participating in national affairs. Acculturation may ease the way for integration, but in actuality it is the vital political and socio-economic factors affecting ethnic relations that account for the rate of integration. In fact, the sharing of the common language and the experience of living together in a nation will eventually lead to a certain degree of integration without the use of undue pressure or force.

Although acculturation has its advantages for ethnic Chinese, it does not always guarantee their full acceptance by the majority. In a sense, it is not easy to be an ethnic Chinese. One has to be competitive in order to survive and to succeed in an environment dominated by the majority. Yet in many countries, success may perpetuate or create envy and ill feeling against the Chinese. Even international politics involving China may affect their relationship with the majority. The experience of the Chinese Peranakan in Indonesia is an example. Even if anti-Chinese riots or campaigns were aimed at alien Chinese, the Chinese Peranakan suffered as well. The experience of the Vietnamese refugees, mostly people of Chinese descent, following the Sino-Vietnam conflict was another tragedy. Even the small minority of Chinese in India suffered discrimination following the Sino-India War in 1962 (Schermerhorn 1978).[12]

Acculturation produces many models of Chinese culture. If we ignore the diversity among the local Chinese customs and traditions brought along by the early migrants to different parts of the globe and regard them as a common theme, then various adjustments on the part of the Chinese to different dominant cultures may be seen to have produced many versions of this underlying socio-cultural theme. All such versions still reflect some common features of this underlying theme, difficult to describe though it may be. Although stressing their respective local identities, the people of Chinese descent understandably are still curious about this common underlying theme, its place of origin, and their own local 'roots'. This should not be held against them, nor should their political loyalty be questioned because of their interest and curiosity. As Ip (1990, 201) points out, China is no longer the motherland and home of Chinese overseas; it has become 'the place where overseas Chinese would pay occasional visits to in order to keep in touch with their ethnic-cultural roots'.

Overall, the ethnic Chinese all over the world are really different communities, each shaped by different forces of change and by diverse responses. They are products of different models of Chinese ethnicity that have evolved, and they belong to different nationalities. Even transnational Chinese in fact reside in countries of their choice, and given time, their descendants will experience localization and acquire local identities. Acculturation is a historical process, and it is not so relevant to ask a migrant of the first generation whether he or she has acquired a local identity or to choose one over another. In fact, most ethnic Chinese are rooted in a particular country or region even if they have acquired more than one nationality. In theory, one may choose not to identify as an ethnic person but as a member of a larger society, such as Indonesian or American. In practice, as Ien Ang (1993) has experienced, others may not think so. She was born a Chinese in Indonesia and became a localized Chinese. Even though she did not want to be Chinese, she was nevertheless treated as one. Thus Chineseness was an imposed identity for her. After living in Holland and trying to identify with the new nationality, people in Europe found it difficult to believe that she was 'Dutch'. When she told them that she was Dutch, they would ask, 'No, where are you *really* from?' (Ang 1993, 9). Thus she felt 'the inescapability of my own Chineseness, inscribed as it was on the very surface of my body' (Ang 1993, 8).

On the whole, individuals negotiate their identities, and their localization experience forms an important part of that negotiation. The more localized they are, the more they have to negotiate their identity.

'Who am I?' and 'To be or not to be Chinese' are often questions asked by such highly localized Chinese, as Ang (2000), Giese (1997) and Shen (2001) have shown in Australian-born Chinese. Being Chinese of a particular type or not being Chinese is also influenced by the attitudes of others. However, most people of Chinese descent who are not products of intermarriage have remained Chinese. It is in situations of discrimination or when being Chinese is a stigma that there may be individuals who choose to reject their Chinese identity, whereas others eventually learn to accept their Chinese status and not feel ashamed of it. There are many accounts in North America about first-generation local-born Chinese American or Canadian students going through a stage of trying to reject their Chinese and minority status in order to be accepted as equal with the white majority. But as they grow up, they learn to accept their Americanized or Canadianized (i.e., localized) Chinese status (*see* for instance the video *Mah Jong Orphan* 1995).

Indeed it is essential that minorities feel proud of their own identities; otherwise, there will be an identity crisis. This is so, too, for the highly localized Chinese. If they feel ashamed of their acculturated Chinese identity, they will have an inferiority complex in relation to the so-called 'pure' Chinese. Individuals will feel the need to mask or leave that status or try to merge with the mainstream Chinese or even try not to be a Chinese, by identifying with the larger national identity. But it is not always possible to do so. Some Chinese American exchange students talked to me about their experience in Hong Kong. They said that in the US they had taken their Chinese American identity for granted, but their encounter with Chinese people and culture in Hong Kong made them feel culturally not Chinese enough or so they were told. In my opinion, the best way to deal with this situation is to understand that there is no fixed Chinese cultural identity. One can be Chinese but can express that identity culturally in different ways, depending on one's socialization and localization experience. People may identify ethnically as Chinese, but there are different types of cultural Chinese. All are Chinese to the extent that they identify as Chinese. Understanding that there are different ways of being Chinese, often a result of diverse localization, helps to understand one's own 'hybridized' status, and one need not accept any fixed definition of Chineseness. In other words, Malay-speaking Babas and English-speaking Chinese Americans do not have to accept the expectation that Chinese should be able to speak a Chinese language. In this way, as most Babas do, they can be Chinese in their own ways.

Instead of seeing acculturation as degrading, such as less Chinese in the case of culturally localized Chinese, one can see it as cultural enrichment, of Chinese incorporating local cultural features and recreating cultural identity. As a result of localization, ethnic Chinese are constantly reshaping their Chineseness. In cultural studies, hybridity has become a common term to describe cultures in the globalizing world. But there is no pure unmixed culture in the first place, as all first-year anthropology students learn. There is always intercultural influence, and globalization intensifies it and makes it more marked. Thus as far as possible, I refrain from adopting the term 'hybridity', despite its popularity. Localization in the form of acculturation brings about very overt cultural change, causing the less localized to see the highly localized as less normal. This creates much space for the politics of identity. Chinese overseas, especially those who do not speak any Chinese language, have to reconcile with their Chineseness. Even the realization that one is an ethnic Chinese who 'did not (does not) have to be so Chinese' (Shang 2001, 199) helps. There are many types of Chinese and there are many ways of being Chinese. The alternative is to give up being Chinese, but this is by no means an easy choice, as Ang (1993) has experienced.

3

Chinese Migration, Localization and the Production of Baba Culture

INTRODUCTION

In this chapter, I use the case of the Baba of Melaka, Malaysia, to examine more closely the production of culture. In the discussion on acculturation in Chapter 2, we paid attention to the major economic and political factors in the larger society that influenced cultural change and ethnic identification. However, the localization of ethnic Chinese does not mean that they are passively being localized. This chapter emphasizes individuals as active agents in reproducing and reinventing culture. My research interest on the Baba began in 1977, when I carried out a year of fieldwork in Melaka. I have continued to visit some of my Baba friends in rural and urban Melaka since then. Briefly, we may describe the Baba as Malay-speaking Chinese who identify themselves as both 'Baba' and 'Peranakan', that is, Chinese 'Peranakan'. Of course in multi-ethnic Melaka, where the majority of Chinese are Hokkien (descendants of Chinese from southern Fujian in China), some Babas can speak Hokkien, too. Their literate language has been English since colonial times, but today the younger generation of Baba is educated in Bahasa Malaysia, the national Malay language. At home, the Baba-style of Malay, called Baba Malay, is the preferred language, and many older women speak Baba Malay only. The Baba of Melaka are similar to the Chinese Peranakan of Indonesia, but there are differences because of the different colonial past and regional cultural differences. In the past, the educated Chinese Peranakans in Indonesia could speak Dutch (and some older people still do) but not those in Melaka, whereas many Chinese Peranakans in Central Java speak Javanese among themselves.[1]

The Babas of Singapore are closer to those in Melaka, especially before the independence of Malaya (now Peninsular Malaysia) in 1957, since many were migrants from Melaka. However, there are many changes today that we have to bear in mind when we discuss Melaka and Singapore Baba. For example, many Babas in Singapore are Christians, whereas in Melaka most Babas still observe ancestor worship, pray to Chinese deities and observe Chinese religious rites. There is still a recognizable community of Babas in Melaka, maintained by an intensive kin network throughout Melaka; in Singapore the community is not so distinct, although there are pockets of Baba concentrations. English is the dominant language in Singapore, and many younger people who claim to be Baba speak little Baba Malay. It is therefore not surprising that there are more attempts at staging 'Baba culture' (such as organizing Baba dramas) in Singapore.[2]

In Penang, the label Baba was very common during the colonial period. Indeed, the label was common throughout the Straits Settlements, the British colony comprising Penang, Singapore and Melaka. However, the Babas of Penang were not the same as those in Melaka and Singapore who identified themselves as 'Peranakan' and still do. The Penang Baba spoke a localized version of Hokkien, which today is popularly referred to as Penang Hokkien. Except for the Chinese Peranakans who migrated from such places as Sumatra and Melaka, the Penang Baba did not use Malay as their home language. Today, few people in Penang regularly identify themselves as Baba. However, since the 1980s, under the leadership of Datuk Khoo Keat Siew, the State Chinese (Penang) Association (formerly the Penang branch of the Straits Chinese British Association) has been cooperating with the Baba associations in Melaka and Singapore to promote cultural activities. Even the label 'Peranakan' has appeared in the name of the association in Malay, i.e., Persatuan Peranakan Cina Pulau Pinang (Tan 1993, 31), despite the fact that the 'Babas' of Penang (except the Malay-speaking ones) do not identify themselves as 'Peranakan'.[3]

Thus the label Baba has different uses with variant meanings in different periods (Tan 1993, Chapter 2; Rudolph 1998). During the colonial period, the label was used in the Straits Settlement to refer to the local-born Chinese (i.e., Straits-born Chinese) in contrast to the China-born immigrants. The Straits-born Chinese had acquired some local and non-Chinese cultural characteristics (such as the consumption of local food, the adoption of Western male attire, speaking Malay etc.), which distinguished them from the new immigrants. Today, the term 'Babas' is also used loosely and derogatorily by the mainstream non-Baba Chinese to refer to those Chinese who cannot speak any Chinese languages, including the English speakers.

However, the 'Babas' of Melaka is an ethnic label, recognized by both the Baba themselves and other Malaysians. Indeed, the Baba of Melaka have become a distinct speech community among the Chinese and may be described as a sub-ethnic group. Since the Baba also identify themselves with such Chinese speech groups as Hokkien, Khek (i.e., Hakka), Teochiu and so on, it is confusing to describe them as another speech group. The majority of the Babas are Hokkien, and thus it is common to come across some Hokkien Babas who claim, ethnocentrically, that only Hokkien Babas are true Babas. Despite the diverse speech-group identification, the Babas generally share certain cultural features that are based on the localization of Hokkien cultural forms. For example, the words borrowed from Chinese in Baba Malay are largely of Hokkien origin, and the Cantonese and Hakka Babas also observe the Hokkien worship of Tī-Kong (God of Heaven) on the ninth day of the Chinese New Year.

The production of Baba culture was brought about by the early migration of Chinese, mainly of southern Fujian origin, to Southeast Asia, and in our case, to Melaka. It is a product of cultural interaction between Chinese and Southeast Asian cultures, especially between Chinese and Malays. Anthropologists have been aware of the phenomena of acculturation and assimilation for a long time (Teske and Nelson 1974), but in this chapter I prefer to discuss localization and production of culture. We will thus examine the continuity and transformation of

Chinese culture. We shall pay attention to not only the forces that have brought about such changes but also to the agents that have played crucial roles in the production of new cultural forms. Although it is convenient to talk about the acculturation of the Baba, it is misleading to say that the Baba are acculturated by the Malays; it is really Baba individuals who experience, select and invent cultural forms, which both the Baba and observers now perceive as 'Babas'.

In studying Baba ethnicity, my approach in 1977 was to see which people identified themselves as 'Baba' and were known to other Babas and their non-Baba neighbors and friends as such. I then examined how the Baba perceived their Baba identity and how they essentialized their culture to project Baba identities. For example, both the Baba and non-Baba Malaysians were conscious of the Babas' use of Baba Malay that made them a distinct category of Chinese, since the mainstream non-Baba Chinese generally did not speak Malay among themselves. The non-Baba Chinese generally used this cultural feature to discredit the Baba as Chinese. However, the Babas also emphasized the practice of 'traditional' Chinese religious rites. Hence my first book on the culture and identity of the Baba emphasizes the need to examine both acculturation (a term I used then) and cultural persistence, as represented by Baba Malay and the persistence of Chinese traditions. This approach of studying identity does not mean that we see the Baba identity as static, for the perception of 'Baba' and its cultural expression of course changes through time and space. There have been variations in the cultural expression of Baba identity in the past and today. Similarly today, the expressions of Baba identity in Melaka and Singapore are different, due to different historical processes and developments in national societies. However, in studying contemporary cultural identities, it is useful and convenient to first identify the people through their own self-identification and then proceed to see how they use cultural features or other means to portray their identity. To this day, the Babas in Melaka still see language (Baba Malay) and Chinese rites as important components of their cultural identities. In this chapter, I discuss the production of Baba culture by examining some of its features.

In Chapter 1, I made a distinction between cultural identity and ethnic identification. In the approach outlined above, the Baba may continue to identify themselves as Baba, but cultural expressions vary through time and space. Thus both Baba and non-Baba Chinese identify themselves as Chinese Malaysians (ethnic identification), but they have different cultural expressions, that is, different cultural identities. The Baba identification is rooted in a distinct local identity. Thus, Babas take their Chinese ethnic identity for granted without having to specify that they are Chinese, as the label Baba already assumes a local Chinese identity. The Malay label *Cina* means 'Chinese', but the Baba generally use that to refer to the non-Baba Chinese; depending on the tone, it can be used rather derogatorily. The distinction of cultural identity and ethnic identity is important to the study of migration and identity. For example, the descendants of the Chinese immigrants in Malaysia and the Philippines may identify themselves as 'Chinese', but they have different Chinese cultural identities. Of course the perception of ethnic identity is also very much influenced by the experience of cultural identity.

In the study of ethnic Chinese who are the descendants of immigrants from China, the adaptation approach is obviously useful for seeing how the Chinese have adapted to different societies and how they have become localized. Scholars (including me) who have used this approach generally have not paid sufficient attention to the active roles of individuals in the reproduction and production of culture. As I continue to think about localization and cultural change, especially in my recent analysis of cultural change and identity through studying food (Tan 1996), I have been drawn to individuals' interpretation of cultural rules. There is the need to combine the adaptation approach with the agency perspective, to take into account human agency in cultural adaptation. I have seen culture according to cultural principles that guide human behavior (Tan 1988c), although for convenience I also use 'culture' to refer loosely to the overall way of life of a people, such as 'Baba culture'. The more persistent cultural principles that give the impression of a persistent style may be called tradition (Tan 1999).

This presentation provides an opportunity for me to outline my thoughts on culture and agency. Both Bourdieu (1977) in his concern with 'strategy' and Giddens (1984) in his analysis of 'structuration' have contributed much to our understanding of the active roles of individuals in the reproduction, genesis, reinterpretation and transmission of cultural rules. My own inspiration has also come from the analysis of the production of Baba food, which has led me to think again about Geertz's (1973, 4) interesting comparison of culture and recipes as a set of control mechanisms that govern behavior. To say that culture governs behavior is too deterministic. However, if we introduce the idea of agency, culture can be compared to recipes that guide rather than govern behavior. The final cultural expression is the outcome mediated by individuals who can decide to follow the recipes exactly, modify them slightly, or add or reduce some ingredients here and there. The final product, while influenced by the preexisting recipe, is unique. Different people have different cooking skills, and food produced from the same recipe may taste different in each instance. At the same time, even if there is a variation in the final cultural expression, there is in fact continuity in transformation. Cultural expression is adapted, the product of one or more cultural principles mediated and practiced by individuals. Over time, a recipe may be so transformed that a new recipe is produced. Individuals exist in a social environment; thus there is the need to see cultural production from an adaptation perspective. Our analysis of food allows us to see culture according to cultural principles mediated by individuals in an environment; hence the need to combine the adaptation approach and the agency perspective in cultural analysis.

PRODUCTION OF CULTURE BY ADOPTION: BABA MALAY AND BABA CULTURAL IDENTITY

Baba Malay as a language of the Baba is an example of the local production of culture through the adoption and development of a local Malay lingua franca. It is a Malay-based Creole developed by the early Chinese immigrants and their local-born descendants. I shall not describe the features of Baba Malay, as these have been described elsewhere

(Tan 1980; Pakir 1986; Gwee 1993). Suffice it to say that the Malay Creole grew out of the cultural adaptation of early Chinese immigrants to the Malay dominant cultural environment in Melaka. Indeed, the early Chinese immigrants had first to adapt by learning either a local language or the local lingua franca, in order to interact with the local people, especially for trading purposes. Baba Malay was developed by the early Chinese immigrants from the local bazaar Malay, the colloquial Malay, which served as the Malay lingua franca in the Malay Archipelago. Thus Baba Malay contains the colloquial structure of the Malay language, marked by the less frequent use of prefixes and suffixes.

Many words are borrowed from Chinese, mainly Hokkien, such as the Hokkien *lu* and *gua* for 'you' and 'I', as well as some Chinese-style expressions. As the Chinese follow the patrilineal principle of descent, unlike Malays who observe cognatic descent, many Hokkien kin terms are retained in Baba Malay to express the Chinese classification of kin, such as *m-peh* for FeB (father's elder brother) and *ng-ku* for MB (mother's brother); both are *pacik* in Malay kinship terminology, which does not distinguish patrilateral and matrilateral uncles. Similarly, Baba Malay contains many Chinese religious terms not available in Malay.

The earliest Chinese immigrants to Southeast Asia must have been traders; the earliest known ancestors of the Baba were traders. For example, I have worked out the family history of a Cheong Baba family in Melaka, tracing to the first ancestor who went to Melaka in the 18th century (Tan 1988a, 96; Tan 1993, 20). He was a trader, so was the first ancestor of the famous Tan Cheng Lock family (Mabbett 1976; Tan 1988a, 96). In the 19th century, the dominant Chinese merchants in the Straits Settlements were Baba, as is evident in Song's (1923) description of the Baba in 19th-century Singapore. The need of the early Chinese immigrants to use Malay was obvious; otherwise, how could they communicate with the local people? In fact, the Chinese were the first to compile a Malay dictionary, in the 15th century (cf. Asmah Haji Omar 1987, 3; Liang 1996, 99–111). To give an example, in 1877, Lin Hengnan published a Malay dictionary entitled *Tong Yi Xinyu* (Chinese-Malay New Words), written in Chinese (Tan 1993, 37).

How did Malay become the language of the Baba? Chinese immigrants to different parts of the world learned to speak at least some local languages, but most did not give up their original language. The Chinese language may be localized by the incorporation of non-Chinese loan words, and the local languages might have Chinese influences. Most Chinese communities have managed to retain their Chinese language, albeit localized in various ways. To understand the use of Malay as an intra-group language among the Babas, one has to note the intermarriage theory. Scholars such as Tan (1988), Skinner (1996, 52) and Rudolph (1998) agree that the earliest Chinese immigrants married Southeast Asian women, such as Malays and Balinese, as no Chinese women were available. The earliest Chinese immigrants were men, so intermarriage must have been important in the 18th, 19th and early 20th centuries — the history of existing families in Melaka can be traced to the 18th century. In time, the local-born Chinese women (called *nyonya*) of such intermarriages became available. The *nyonya* were in high demand as wives by both the local Chinese men and the China-born immigrants. With the increase of Chinese migration in the 19th century, the local Chinese were able to find Chinese husbands for their daughters. In fact, when I began my research in 1977, some older Babas still knew of their grandparents and parents *beli kiā-sai*, 'buying sons-in-law' (see Chapter 4). This also contributed to the development of matrilocal marriage among the Baba.

The migration of Chinese women to the Straits Settlement began only in the mid-19th century (Lim 1967, 66). It is thus obvious that before then, especially in the 18th century, those Chinese settlers who married had to marry local non-Chinese women, and even up until the mid-19th century, many poorer ones could not find a wife (Siah 1848, 284). This early intermarriage with non-Chinese explains how the Chinese language was lost so easily and explains the creation of the crucial Baba identity as Malay-speaking. Chinese husbands had to speak Malay to their wives; children, who spent more time with women and interacting in the then predominantly Malay-speaking environment of Melaka, grew up to speak Malay naturally. This was accurately described by Newbold (1839, 172):

'... The colonists (the Chinese) are constrained to intermarry with the people, among whom they settle; in the Straits generally with Malays and with their descendants, consequently the Malay language is the one commonly spoken in their houses, and becomes the vernacular of their children, to whom the later acquirement of Chinese must become a matter of time and difficulty.'

This easy adoption of Malay in one or two generations could still be observed when I began my research in 1977. In Bukit Rambai Village, where I stayed for a year to conduct my research, I knew very well two non-Baba Chinese, an older man and a young man, who married Baba women (*nyonya*) and lived matrilocally. The young man married the older man's daughter. Both of these non-Baba Chinese spoke Baba Malay in the family, as their wives spoke only Baba Malay. In the dominant Baba environment (the family and the network of Baba kin), the young man's children spoke Baba Malay, too.

Thus we have a scenario of local-born Chinese people speaking Malay and acquiring other very localized features such as food and Malay-style dress, even before the people called themselves Baba. In other words, the perceived Baba culture was developed before the existence of the Baba (ethnic) identity. It is not possible to pinpoint when the Baba became a conscious distinct community. The term became popular in the 19th-century Straits Settlement to refer to local-born Chinese (having local cultural characteristics) in contrast to China-born immigrants (Tan 1988a, 45). Although the term was used generally to refer to Straits-born Chinese, those in Melaka and Singapore (the early generations of Babas in Singapore were mostly migrants from Melaka) became a distinct Chinese community. However, the Babas did not all originate from a common period. From the very early Chinese settlement in Melaka, we note that a Chinese family could comprise a China-born father who spoke and wrote Chinese, a *nyonya* who spoke only Malay, and children who might or might not speak Chinese. Thus if we take the present people who consider themselves Baba, families became Baba at different stages. The history of the Baba as a distinct community might not be as long as generally assumed or claimed, for in the early period, the label was used in the general sense as a contrast with the China-born immigrants rather than as one used by a self-conscious ethnic community.

We have seen how Malay became the home language of the Baba, but the Baba have remained Chinese who follow certain Chinese traditions. Thus individuals made adjustments so that the Malay adopted could also express Chinese traditions; hence the formation of the Baba Malay which contains words borrowed from Chinese and expressions of Chinese kinship and religious views.

THE CIRCUMSTANTIAL PRODUCTION OF LOCAL CULTURE: BABA MATRILOCAL RESIDENCE

The early Chinese immigrants (men) obviously tried to ensure the continuity of the Chinese as a community. Although men might marry local non-Chinese women, they did not allow their daughters to marry non-Chinese. As the well-known Straits Chinese Dr Lim Boon Keng (1917, 876) wrote, 'The female children of Chinese fathers were never permitted to marry the natives of the country'. Chinese immigrants in other lands also generally practiced this norm of not allowing their daughters to marry non-Chinese. Lai (1985, 48) writes about Wong Aloiau, the 19th-century Chinese immigrant in Hawaii, who insisted that his daughters marry Chinese men. When it was pointed out that he himself had married a Hawaiian-German, he said, 'That's different. When Emma married me, she took my name and became Chinese. Now, when you marry a foreign devil, you take his name and become a foreign devil, yourself.' That was the attitude of the early Chinese immigrants. This reluctance to allow their daughters to marry non-Chinese, although the men could intermarry with non-Chinese and bring them into the Chinese community, helped to establish a local Chinese community. For Melaka, it caused the formation of a people called Baba.

Since the 'Baba' daughters were not allowed to marry non-Chinese, they had to depend on the local-born Chinese immigrants for husbands. When Chinese immigration increased in the 19th century, the *nyonya* could also marry China-born men. After the formation of a distinct Baba community, the preference for marrying within the community due to linguistic consideration resulted in an intensive kin network. I was still able to observe this practice in 1977. Many Babas married relatives as long as they were not patrilateral relatives. I have discussed elsewhere (Tan 1984) the effects of this on the maintenance of the Baba identity and the socialization of children to become Baba.

The Chinese immigrants observed the patrilineal principle of descent, and surnames were passed down patrilineally, from father to son. Nevertheless, individuals in practice may modify or reinterpret cultural rules. Until about the Second World War, in addition to the usual Chinese principle of patrilocal residence, the Baba practiced matrilocal marriage. Other writers such as Minchin (1870) and Freedman (1962) also reported this. My description of the Baba selecting China-born immigrants as sons-in-law explains the origin of this new cultural practice. The less established immigrants had a good incentive to marry into the more established Baba families. Furthermore, up to the first part of the 20th century, most of the successful merchants in the Straits Settlements were Baba. The élite Babas could also insist that their Baba sons-in-law married matrilocally, at least at the initial stage of marriage. However, the surname was passed down patrilineally, even if a man continued to stay in his wife's residence.

Thus the matrilocal residence rule at the time of marriage became accepted as a Baba practice, alongside patrilocal residence. We do not know how widely practiced it was, but during my research in 1977, I found that older Baba informants talked of matrilocal marriage as if it were common practice in the past. I was told that representatives of both families involved in a marriage would agree on the residence before the marriage took place. Thus both patrilocal and matrilocal residences were acceptable, but the choice would depend on mutual agreement, and of course family status.

With the decline of the Baba community, certainly since the Second World War, the Baba ceased to practice matrilocal marriage, following the patrilocal rule of the mainstream non-Baba Chinese whom many

Babas now marry. However, in the 'old-fashioned marriage' (*kahwin dolu-kala*), which a few Baba families still practiced in 1977 and some do to this day, the bride is brought over to the groom's house on the eve of wedding while the groom leaves his own house temporarily. On the wedding day, the groom goes to his own house, where the bride now resides, as if to marry matrilocally. Most Baba weddings, like those of other Chinese, are now conducted in the modern fashion, the groom wearing a Western suit and the bride a white gown. At an old-fashioned wedding, an attempt is made to imitate the past Chinese-style wedding (perceived by the Baba as a Baba wedding), which involved wearing traditional Chinese wedding attire and conducting tedious Chinese religious rites.

The discussion here shows that migration and local settlement led to the development of a new cultural practice, made possible by the new political economy that allowed wife-givers a bigger say in the marriage residence. The traditional patrilocal residence rule was not discarded; instead, matrilocal residence was accepted, too. The shortage of Chinese women and the economic status of Baba families made it possible for the reinterpretation of a cultural rule to produce a new cultural practice. After Chinese women became easily available, and the Babas had lost their economic dominance, the traditional rule was fully observed again. This also shows the importance of relating adaptation and agency to political economy.

CULTURAL PERSISTENCE AND REPRODUCTION OF CULTURE

Outside observers tend to see more of the localized aspects of Baba culture. In fact, much continuity of Chinese cultural principles exists in Baba culture. There is continuity in transformation, mediated and reproduced by Baba individuals, albeit in localized forms. Cultural rules are not imposed or followed blindly. Individuals negotiate rules for practical situations that depend on the environment. However, most of the time they perpetuate rules that accord to their experience of socialization. For example, through participation in worshipping deities and ancestors, Baba individuals learn that the number of joss sticks offered to deities must be odd (such as one or three), and ancestors must be offered an even number. Not all Babas know why this should be so, but it conforms to the general Chinese practice, which is guided by the Chinese *yin-yang* principle; an odd number is *yang* and an even number is *yin*. Youngsters learn this when they are asked to pray at home and in the temple. In normal circumstances the known cultural principles are followed, but there may be consultation when one is not sure; when a 'mistake' is made, this may be pointed out by others and corrected. This is how certain traditions are perpetuated with very few changes.

I have often observed this mutual consultation or correction when family members (including married sisters who have returned specially) perform religious rites. For example, an important item of offering at major rites is the trinity of offerings called *sam-seng* (*sansheng* in Mandarin). This is the tray or plate of offerings comprising a piece of blanched pork or pig's leg, flanked by blanched whole chicken and duck. There was often discussion among individuals, especially less experienced ones, about whether the duck should be on the left or right; usually a more knowledgeable one would point out that it should be on stage left, which is ritually superior to stage right. When worshipping ancestors, the *sam-seng* is arranged to face the altars; that is, the heads of the chicken and duck face the altars. In Baba families, the statues of deities are generally installed in the living room facing the main entrance. When worshipping deities, the *sam-seng* is arranged to face this entrance rather than the deities' altars. Knowledgeable Babas would point this out to the less experienced who may have arranged their offering 'wrongly'. I was not aware of this even after observing a number of rites, until one day an old Baba kindly pointed it out.

The point is that cultural rules are not passed down blindly; they are consciously observed and debated as the situation occurs. Nevertheless, there is an attempt to follow tradition. When circumstances make it difficult to follow closely, rules may be negotiated. For instance, the Babas and indeed other Chinese Malaysians who worship deities at home, would have installed a small altar on the stage left side of the wall or post (if any) on the front verandah of the house. This is the altar for the Heavenly Official (*Tianguan* in Mandarin). To begin domestic worship, one holds the lit joss sticks while standing on the verandah, facing skyward, and prays to the God of Heaven. Either one or three joss sticks are then placed at the small altar on the left side of the wall, after which one goes into the house to pray at the various altars of the deities and ancestors. In a terraced house, the neighbors on the stage left side may be a Muslim family, and it would not then be appropriate to place the Heavenly Official's altar on that side; therefore, some families would install the altar on the wall on the stage right side. This is an example of how a cultural rule is adjusted to the needs of multi-ethnic and multi-religious living in Malaysia.

Individual Babas perpetuate Baba culture through their practice in daily life and in ritual participation. In fact, both cultural continuity and transformation are expressed. Certain agents are crucial in perpetuating Chinese cultural traditions, which the Babas in their consciousness think of as Baba. Baba parents play crucial roles in the socialization of children to observe traditions. Even at the time of an impending wedding, there is often a struggle of opinion between parents and the son who is to be married over the style and details of wedding. Parents may insist on holding an old-fashioned wedding, but the son may want a simple modern one. The final outcome may be a compromise, such as only part of the wedding is conducted in the old-fashioned style. Nevertheless, even if the modern style of wearing a Western suit and a wedding gown is adopted, certain traditions such as the ritual offering of tea to parents and relatives are retained.

In wedding and funeral rites, specialists play important roles of perpetuating as well as interpreting traditions. Even the mainstream non-Baba Chinese depend on funeral specialists such as Daoist priests, monks and specialists from a funeral home to direct the performance of rites. There are always knowledgeable older people (sometimes even younger ones) who can advise or who are more than willing to suggest what to

do and which practice is proper. In the course of my research on the
Baba, I have observed lots of discussion, consultation and debate on
the 'proper' practice of culture. Anthropologists, in their eagerness to
describe the ethnography of a cultural practice, often write about the
final outcome but neglect the process of practicing a tradition, which
involves the mediation of individuals. In this process, a cultural principle
is interpreted, reinterpreted or modified. Even the perpetuation of a
cultural practice is never practiced as it was in the past: Only the
underlying principle is observed or considered. For example, my Baba
informants said that one should use the kind of banana called *pisang
raja* when making offerings at certain religious rites. The significance
lies in the Malay word *raja*, meaning 'king', or *ong* in Hokkien, which is
homonymous with the word for prosperity. In practice, I found that if
on the day of worship one did not have *pisang raja*, other kinds of banana
were used instead. This does not mean that the individuals concerned
had rejected the rule of using *pisang raja*; they were guided by the rule
but had for practical reasons made an adjustment on that occasion. Of
course, in the long run, constant reinterpretation and non-practice may
lead to the change of a cultural rule.

In fact, because of the needs of individuals to adapt to the changing
'modern' situation, some cultural rules are either reinterpreted or even
phased out through non-practice. For example, after the actual wedding,
the Baba bridal couple, like the Hokkien in general, has to pay a ritual
visit to the bride's family. In the past this used to take place on the third
day, but nowadays it happens on the wedding day, in the afternoon
before the evening wedding banquet. On returning to the groom's house
(on the same day of course), the bride's parents give the bridal couple,
among other things, a cock and a hen. On reaching the groom's house,
tradition says that the chickens should be released under the bridal bed
to see which one emerges first. If the cock comes out first, the first child
will be a boy, if the hen, a girl. When one interviews knowledgeable
Baba individuals, one is told of this tradition. In practice, most people
do not release the chicken under the bed any more, as they do not want

the chicken to defecate on the floor. Furthermore, many modern beds do not have a space underneath. Thus, even in 1977 I observed the change in this custom. To this day, if a Baba were asked about this practice, he or she would most likely describe the ritual release of chickens under the bridal bed. This was a common Hokkien practice, but today not all Hokkiens actually release them under the bridal bed. Thus the ritual gift of a chicken by the bride's parent has become just another gift, and in future it may even be phased out. Here is an example of the need to view both adaptation and agency of individuals in order to understand the production as well as the discontinuation of culture.

On the whole, we see that the production of Baba culture from the early days of Chinese immigration to Melaka has resulted in two interesting and contrasting dimensions: speaking Baba Malay and practicing Chinese rites, both of which are perceived by the Baba as 'Baba'. We can argue that the loss of the Chinese language resulted in the Melaka Baba stressing Chinese customs and rites. Indeed, among the Peranakan-type Chinese in Kelantan and Terengganu, Malaysia, there is a strong emphasis on displaying Chinese symbolism. The Peranakan-type Chinese do not call themselves 'Baba' or 'Peranakan', but they are so localized that they are culturally very much like the Chinese Peranakan of Melaka; hence the label Peranakan-type Chinese.[4] Like the Baba, the Peranakan-type Chinese are more serious than the non-Baba Chinese about putting up Chinese couplets called *lian* on their front doors and window shutters.

During my research among the Babas of Melaka, I was often asked by my friends to explain the meaning of the Chinese characters displayed on their doors. The *lian* symbolize Chinese identity and it does not matter if the occupants of the house do not read Chinese. This is especially important in Terengganu, where the outward appearance of a Peranakan-type Chinese house may not be very different from that of a Malay house; the Chinese couplets show that it is a Chinese house. The perpetuation of a Chinese tradition here has special symbolic significance to the local Chinese.

THE METAPHOR OF FOOD

In this last section before the conclusion, I discuss Baba food to further illustrate cultural principles, agency and cultural production, and reproduction. In a way, Baba food reflects general Baba cultural identity, which contains both the very localized components and 'traditional' Chinese culture. To many non-Baba Chinese, Baba food is Malay-like, characterized by much use of chili; to the Baba, it is distinctively Baba, not the same as non-Baba Chinese food, nor is it Malay. Indeed, the marketing and tourist promotion of Baba food, especially in Singapore, has made the Babas even more conscious of the uniqueness of their food. It is one cultural feature that generally all Babas feel proud of as their tradition, irrespective of their religious background. My Baba informants often talk of their food as special, in anthropological language, a crucial component of Baba cultural identity.

In Malaysia and Singapore, Baba food is often referred to as *Nyonya* food, emphasizing the female contribution to the development of its cuisine. Indeed, the production of the delicious Baba food is connected with the patriarchal emphasis in the past that women should stay at home and learn to cook. My older informants experienced this kind of patriarchal culture when they were younger, and it must have been even stricter earlier in the century. The *bibi* (address for older *nyonya*) often mentioned that in the old days, by listening to the way a woman pounded chili, an experienced observer would know if she was a good cook and would be a good daughter-in-law. Pounding chili was an art that required patience to produce fine paste.

Baba food is produced by the combined use of both Chinese and local non-Chinese (mainly Malay) principles of cooking. It is a reflection of the local Chinese adapting to the local environment to produce a new food culture. There is much use of food ingredients that were and still are available in the multi-ethnic environment of Southeast Asia. There is, for example, much use of candle nuts (*buah keras*), coriander seeds (*ketumbar*), galangal root (*lengkuas*), *kesum* (*Polygonum minus Huds*) leaves, lemon grass (*serai*), lime leaves (*daun limau perut*), tumeric roots and leaves (*kunyit*), tamarind pulp (*asam jawa*) and others, which make Baba food quite different from mainstream Chinese food. The Baba also use ingredients commonly used in Hokkien cooking, such as soy sauce, preserved soybean paste (*taucheo*), shallot, garlic, and of course ginger and others. Even these may be used in such a way as to create distinct Baba food. For example, much soybean paste is used in the preparation of the delicious chicken dish called *pongteh* and the fried noodles called *mi siam*. Although the non-Baba-Hokkien often use some shallots in their cooking, they, and for that matter Malays, would be shocked to learn that for a dish of *pongteh* using one chicken, around 30 shallots and two bulbs of garlic are used, peeled and ground separately.

A *nyonya* dish may be delicious to eat, but it requires much effort in the preparation of various ingredients. I did not understand why in the past the preparation of a Baba wedding feast was preceded by *kopeh bawang*, peeling shallots, until I actually observed and learned to cook some *nyonya* dishes. Much time is needed to peel many shallots and to pound them, as well as to pound chili and other ingredients. If there are Babas who complain that women nowadays do not cook such delicious food as their mothers and grandmothers did, it is not surprising, since the girls go to school and, when they are women, have careers outside the home. They do not have the time to learn to cook Baba food through the experience of trial and error, which is a process of creation. Many now depend on cookbooks.

However, the men contributed to the development of Baba food, too. At the early intermarriage period, the local non-Chinese women obviously introduced the local food that they were familiar with. But the men must have also cooked, to pass down the Chinese way of cooking. A description in Lai's account of Aloiau, the early immigrant to Hawaii, is most illuminating on the subject of Chinese migration and the cooking of Chinese food. Wong Aloiau married Emma, a half-white Hawaiian woman. There was the problem of adjustment in food habits. Emma preferred her fermented *poi*, whereas Aloiau preferred rice. 'He soon grew tired of her cooking methods, limited to boiling and occasional use of an *imu* (an underground oven). Before long he was at the *wok*, stir-frying vegetables from his garden with slices of chicken, beef or pork' (Lai 1985, 37). This must be a common experience of early immigrants who married indigenous women. Men's Chinese cooking and women's indigenous cooking formed the basis of the later development of a localized Chinese cuisine.

It is not useful to think of today's Baba food as a result of Chinese food culture acculturated or assimilated by the Malays. It is more enlightening to see it as the product of descendants of Chinese immigrants (now Baba) using knowledge of both Chinese and Southeast Asian food preparation, and in the process creating a new cuisine. Baba food is a product of adaptation in a multi-ethnic environment. Southeast Asian influences are not just confined to those from the Malays of Melaka but also from the Chitty (Malay-speaking localized Indians) with whom the Baba have much social interaction, the Portuguese Malaysians, Indians and others, as well as influences from Indonesian islands. The use of *buah keluak*, a kind of nut whose black seed is used in cooking, is of Indonesian origin, and one can expect an 'authentic' Baba restaurant to have dishes such as 'chicken cooked with *buah keluak*'.

Food is thus a useful metaphor for describing Baba culture. The production of Baba culture is very much like the production of its food. It involves individuals in the multi-ethnic environment of Melaka using knowledge of Chinese culture and of local indigenous cultures to produce a distinct local culture and identity.

Conclusion

Baba cultural identity is to be understood in a holistic perspective. Non-Baba Chinese who want to emphasize the non-Chinese aspect of Baba identity emphasize the localized 'non-Chinese' aspects, whereas observers and the Baba themselves, who want to emphasize Chinese cultural continuity, emphasize the 'traditional' Chinese cultural features. Depending on the context of discourse, Baba individuals will emphasize different aspects of their cultural features to project their Baba cultural identity. Many Babas in Melaka still emphasize participating in Chinese religious rites as an important component of Baba identity, but this cannot be so in Singapore, where many Babas are Christians. As mentioned, Babas regard their food as a common Baba cultural feature. In fact, in Singapore where food is also promoted for tourism and Singapore identity, it approximates a national cuisine in a society where foods are ethnically based. I have shown that Baba food actually reflects Baba culture as a whole, comprising both the very localized aspects and the 'original' Chinese aspects; but as a whole it is really a local production of culture in a changing multi-ethnic environment.

Indeed, the production of Baba culture takes place in a changing multi-ethnic environment. Historically, Melaka has been a meeting point for diverse cultures. The early Chinese immigrants did not merely adapt to the local Malay society; they interacted with not only the local people but also with immigrants of different origins. For instance, the Indonesian influence is still evident in Baba Malay and in Baba food. Early intermarriage with Balinese and other women from Indonesian islands (cf. Abdullah 1970, 184), as well as subsequent interaction with people of these origins, must have contributed to the Indonesian influence in Baba culture. The terms of address *bibi* for older women (equivalent to auntie) and *wak* for older people are Indonesian in origin; *wak* is in fact a Javanese word. The use of *cangkir* rather than the usual local Malay usage of *cawan* for cup is another example of Indonesian linguistic influence. From the early days of the immigrants, the local-born Chinese descendants have been adapting to a very multi-ethnic environment, a point that one has to bear in mind when talking about localization and cultural innovation. We should also not forget that since the 19th century especially, the local-born Chinese have been exposed to Western cultural influences and have been receiving the effects of Western colonialism. Thus Baba cultures have been changing over time, and today, just like other people, they are also exposed to global cultural influences.

I have discussed the significance of individuals as agents in the production of culture. In the early days of immigrants, traders played important roles in the perpetuation and transformation of Chinese culture. Throughout the 19th and early 20th centuries, Baba business people and planters, i.e., the élite, were dominant players in the shaping of Baba culture and in fact in the formation of the Baba as a distinct Chinese community. To this day, the élite aspects of 'Baba' culture, as expressed in 'Baba' material culture such as silverware, porcelain and Chinese antique furniture, is still stressed by many Baba as part of their Baba heritage. It is this aspect of Baba culture that is most prominently displayed in museums in Kuala Lumpur and Singapore.

In fact, all ordinary Babas have played their part in the perpetuation and production of Baba culture. The roles of *nyonya*, Baba women, deserve special mention. From the very early period of intermarriage, women already played crucial roles in introducing the local non-Chinese cultural elements into the local Chinese community. The Chinese identity of early Chinese immigrants and the indigenous identity of the local women are reflected in Baba culture. As we have seen, the women wore Malay-style dress and the men wore Chinese-style dress, and élite Baba men also wore Western-style attire. Women also contributed to the socialization of children to speak Malay, and of course they contributed tremendously to the development of Baba food. Thus women, from the early non-Chinese women of the early immigration days to the later *nyonya*, have contributed much to the production of Baba culture.

This chapter discusses migration, agency and Baba identity, but the focus is on cultural reproduction and invention rather than on ethnic identity. To answer why the localized Chinese in Melaka, Singapore and Penang identified themselves separately as Baba but the localized Chinese elsewhere in the Malay Peninsula did not would require discussing the effect of the colonial political economy. The prominence of Baba business people in the 19th century and the roles of Baba compradors in the colonial economy, as well as the political recognition of Straits Chinese (mainly Babas) as a special category of Chinese, are important factors to be considered. Similarly, explaining the emergence of Chinese Peranakans in Indonesia, Malaysia and Singapore would require us to examine not just the cultural diversity between the Chinese and the indigenous people (such as non-Muslims versus Muslims), but more significantly the political and economic factors that encouraged the acculturated Chinese to become a separate category of Chinese. I have discussed this in Chapter 2.

Overall, the adaptation and agency approaches are useful for the study of Chinese overseas, especially the study of the production of local Chinese cultures. The experience of the Baba is actually quite common among Chinese overseas; it is only a matter of degree of localization. The loss of the Chinese language and the formation of a distinct Baba community were due to historical circumstances. Most localized descendants of Chinese immigrants have not formed as distinct a community as the Baba have. Also, the fact that the Baba speak Malay has received more attention than Chinese who speak English. This is a result of English being a prestigious language during the colonial era and today the world language. Thus people are surprised at Chinese-speaking Malay among themselves but not so surprised at Chinese Americans or Chinese Canadians or even Chinese Singaporeans speaking English. In the context of Malaysia, English has become an ethnically neutral language, so it is more acceptable than Malay as an intra-group language among the Chinese.

Lastly, the distinction of cultural identity from ethnic identity allows us to examine how Chinese people everywhere express their cultural identities. Even within a country, Chinese of different regions have different expressions of their respective cultural identities that reflect their adaptation to their respective social environments. This is not to say that cultural and ethnic identities are unrelated; they are. Perception of an ethnic identity is influenced by the kinds of cultural identity held. The Baba cultural identities affect how Baba and non-Baba perceive the Babas' Chinese ethnic identification. Among themselves, the Melaka Baba think of themselves as Baba or Peranakan, by which labels they identify themselves as localized Chinese. It is a localized ethnic identity that expresses changing localized cultural identities. It is a product of migration and localization.

4

Chinese Identities in Malaysia

INTRODUCTION

The Chinese comprise 28% of the citizens of Malaysia (Department of Statistics 1995, 39). They are a heterogeneous category of people. All of them identify themselves as 'Chinese' or *Huaren* in Mandarin (*Teng-lang* in Hokkien, *Tohngyahn* in Cantonese, etc.), but they also identify with their respective speech-groups such as Hokkien, Hakka, Cantonese, Teochiu, Hailam (Hainanese), Hokchiu, Kongsai, Henghua, Hockchia, and others. All of them bear the historical continuity of identities that are, however, transformed by their localization experience in Malaysia. In fact, some of them have become so culturally localized that they acquire new local Chinese identities.

This chapter describes the types of Chinese identity in Malaysia. Their identities reflect historical continuity as descendants of migrants from China and local transformation as a result of adaptation to living in Malaysian society. Anthropologists have debated on the relevance of culture to ethnic identification. The static view that ethnic identity is defined by cultural traits is now rejected. Since Barth's seminal paper (1969a), many have focused on ethnic boundary: how people organize themselves to form an ethnic group, i.e., how people categorize themselves and distinguish themselves from others. This approach has also given scope to the 'rational choice' theory of ethnicity (cf. Banton 1983). However, as I argue, in many instances, people are socialized to certain identities. My own research on the Baba, a Malay-speaking group of Chinese in Malaysia, shows that socialization is basic to identifying with an ethnic or a sub-ethnic group, although individuals are active in interpreting that identity and deciding when to emphasize or not to emphasize its public expression. In this chapter, I discuss Chinese identities in Malaysia and show the role of socialization in ethnic identification.

TYPES OF CHINESE MALAYSIAN IDENTITY

An ethnic identity has a history, and often the label is derived from a people's place of origin. The Chinese in Malaysia are descendants of migrants from different parts of China, especially Fujian and Guangdong, thus bearing the identities of Hokkien, Teochiu and so on. These are ethnic identifications, which, in the case of the Chinese in Southeast Asia, have nothing to do with identifying with China. It is like the Malays of Javanese origin still identifying as Javanese ethnically or, rather, sub-ethnically, but they are people of Malaysia rather than Indonesia. In China, a Cantonese and a Hakka belong to different ethnic categories, but in Malaysia, all Chinese see themselves as belonging to one ethnic group *vis-à-vis* the Malays and other Malaysians. The Cantonese and Hakka are usually described as 'dialect groups or speech-groups'.

The majority of the Chinese immigrants to Malaysia were from southern Fujian, and they identified themselves as Hokkien (i.e., Fujian people); hence, today, the word 'Hokkien' in Malaysia and other parts of Southeast Asia refers, in general, to Chinese whose forebears came from southern Fujian. Those whose forebears came from Xinghua and Fuzhou, farther north along the coast of Fujian, are known specifically as Henghua and Hockchiu in the Hokkien 'dialect'. The Hakka, also called Kheh, are the second largest category of Chinese in Malaysia. Their forebears came from Guangdong Province, though some of them originated from southwestern Fujian. Like the Hokkien, they are found all over Malaysia, but in Sabah, where they are in the majority among the Chinese, Hakka is widely spoken. 'Cantonese' is the English label for the 'Kongfu' people, whose ancestors came from around the region of Guangzhou (the capital city of Guangdong Province) and its rural surroundings. Their language has become the Chinese lingua franca in such urban centers as Kuala Lumpur, Ipoh, Kampar and Seremban. Teochiu, although linguistically belonging to the Min (Fujian) group, are descendants from that part of Guangdong around Shantou (Swatow). The Hainanese are, of course, descendants of people from Hainan Island in south China. There are some Kwongsai people whose forebears came from Guangxi Province. Not many Chinese migrants came from north China, although there are some Shanghainese and Shandong people in different towns in Malaysia. In Sabah, there is a community of Hebei people who originally came from Hebei Province in north China (Tan 1997a).

Thus, Chinese Malaysians still identify with their respective speech-groups and are linguistically rather diverse. However, they use Mandarin (locally called *Huayu*) as the common Chinese language; in Chinese education, the medium of instruction is Mandarin rather than a speech-group dialect. Chinese Malaysians are generally multilingual, speaking more than one Chinese dialect as well as Malay. Many can speak English, too. In the context of Malaysia, speech-group identities are in fact sub-ethnic identities rather than autonomous ethnic identities.

In addition, there is a unique sub-ethnic Chinese identity that is the product of cultural change as a result of long-term direct interaction with the indigenous people of Malaysia, especially Malays. These are the Baba, who are Malay-speaking, although many of them also speak English among themselves. Baba culture was originally formed as a result of early Chinese immigrants marrying local women and their offspring acquiring Malay as their mother tongue. It was a product of Chinese cultural localization. The adoption of some local lifestyles, such as the women wearing the Malay-style dress and the people eating both Chinese and Malay-style food as well as those they innovated locally, further distinguished the Baba from later immigrants. In the Straits Settlements (Melaka, Penang and Singapore) in the 19th century, Baba became a category of local-born Chinese, in contrast to Sinkheh, the new immigrants from China.

However, the Babas in Penang, although having acquired local cultural features (which include the wearing of sarongs by the women) continue to speak Hokkien, albeit a localized version. It was in Melaka and Singapore that there was a category of Malay-speaking Chinese who identified themselves as 'Peranakan' (i.e., Chinese Peranakan), as well as 'Baba'. To this day these Baba identify as 'Peranakan' and continue to see themselves as a separate and unique group of Chinese. Anyway, speaking Malay (although it is the Baba-style of Malay) distinguishes the Baba from the mainstream Chinese, who speak at least one Chinese dialect among themselves. Baba Melaka (i.e., Melaka Baba) today form a sub-ethnic category of Chinese; so do Singapore Baba. However, the Babas also identify with their respective Chinese speech-groups, and most of them are Hokkien who are proud of this identity and even a sub-ethnic identity such as 'Eng-Choon' (i.e., Hokkien of Yongchun origin). The Baba identity is a culturally localized Chinese identity.

LOCALIZATION, CULTURE AND PERCEPTION OF IDENTITIES

Although ethnic identification is subjective, identity is usually perceived through cultural expression. In this respect, different local cultural adaptation gives rise to different perceptions of local identities. Localization contributes to regional Chinese identities. The level of cultural localization, for example, forms a basis of distinguishing a more localized group of Chinese from the less localized ones. The Baba have become so localized that they have even acquired Malay as their mother tongue, replacing the original Hokkien language. In northeastern Kelantan and parts of rural Terengganu (such as Tirok), the Chinese have also become as culturally localized as the Baba, but they are influenced by the Malays of Kelantan and Terengganu. The Peranakan-type Chinese (to distinguish them from the Melaka Baba) of Kelantan speak Kelantan Malay fluently, and the young people often speak to each other in this language. Many can speak the local Thai, too. It is common for both men and women to wear sarongs, especially in the villages, and the men in the rural areas even put on the local Malay-style headdress called *semutar* (Tan 1982). To the mainstream, less localized Chinese, they are rather Malay-like. However, the Kelantan Peranakan-type Chinese do not call themselves Baba and, unlike the Baba, they still speak Hokkien but a kind which has been influenced by Kelantan Malay and the local Thai. It contains Kelantan Malay loanwords. The Peranakan-type Chinese in Terengganu are like those in Kelantan except that they are influenced by the Terengganu Malay dialect and are not much influenced by the Thai.

Of the more localized groups, only the Melaka Baba form a distinct sub-ethnic identity. The Peranakan-type Chinese of Kelantan and Terengganu merely identify themselves as *Teng-lang*, which is the Hokkien label for 'Chinese'; that is, they do not identify with a separate localized identity. Why do the Baba form a separate local Chinese identity? This has to do with the fact that during the 19th century, most of the business people in the Straits Settlements were Baba, and so they formed a prestigious class of local people. Losing their Chinese mother tongue and speaking only Malay (and later English) set them apart from the other Chinese. The immigrant Chinese and their Chinese-speaking descendants saw them as different; so did the Baba themselves. Thus, drastic cultural differentiation (there were Chinese who could not speak any Chinese language) and economic status led to the Baba forming a separate Chinese identity. This separate identity enabled the Baba to justify their not speaking any Chinese. The economic status of the Baba and their higher social status relative to the local population in the colonial society of the Straits Settlements must have distinguished them from other Chinese. In the case of the Peranakan-type Chinese of Kelantan, they did not lose their Hokkien language, but their class position of rural peasant background did not help them to establish a separate sub-ethnic category.

In contrast, the Baba of the Straits Settlements looked down upon the new Chinese immigrants, who had a low status background. In fact, the Baba called the immigrants *Cinageh* (pronounced cinagə), sort of like 'Chinamen' in the derogatory sense. To this day, the Baba, when they mean to be derogatory, call the culturally less localized mainstream

Chinese (non-Baba Chinese) *Cinageh*. This term may be related to the term *Pak Saga*, meaning 'Stingy Uncle', which some Baba used when referring to the China-born Chinese. In fact, my older Baba informants told me that until about World War II, established Baba families could 'buy' Chinese immigrants as indentured workers, who had to work for the families for a number of years. In Hokkien, this was called *bue Sinkheh*, or *beli kepala* (literally, 'bought heads') in Baba Malay. In my July 1997 visit to Melaka, a 72-year-old *nyonya* (Baba woman) compared the situation to the present employment of Indonesian maids and workers in Malaysia. Her father-in-law, who reared pigs, 'bought' a Chinese immigrant to help him. The low status of Chinese immigrants also explained why the established Baba families in the 19th and the pre-war 20th century were able to *beli kiā-sai* or 'buy sons-in-law'; that is, the China-born Chinese who wanted to marry a *nyonya* were asked to move in with the Baba family. Thus, matrilocal marriage became an acceptable practice among the Baba in the Straits Settlements (see Tan 1988a, 182). With the decline of the Baba communities after the war and especially after the independence of Malaya, the situation was reversed. Many Baba are now married into non-Baba Chinese families, and matrilocal marriage is no longer acceptable even among the Baba themselves. Today, the Baba are generally looked down upon by the non-Baba Chinese. Although in colonial days the China-born Chinese despised the Baba, too, for not speaking Chinese, the economically established Baba occupied a higher social status. Today, the mainstream Chinese, especially the cultural nationalist ones, regard the Baba as an example of what the Chinese should not be.

In Malaysia, the Chinese have always been free to speak their own languages, and mainly because of the large population of Chinese, it has not been the norm for the Chinese to speak Malay among themselves. This is why the Baba identity is not acceptable to the 'purist' Chinese. However, with the successful implementation of Malay as the national language, today Malay is spoken as an official language even among some younger Chinese, such as between a university lecturer and his or her students. However, speaking Malay and losing the Chinese language is a distinct contrast among the Chinese. Thus, the Baba have remained a separate category of Chinese. In Penang, the Chinese have acquired many local features, and the 'Penang Hokkien' dialect is a distinct Hokkien that contains quite a number of Malay loanwords. The localized Penang Chinese food, too, reflects local cultural influences. Thus, Penang Chinese, as well as the Chinese from Kedah and Perlis, are culturally distinct from Chinese Malaysians elsewhere. Although the localized Chinese in Penang were called Baba (specifically, Penang Baba) in the past, the Chinese there today do not identify ethnically as a separate category of Chinese. Nevertheless, the regional cultural distinction is maintained.

Similarly, Chinese Malaysians in different regions have different localization experiences. Their Chinese identities are perceived differently both by them and by the Chinese from other regions, even though they are all Chinese. For example, the Chinese from Iban majority regions in East Malaysia, who can speak Iban and who eat some local non-Chinese food, are perceived differently from the Chinese in Kuala Lumpur.

Other than overall cultural change, language and education influence the perception of Chinese identities in Malaysia. As English has been perceived as a neutral language in multi-ethnic Malaysia, speaking English among the Chinese is perceived as less un-Chinese than speaking Malay among the Chinese. Partly because of the importance of English education in the past, there have been Chinese who are English-speaking or who speak English more regularly than a Chinese language. There are, thus, English-speaking Chinese, but unlike the Malay-speaking Baba, they do not form a separate category of sub-ethnic Chinese. Those who have received Chinese education are the Chinese-educated Chinese, but these include those who have been educated in Chinese throughout their years of schooling and those who have received Chinese education for only part of their years of schooling. In Tan (1988b), I have classified Chinese Malaysians according to language and education into various types of Chinese-educated Chinese, English-speaking Chinese and Malay-educated Chinese. Most of the

Chinese speak a number of languages, usually more than one Chinese language, and Malay as well as English. However, it is their language of literacy that has the greatest influence on their cultural taste and on identity.

Overall, in cultural identity, Chinese Malaysians fall into a continuum of the most localized culturally on the one hand, as represented by the Baba, and the least localized culturally on the other hand. Of the least localized, the extreme examples are those who not only believe that all Chinese should be able to speak and write Chinese but also reject all kinds of localization. These are the Chinese cultural nationalists, some of whom are rather ethnocentric. Most Chinese are between these two polarities of cultural types. In Indonesia, such cultural contrasts of the Chinese are known as *Totok* ('pure' Chinese) and Peranakan (i.e., the Baba). In Malaysia, the Chinese do not have an equivalent label for the so-called 'pure' Chinese. Rather, the perception is according to whether the Chinese are Baba-like or not. For the mainstream Chinese, the Baba model is negative. Thus, the term 'Baba' is not just a sub-ethnic label for the Melaka Baba but is also used as a descriptive term for any Chinese who have 'lost' significant aspects of Chinese culture as a result of a high level of cultural localization. The Baba are today despised. Nevertheless, most of them are still proud of their Baba identity.

Although the specific Baba identity is rejected by the mainstream Chinese, being local in the sense of having a general Malaysian way of life (in contrast to non-Malaysians) is viewed positively by Chinese Malaysians. In general, even the present-day non-Baba Chinese do regard the localized status as positive, as long as one does not lose the relevant Chinese language. The Malay term *Cina* means 'Chinese', but when stressed in a certain way, as used by the Malays, the Baba and the Peranakan-type Chinese, it has the negative sense of 'totally un-localized Chinese', something like 'Chinaman'. In Hokkien, *Teng-suã A-peh* (literally, 'uncle from China') is used to tease another Chinese person as being too 'Chinaman' in behavior or attitude. Furthermore, compared with the Chinese from China and other countries, Chinese Malaysians, whether Baba or not, have local Malaysian characteristics which make them distinct from non-Malaysian Chinese. Compared with the ethnic Chinese from other countries, Chinese Malaysians do have certain Malaysian characteristics such as language usage, food habits, overall experience of living in the multi-ethnic Malaysian society and others. They have all experienced localization, and among them they differ only in the nature and intensity of localization.

SOCIALIZATION AND IDENTITIES

This discussion highlights the influence of ethnic and regional identification. My research on the Baba shows that the Baba become Baba 'not so much because their parents are Baba or it is more advantageous to be one, but because of the way they are socialized to be what they are' (Tan 1988a, 7). As explained in Tan (1988a, 94–5), if a person is brought up in Melaka to be a Baba and to speak Baba Malay, he or she is likely to grow up to identify himself or herself as a Baba. When a Baba marries a non-Baba Chinese, whether the offspring grow up to identify themselves as Baba or not depends on whether they are socialized more to be Baba or non-Baba. If they have learned to speak a Chinese language and interact more with their non-Baba Chinese relatives, then they may not find it meaningful to identify as Baba. After marriage, an ambiguous identity may be clarified; if an offspring of such a family marries a non-Baba Chinese, it is likely that the decline in Baba identity may be consolidated, but if the offspring marries a Baba and continues to interact with the Baba kin, then he or she is likely to continue to identify as a Baba. Offspring from a mixed marriage between Baba and non-Baba Chinese have a chance to acquire a Chinese language, and so it is easy to relinquish the present less prestigious Baba identity if they so wish. But the eventual identification of the Baba in Melaka is very much influenced by one's experience of socialization rather than purely by rational choice.

As a group, the Baba could claim to be descended from the earliest Chinese migrants to Malaysia, but it is not true that all Baba are descended from the earliest migrants. For instance, there is a well-known

Baba whose father was China-born. When interviewed, he stressed his long Baba line of descent through his mother. This is quite a common pattern, for many Melaka Baba I have interviewed claim to have a long history of settlement in Melaka. Often this was assumed to be on the mother's side, for the earliest ancestor might be a Chinese migrant of the grandfather's generation or great-grandfather's generation. There were informants who did not know at which generation the first Chinese ancestor came to Malaysia. Like other Chinese, the Baba observe patrilineality in tracing descent and passing down surnames. However, in claiming a long Baba family history, they do not hesitate to say that, 'on my mother's side, we have been Baba for many generations'. Of course, there is no proof of an actual line of descent through the women, since the patrilineal bias means that the history on the mother's side is generally not recorded. The point is, Baba identification is basically a product of socialization, so the history of settlement is not very relevant except for prestige. However, whether one is accepted by the Baba community as Baba is not just a matter of claim but the ability to exhibit core Baba cultural features. Foremost is the ability to speak Baba Malay, that is, the creolized Malay dialect spoken by the Baba and which differs in various ways from other Malay dialects (*see* Tan 1988a, 120–43). The Baba I mentioned earlier, a first-generation local-born on his father's side, speaks Baba Malay and English but very little Hokkien. He is also knowledgeable about Baba heritage. What we should note is that in his experience of socialization, he feels Baba, is more used to being Baba, and assumes the Baba identity naturally. After all, ethnic identification is very much a matter of feeling, for instance, having the feeling of being an ethnic Chinese or a Baba specifically.

The Chinese in Malaysia are generally socialized to be Chinese. This is very clear in Malaysia, where each Malaysian is expected to have a distinct ethnic identity, such as Malay, Chinese, Indian, Iban, Kadazan, and so on. Only the offspring of intermarriage may have problems fitting into these clear-cut categories. For instance, the offspring of a Chinese-Indian union may be culturally socialized to be more Chinese or more Indian and may feel to be more one than the other. However, the patrilineal principle requires them to identify with the ethnic identity of their father. This may be socially problematic if one looks physically South Indian but has to identify as Chinese, for instance. One can identify as Malaysian but in an ethnic-conscious society, one still requires the ability to specify a distinct ethnic identity. For offspring of marriages across Chinese speech-groups, the general rule is to identify with the father's speech-group. There is not much problem here, since one is still Chinese; speech-group identity is merely a sub-ethnic identity which one can choose not to emphasize. A Cantonese who grows up in the dominant Hokkien cultural environment of Penang may speak 'Penang Hokkien' rather than Cantonese, but socially among the Chinese there is generally no pressure to declare one's speech-group identity. When asked, one can explain that one's father is Cantonese and mother Hokkien, although one may be culturally Hokkien in every respect. Of course, in this case, there is no strong identification with the Cantonese, which, for this person, is merely, if anything, a marginal identity.

Having various levels of identity allows one to emphasize an identity situationally. The pan-Chinese identity is most relevant generally, but among the Hokkien, a person's Hokkien identity is relevant and is assumed through one's language use and discourse. In the case of a 'Babaized' identity, which is despised and not understood outside Melaka, Kelantan and Terengganu, a Baba or a Peranakan-type Chinese from Kelantan will choose to emphasize only the general Chinese identity and may even camouflage the 'Baba' identity by conversing with non-Peranakan-type Chinese in English. Among themselves, they will speak in Baba Malay or, among those from Kelantan, Kelantan Malay. A Baba is a Chinese, only a different kind of Chinese. Socialization makes Baba the kind of Chinese they are, but the identities are culturally relevant to those who have been socialized to assume them.

A concrete example helps to illustrate the issue here. I have known the family of Mr and Mrs Bong in a village in Melaka for over 25 years, since 1977 when I first began my research among the Baba. In 1977, the eldest son was in primary school, but now he works in Kuala Lumpur. The only daughter and the second son are now in their late and early

20s respectively, and they work in Melaka Town. The youngest son is a lower secondary school student. All of them speak Baba Malay at home. Because of the personal experience of being teased by non-Baba Chinese for their inability to speak any Chinese language, Mr and Mrs Bong decided to send the eldest son and daughter (second child) to a Chinese primary school. This turned out to be rather inconvenient, as the parents could not help with their children's homework; at the same time, whenever they received a circular from the school they had to find someone to read it, and I was often consulted in 1977. Hence, they decided to send their third and fourth children to a Malay-medium school.

Here, the education received influenced the cultural identity of the children, for now the eldest son and the daughter can speak Mandarin and read some Chinese. Knowing Mandarin is particularly useful to the eldest son, who works in a bank and can speak to his Chinese friends in Kuala Lumpur (who are not Baba) in either Mandarin or English. Anyway, all of the children see themselves as Baba, including the two who can speak Chinese. This is natural, as they have been so socialized and have their close network of Baba relatives. Given the negative attitude of the mainstream Chinese, the Baba, like the eldest son here, can choose not to highlight their Baba identity while outside of Melaka, for instance, in Kuala Lumpur, by speaking Mandarin and English. This does not mean that they feel less Baba, only that it is not relevant or advantageous to emphasize their Malay-speaking Baba identity in certain situations. Now, if Mr Bong's eldest son marries a non-Baba Chinese in Kuala Lumpur, then whether his children will identify as Baba will depend on whether they will have the chance for continuous interaction with the Baba kin in Melaka or whether they are consciously socialized not to be Baba and have more interaction with their non-Baba relatives.

Speaking Baba Malay is taken for granted in Mr Bong's family. *Nyonya* food (Baba food), however, is common rhetoric of both the older and younger Baba when relating with the non-Baba Chinese and Malays. They view *nyonya* food as delicious and a unique Baba cultural product. For Mr and Mrs Bong, as is true of the older Baba, worshipping ancestors and Chinese deities is also essential to being Baba and, in essence, being Chinese. This is despite the fact that some Babas are Christians. Mr Bong cleans the family altars every morning and offers joss sticks to the deities every morning and evening. His daughter and second son also offer joss sticks to the deities in the morning before going out to work. Here is another aspect of socialization at work. During my stay with the family in July 1997, Mr Bong talked alarmingly about a charismatic Christian sect called Gateway, which preached rather aggressively. Because of some success of its members' preaching among the Baba, I soon found that most Babas in Melaka knew the name 'Gateway' and were rather worried about its activities among the Baba. Here we see that the informants generally essentialized their identity, and most of the older Baba in Melaka were beginning to find that their association of Baba identity with worshipping ancestors and Chinese deities, among others, was being threatened by the new Christian 'onslaught'. This explained their exaggeration that many Babas had converted to Christianity — in fact there was only one Baba Christian family in Bukit Rambai in July 1997 when I revisited the village. Christians are still a minority, albeit an increasing one, among the Babas of Melaka.

From the etic point of view, identity is dynamic and different symbols can be mobilized and associated with an identity in a changing situation. Unlike in Melaka, many of the Babas in Singapore are Christians and, obviously, worshipping ancestors and Chinese deities is not part of their essentialization of Baba identity. Overall, people do use cultural symbols to essentialize their identity. After having associated with many Baba over the years, I can say what is essentialized generally, even though specifically the individuals may differ somewhat in their emphasis of cultural symbols because of their diverse experiences.

CHINESE AS MALAYSIANS

It is the socialization experience that makes the Chinese in Malaysia Chinese Malaysians. They are culturally different from the Chinese of other countries. Part of the difference is the result of localization in Malaysia, the transformation and recreation of 'Chinese' ways of life in Malaysia. There is also the influence of the 'national culture' (Steward 1973, 48–9) of Malaysia, as well as the experience of living in the multi-ethnic Malaysian society. This is reflected in their ways of life, including the love of Malaysian food and certain attitudes. They display, for example, more sensitivity towards the feelings of Malays — the majority people — than, say, Chinese Singaporeans, who live in a Chinese majority multi-ethnic society. Thus, in contrast to the Chinese from other countries, Chinese Malaysians are culturally and attitudinally distinct in a number of ways.

Within the country, the national Chinese identity is taken for granted. As citizens, Chinese Malaysians identify with other citizens as Malaysians, but they do not necessarily 'imagine' (cf. Anderson 1983) the Malaysian nation similarly as non-Chinese citizens. In fact, as citizens, Chinese Malaysians are united in their views that there should be equal opportunity for all citizens, and they share common sentiments against any form of discrimination, such as the use of quotas for university admission or for issuing permits. This is despite the fact that some of them may agree that some kind of affirmative action policy is necessary to help the economically disadvantaged indigenous people and the poor in general.

Because of the diverse socialization experiences and perceptions of Chinese identities, Chinese Malaysians have diverse views about nation building. The Chinese-educated, especially the Chinese cultural nationalists, are very concerned about Chinese education, which they see as crucial for a 'pure' Chinese identity. The Baba, while appreciating the usefulness of learning Chinese, are understandably not so affected by whether a separate Chinese school system survives in Malaysia or not, or whether the establishment of a Chinese-medium university can be realized. Thus Chinese Malaysians are diverse in their cultural and attitudinal expressions, but as Chinese Malaysians, they are united in matters concerning their common interests.

The significance of socialization to ethnicity is that it cultivates in a people certain cultural habits and attitudes. It reproduces cultural identities. Within a country, it reproduces different Chinese cultural expressions, depending on the nature of local Chinese cultural continuity and transformation as well as local cultural innovation. Adaptation and socialization vary in different societies, and this makes the Chinese heterogeneous. Nevertheless, the need to adjust to multi-ethnic Southeast Asian societies, and to the indigenous majority in particular, also result in the Chinese sharing similar concerns and attitudes. Many Chinese Malaysians and Chinese Filipinos are conscious of the need to establish good relations with the indigenous peoples. It is this common experience of the wish to emphasize local national Chinese identities and to have good relations with the indigenous people that accounts for most scholars of Chinese origin in Southeast Asia rejecting the label of 'Overseas Chinese'. The Chinese in Malaysia and Singapore, for example, generally use the term *Huaren* (ethnic Chinese) to refer to themselves in Mandarin, rather than *Huaqiao* (Overseas Chinese) or even *Zhongguoren* (Chinese, especially the people of China). The change of identity from *Huaqiao* in the past to *Huaren* today reflects the process of localization as experienced by the Chinese in Southeast Asia, making it meaningful and necessary to emphasize their local Chinese identities.

Transnational migration is a common feature of the present era. The transmigrants are involved in different national societies and in the process build 'social fields that link together their country of origin and their country of settlement' which Schiller, Basch and Blanc-Szanton (1992, 1) refer to as 'transnationalism'. Many Chinese Malaysians have gone to Japan, Taiwan and even the United States in search of better opportunities, returning to Malaysia only now and then. Most continue to be Malaysians, and their Chinese Malaysian identities remain relevant. The experience of being Malaysian and Chinese Malaysian influences one's cultural habits. I am a Chinese Malaysian now teaching in Hong Kong. When asked how I feel about living in Hong Kong, my answer is, 'I miss Malaysian food'. By that I mean both Malaysian food in general and Chinese Malaysian food in particular, for the Chinese in Malaysia, as elsewhere, have developed their own local Chinese food. The cultural habits and interests are of course influenced by years of socialization, which cannot be erased easily even when living elsewhere.

Some scholars writing about the Chinese diaspora tend to assume homogeneity among the diverse Chinese populations, and over-stress or assume discontinuity. Chinese Malaysian transmigrants are different from Chinese migrants from elsewhere. At the same time, the 'temporary' transmigrants should be distinguished from those migrants who intend to migrate for good or who have decided to settle in a new country. The temporary Malaysian transmigrants still keep their Malaysian identity, but those who migrate for good try to acquire a new nationality. Even then, their socialization experience continues to influence their cultural habits, although they may choose to emphasize a new national identity and a new Chinese identity. Generally, it is their children, who grow up in a new society, who assume a new Chinese ethnic identity, one associated with a new national society. The generation factor is important, but post-modernist writers on the Chinese in diaspora often ignore this. Surely when discussing the identities of the Chinese in transnational settings, there is a need to distinguish transmigrants who are first-generation migrants from those who have a history of more than one generation in a new society.

In a transnational setting, one can choose to drop or suppress the nationally based ethnic identity. This is especially so if one wants to acquire a new national identity. For people of Chinese origin, it is a generalized Chinese identity, however privately perceived, which is enduring. The sub-ethnic identity such as being a Baba or a Hakka can be emphasized or de-emphasized situationally, whereas in transnational contexts the national identity (such as being a Chinese Malaysian) can also be emphasized or played down, or even dropped in favor of a new national identity. But being Chinese is meaningful to Chinese individuals in different contexts, whether as a local Chinese in Kelantan or as an ethnic Chinese without reference to any nationality in Hong Kong or Australia. Chinese Malaysians are a heterogeneous category of Chinese who identify themselves as ethnic Chinese generally (*Huaren*), as Chinese Malaysians (or Malaysian Chinese), and as Chinese of different localized identities. As subgroups and as individuals, they can have different expressions of being Chinese.

Conclusion

Socialization influences the way in which individuals find a certain ethnic identity meaningful and natural. Identity is a basic characteristic of human beings; ethnic affiliation is a powerful identification beyond the family, as it links individuals to a larger group of 'similar' people sharing a history (even if it is a myth) and the meaningfulness of cultural heritage, such as speaking a common language. The diverse experience of life, of socialization, influences the perception and meaning of an ethnic identity.

In my research on the Baba, I have found it useful to analyze identity according to three components: the label, the subjective experience of identification, and the objective expression of identity (Tan 1988a, 4). Socialization is crucial to the understanding of the subjective component, and even the adoption of a certain label and the objective expression of identity, such as the use of a certain language or wearing a certain kind of dress, is influenced by one's experience of socialization.

It is important to understand the politics of labels and the meaning people attach to ethnic labels. Of course, the use of label is necessarily part of the discussion on subjective identification, and in this respect, it need not be singled out as a separate component. Nevertheless, treating it separately allows one a more comprehensive discussion of the various labels used by the people themselves and by others. There are, for example, different Chinese labels for the English label 'Chinese', each with a different political connotation. Chinese Americans who originate from Southeast Asia have different labels, such as Chinese Americans, Chinese Vietnamese Americans, Vietnamese Americans. Many of these Chinese of Southeast Asian origins have found it convenient to identify with the larger Chinese American 'community' as Chinese Americans, although for other purposes they may emphasize their specific Southeast Asian origins (cf. Bao 1999; Wang Ling-chi 1991). The Babas perceive 'Baba' to be a special kind of identity, but the non-Baba Chinese not only have a different perception, they have different usages, too. They may also refer to other Chinese who have lost, in their view, Chineseness (not speaking any Chinese), as Baba.

By paying attention to socialization, one can avoid the polarized approach in the study of ethnic group and ethnic identity, between the primordial approach and the instrumental approach (cf. Bentley 1989, 25). The primordial approach of emphasis on emotion can lead to the mistaken view of ethnicity as innate, though in fact it is a product of socialization. A different style and intensity of socialization may have a different effect on the form and intensity of ethnic emotion. In some societies, individuals are socialized to their religion in a very exclusive way. Socialization experience also includes the experience of living with other peoples and in a nation-state. Where a people are culturally oppressed or where resources are distributed along ethnic lines, ethnic consciousness is bound to be high.

Because of the emphasis on circumstantial manipulation of ethnicity, those who adopt the 'instrumental' approach tend to ignore the effect of socialization and, as a result, fail to take into consideration the emotional and habitual dimension of ethnicity. The socialization approach can bridge the two approaches. Similarly, the transactional theory of Barth (1969a) and the rational choice theory (cf. Banton 1983), while orienting attention to choice, tend to ignore the emotional dimension of human action. Paying some attention to socialization should help to reduce this bias. For Chinese Malaysians, Chinese ethnicity is shaped by both the socialization of the Chinese at home and in the larger multi-ethnic society. The Chinese ethnicity vis-à-vis the Malays is obviously shaped by the nature of ethnic relations between the Chinese and Malays, such that all Chinese of different speech-groups (that were originally different ethnic categories so to speak) see themselves as one ethnic group with regard to the Malays. However, the expression of specific Chinese Malaysian identities is influenced by their regional and national experience of localization. Thus, Chinese Malaysian identities have multi-levels and are multifaceted.

Lastly, Chinese Malaysians are both ethnic Chinese and Malaysians. As regards labels, they see themselves as *Huaren*, as ethnic Chinese. As *Huaren*, they need not be territorially bound. Due to their experience of localization, the Chinese in Malaysia do see themselves as Chinese of Malaysia in contrast to Chinese of other nationalities, although they can also relate to them as *Huaren*, the unbounded Chinese identity. In English, the Chinese in Malaysia are often described by Malaysians and non-Malaysians as 'Malaysian Chinese', although 'Chinese Malaysians' may be used to reflect the Malaysian-bound identity. Identities need not be exclusive, and being Chinese and being Malaysian are not exclusive and should not be analyzed as such. For Chinese Malaysians, being Malaysian is expressed through being Chinese in the Malaysian context. Within Malaysia, there are various Chinese speech-groups and regional Chinese identities. The main contrast is between the least localized Chinese model and the Baba model of Chineseness. In fact, all Chinese Malaysians have experienced localization, differing only in degree. Even the language of the non-Baba Hokkien, for example, contains some Malay loanwords such as *su-kah* (Malay, *suka*) for 'to like' and *ba-luh* (Malay, *baru*) for 'just' as in *ba-luh lai* or 'just arrived'.

I have discussed the objective and subjective aspects of Chinese identities. Analytically, the two components can be distinct, and one can distinguish between ethnic identity and cultural identity. However, informants may not make nor necessarily see the distinction. I have discussed the older generation of Baba in Melaka, who associate the observance of Chinese religious rites with Baba identity. Over time, however, the cultural expression of an identity changes. For example, the concept of 'Baba' changes over time (*see* Tan 1991). Nevertheless, a researcher should pay attention to his or her informants' essentialization of culture and identity. In this post-modernist academic climate, there is much criticism against essentialism. Yet to ignore the people's essentialization may lead to merely having an exercise of the analyst's own rhetoric without the informants' rhetoric. An anthropologist should understand his or her informants' essentialism and at the same time transcend it in order to have a more concrete and dynamic analysis of ethnicity and identity.

Chinese Malaysians will, in general, continue to be ethnic Chinese, but their identities will change over time. They are both ethnic Chinese and Malaysian. Their identities are both bounded and unbounded. The unbounded identity as *Huaren* is best observed in the transnational context or when they migrate to live in another country. But as Malaysians, they express a territorially bounded Chinese identity through their participation as citizens of and identification with the Malaysian state.

Photograph 1   Flower girl (who accompanied the bride) and boy (who accompanied the groom) at a Baba wedding in Melaka, Malaysia. Courtesy of the late Mr Cheong Sian Chiang, June 1997.

Photograph 2   A Chinese temple in Surabaya, Indonesia with a banner wishing Muslims a Happy Idul Fitri (End of Fasting Month) celebration. Chinese temples in Indonesia are an important symbol of Chinese identity. Photograph by author, December 2002.

Photograph 3   Preparing for the communal *pudu* celebration at a hawkers' center in Batu Pahat Town, Johor, Malaysia. Photograph by author, August 2000.

Photograph 4 *Pudugong* or the Lord in charge of ghosts during the Hungry Ghost festival in Ayam Suloh Village, Johor, Malaysia. Photograph by author, August 2000.

Photograph 5 The communal *pusi* (called *pudu* in Malaysia) worship in a village in Yongchun, Fujian, China. Photograph by author, August 1999.

Photograph 6 *Pusi* worship in a residential area in Quanzhou City. Photograph by author, August 1999.

Photograph 7   Ancestral altar in a Baba house in Kandang, Melaka, Malaysia. Photograph by author, July 1997.

Photograph 8   A Baba invitation form of ancestor worship on a death anniversary, Bukit Rambai, Melaka, Malaysia. Photograph by author, July 1997.

Photograph 9 *Nyonya* (Baba women) making *kuih* (sweets), Bukit Rambai, Melaka, Malaysia. Note the woman on the right wearing sarong. Photograph by author, July 1997.

Photograph 10 A Peranakan-type Chinese (wearing sarong) and his granddaughter at the verandah of his house in Tirok, Terengganu, Malaysia. Photograph by author, November 1994.

Photograph 11 Localized and still Chinese: A Peranakan-type Chinese at his house in Kelantan. Note the Chinese couplets (*lian*) at the main entrance. Photograph by author, February 1982.

5

Ethnic Chinese: Language, Nationality and Identity

INTRODUCTION

In Chapter 2, I have discussed briefly language and localization. In this chapter, I shall further explore the issue of language, nationality and identity. The ethnic Chinese belong to different nationalities, and have adjusted socially and culturally to their respective local communities and national societies. In fact, they speak the dominant language or languages of their place of residence, although many still speak one or more Chinese languages. Even then, the Chinese languages that they speak may have been acculturated by the dominant local languages. It is thus interesting to examine the relationship between language and linguistic change, and relate to ethnic and national identities. The different experiences of the ethnic Chinese in the larger ethnological field make such a comparative study worthwhile.

Language is undoubtedly an important indicator of ethnic identity. Since ethnic Chinese have adjusted to different socio-cultural environments, I shall first examine the effects of acculturation on ethnic identity. The different levels of acculturation, especially linguistic acculturation and assimilation, give rise to different types of Chinese identities. In addition to acculturation, we also have to distinguish the Chinese who can read and write Chinese from those who cannot. I shall therefore examine the relation-ship between literacy, ethnicity and national identity. I shall also explore the implication, if any, of language and pan-Chinese identity.

We shall bear in mind that within an ethnic identity there are various modes and levels of identification. There is Chinese ethnic identity and there are various types of Chinese identities. While ethnic Chinese worldwide are identified as Chinese, their subjective experiences of identification and perception of their identity are not the same, and they do not necessarily emphasize the same cultural features as symbols of identity. We should also bear in mind that Chinese as an ethnic group or more accurately, an ethnic category, is meaningful only in relation to other ethnic categories in a larger society. When we speak of the Chinese in Malaysia, we assume either consciously or unconsciously that they form an ethnic category in relation to other ethnic categories in Malaysia. Between countries, the people of Chinese descent constitute Chinese of different nationalities.

LANGUAGE, ACCULTURATION AND IDENTITY

When Chinese migrated and settled in foreign lands, one of the first things that they had to adjust to was learning to understand and speak the local lingua franca. In some cases like the Chinese Peranakan — the Malay-speaking Chinese in Southeast Asia — the local language was in fact adopted, albeit in a creolized form, as their own language. In time to come, the Chinese in diaspora, due to their linguistic and other socio-cultural adjustments to the local communities and national societies, attained distinct cultural identities and Chinese ethnic identities.

The case of the Baba of Melaka provides a good example.[1] The Baba who also identified themselves as Peranakan are Chinese but their language of intimacy, i.e. the language used in the sphere of immediate family and close friends (Oetomo 1988: 98) is no more Chinese; it is a creole Malay which may be called Baba Malay (Shellabear 1913, Tan 1980). The earliest Chinese settlers had to interact with the local people and those who married actually married local women such as Malay, Siamese and Balinese women, as well as the offspring of such unions. It was thus not surprising that a category of Malay-speaking local-born Chinese emerged. They were proud of their local identity and even looked down on the *sinkheh* or 'new guests' — the later immigrants from China. This was despite the fact that the *sinkheh* despised the Baba for not speaking Chinese.

The Baba identity was a prestigious local identity in relation to the lower ranked *sinkheh* identity. Furthermore, in the 19th century, Baba merchants dominated the local trade in the British colonized Straits Settlements comprising Singapore, Melaka and Penang. By the 20th century, however, the *sinkheh* had taken over the dominance of the local trade.

British colonization resulted in the Baba, especially the urban ones, learning English. Today numbering about 5,000 or more in Melaka, the Babas speak Baba Malay as their own language while many also speak and write English. Since they speak Malay, the 'pure Chinese' see them as being like Malays. While they are acculturated by the Malays in certain ways, the Baba retain much traditional Chinese culture, some features of which are no more observed by the so-called pure Chinese, i.e. the less acculturated Chinese. Due perhaps to the loss of their original Chinese language, the Baba today emphasize traditional Chinese customs and religion and to this day a traditional style of Chinese wedding (or versions of it), which involves the wearing of 'old-fashioned' Chinese wedding costumes, is observed by some Babas.

The point that we are interested in here is that while language is a crucial symbol of ethnic identity, its loss does not necessarily mean the loss of an ethnic identity. The Babas have remained Chinese despite not speaking a Chinese language. However, it does affect the nature and the perception of the identity. While the label 'Cina' or 'Chinese' persists, the meaning of that label has changed — the Babas have become a different kind of Chinese. As Baba, they have become a sub-ethnic category of Chinese. At the same time, those of Hokkien origin, as most Babas are, also identify themselves as Hokkien.

There is thus the need to distinguish cultural identity from ethnic identity. One can remain a Chinese even though one does not speak a Chinese language. In the context of Malaysia, where Chinese do not normally speak Malay among themselves, the Babas stand out as a separate category of Chinese.

In fact, within Malaysia, Chinese of different regions have different identities as a result of linguistic acculturation. In northeast Kelantan, for example, there are Chinese who speak a Hokkien dialect that is very much influenced by the local Malay and Thai dialects. They also speak Malay as a language of intimacy and many speak Thai too; while the young people actually prefer to speak to each other in Kelantanese Malay. The 'pure Chinese' refer to them derogatorily as 'Poà-Teng-Siam' (half Chinese, half Siamese). The people refer to themselves as 'Teng-Lang' which is the local Hokkien way of saying 'Chinese' (Tan 1982).

The Chinese in Penang, who are mostly of Hokkien origin, speak a unique version of localized Hokkien popularly referred to as Penang Hokkien. It contains more Malay loanwords than the Chinese elsewhere in Malaysia, and it has some Thai influences, too, in the style of speech. While the Hokkien Chinese in Penang have other acculturated features like the regular wearing of sarongs by the older women, it is the Penang Hokkien dialect which distinguishes the 'Penang Chinese' from the Chinese in other parts of Malaysia.

Similarly, if we travel to Sarawak and Sabah, the use of the local lingua franca distinguishes the Chinese there from Chinese Malaysians elsewhere. For example, the Chinese in Kapit (Sarawak) can speak Iban fluently while the Chinese in Belaga (Sarawak) can speak Kayan. Thus, what language or languages the Chinese use as the language of intimacy and as intra-group language as well as the language or languages used when interacting with non-Chinese shape the perception of Chinese identities among the Chinese.

In the transnational context, the main objective feature that distinguishes the Chinese of one country from those of other countries is the languages they speak. This is how we perceive the Chinese in Indonesia (at least from reading about them) who speak Indonesian fluently, or the Chinese in Thailand who speak Thai, or the Chinese in the Philippines who can switch so easily between Chinese (Hokkien or Mandarin), Tagalog and English (Philippine style). Similarly, the local-born Chinese Americans speak the American style of English, and are often considered as too American by the Chinese from Southeast Asia.

To summarize, being Chinese is in the final analysis a matter of subjective identification. Subjectively, whether one speaks a Chinese language or not, does not make one less Chinese. In fact, the Baba can claim to be a different type of Chinese by emphasizing that they speak Malay! They can also claim to be more Chinese by emphasizing that they still observe certain customs which the non-Baba Chinese (the 'pure Chinese') do not observe anymore. However, the language or languages that ethnic Chinese speak differentiate them from other categories of Chinese. There is thus a close relationship between language and Chinese identities. I should like to add that the experience of the Baba is not as unique as it appears; it is actually common to all people of Chinese descent, involving only a question of degree. The Babas, having been linguistically assimilated by the Malays, represent one type of Chinese identity.

CHINESE LITERACY AND IDENTITY

Among ethnic Chinese, some are more acculturated than others. This gives rise to the perception of 'pure Chinese' versus the acculturated Chinese. In actual fact, there are no pure Chinese whether biologically or culturally. Even within a national society, the 'pure Chinese' are 'pure' (*chun*) only in the sense of being less acculturated. For example, in Malaysia, the non-Baba Hokkien Chinese consider themselves purer than the Baba whom they consider like Malays. But when they speak Hokkien (*Minnanhua*) to the Taiwanese, the latter may find it a bit *fan* (not so Chinese, influenced by non-Chinese); for the so-called pure Hokkien Chinese in Malaysia also use some Malay loan words like *kau-yin* (from Malay *kahwin* for '*marry*'), *pun* (meaning 'also' in Malay) and others. A Chinese Malaysian friend told me that when he first went to Hong Kong, he asked the bus conductor '*gei-do lui?*' (how much money?). The conductor looked at him and commented that he must be from Singapore! My friend then realized that the Cantonese that he spoke was rather Malaysian for it contained the Malay loan word *lui* from *duit* in Malay for 'money'.

The 'pure Chinese' perception is of course a myth propagated by those who wish to place one category of Chinese on a higher status than others. 'Pure Chinese' is a matter of definition by people who consider themselves culturally superior to others. Furthermore, how can one objectively define pure Chinese culture? In the first place, there is no one Chinese culture to speak of. Compared to the Taiwanese, Chinese Malaysians seem not so 'pure' after all, but neither are the Taiwanese. The 'pure Chinese' in Southeast Asia associate chewing betel leaves and areca nuts (*pinang* in Malay) with the indigenous people, and consider these habits as un-Chinese (*fan*). Chinese Malaysians who go to Taiwan for the first time will be shocked to see so many Chinese there chew betel nuts!

Ethnic Chinese who claim to be 'pure Chinese' (in the cultural sense) comprise two categories, that is, those who can speak at least a Chinese language but cannot write in Chinese and those who are also literate in Chinese, that is who can speak Mandarin and write Chinese characters. Speaking at least a Chinese language is the minimum claim to being a 'pure Chinese' and not a Baba, so to speak. In the United States, there are Chinese Americans who can speak at least a Chinese language, and there are those who can speak only English, the latter may be considered the 'Baba' of America.

If the Babas are at one end of a continuum (the more acculturated end), the Chinese who are literate in Chinese are at the other end. For convenience, I call the latter Chinese-educated irrespective of their level of literacy in Chinese and whether they have been fully Chinese-educated or not. Everywhere the Chinese-educated generally see themselves as 'pure Chinese' and as guardians of Chinese language and culture. Not surprisingly, the more chauvinistic Chinese come from this category but it would be wrong to assume that all Chinese-educated Chinese are chauvinistic.

Literacy in Chinese makes one a different kind of Chinese, a Chinese that can read Chinese and have direct access to the Chinese literary heritage with the opportunity to learn more about Chinese history, philosophy and civilization in general. They can share similar interests in Chinese music, theatre and Chinese arts in general. The Chinese-educated Malaysians are interested in Chinese music and songs that are produced locally as well as those produced in Singapore, Hong Kong, Taiwan, China and elsewhere, if any. The Chinese-educated Chinese in Malaysia have always been contrasted with the English-educated Chinese: they do have different attitudes towards identity and cultural interests (Wang 1970; Tan 1988b).

In Malaysia, the leaders of the major Chinese communal associations, especially those who champion Chinese education, are vocal and influential in defining as well as safeguarding Chinese culture and identity. To them, all Chinese must be able to speak and write Chinese. A logical follow up to this thinking is that it is natural that they believe that Chinese should send their children to Chinese-medium schools. The survival of Chinese-medium education is seen as crucial to the survival of Chinese culture and the persistence of Chinese identity. Given the communal politics in Malaysia, the linkage of Chinese language to the survival of Chinese culture and Chinese identity provides the most crucial basis of mobilizing political support among the Chinese. If religion (i.e. Islam) is the most important principle of mobilizing Malay support, language (Mandarin) is the most important mobilizing principle among the Chinese — and both religion and language are emotionally loaded once they enter the political arena; hence whoever governs has to handle these two areas with much caution.

The Chinese in Malaysia can send their children to either Chinese-medium or Malay-medium primary schools, both are government-run. At the secondary level, the students have to choose either to go to Malay-medium government schools (with the opportunity to study a subject in Chinese) or Chinese-medium independent private schools (Tan L.E. 1988). As the Chinese-medium primary schools are crucial for the continuation of Chinese education, the survival of Chinese primary schools is a constant issue, and no Chinese-based political party can afford to be seen or depicted as not caring for the survival of Chinese-medium education.

The issue of language and education poses a dilemma to all Chinese

5

parents in Malaysia. To send a child to a Chinese-medium primary school or a Malay-medium school is a matter of serious concern — for it will affect the child's cultural identity as well as his or her upward mobility. The dilemma is that being a Malaysian, a Chinese has to study Bahasa Malaysia (Malay), which is the national language, but for access to more socio-economic opportunities and also for transnational mobility, he/she has to study English. At the same time, most Chinese parents want their children to be able to speak Mandarin as well as read and write Chinese — for the sake of Chinese identity as well as because of the recognition that Chinese is a useful language, more so now that China is doing well economically. While the students in certain national Malay-medium primary schools have the opportunity to study Chinese from Standard Three onwards, the program is weak. On the other hand, there is the fear that students who attend Chinese-medium primary schools and who are average and below average in their performances will lose out when they attend the Malay-medium secondary schools. At the secondary level, most Chinese send their daughters and sons to the government schools rather than to the Chinese-medium independent and private schools (whose certificates are not recognized by the government), and which are thus not considered to be as good for the later upward mobility of the children who will live and work in Malaysia.

The opportunity for studying Chinese depends on government policies as well as the numerical and political strength of the Chinese. This affects the cultural identities of the Chinese in different countries. Not many people realize that Malaysia is the only country where Chinese education has survived best outside of the Mainland China, Taiwan, Hong Kong and Macao. The use of Mandarin is much more widespread and deeply rooted than even in Singapore. There is still a strong tradition of reading Chinese as indicated by the presence of Chinese newspapers and magazines, as well as the wide range of Chinese books in Chinese bookshops. This is despite the fact that Singapore had an official 'Speak Mandarin campaign'[2] and Chinese is taught as a major second language. In Malaysia, there are Chinese-medium primary schools all over the country and there are still 60 independent (private) Chinese secondary schools (UCSTAM 1984: 104).

All countries in Southeast Asia curb Chinese education in one way or another to shape the cultural identities of their Chinese citizens. Even in Thailand, where so much has been written about Chinese integration into Thai society, the Thai governments have always curbed Chinese education severely, limiting the hours that Chinese can be taught. The Chinese find it more advantageous to attend Thai schools (cf. Coughlin 1960: 145, Bao 1999: 100–1). In the Philippines, Chinese education has been curbed, too, especially under the Filipinization of schools policy introduced in 1973, among which the teaching of Chinese is limited to two hours per day. However, the deterioration of Chinese education is also due to internal factors such as the shortage of Chinese language teachers and proper textbooks (Chinben See 1992, Teresita Ang See 1997: 93–104). Indonesia under the Suharto regime in fact adopted an assimilation policy. All Chinese language schools were closed down in 1966 (Mely Tan, 1987) and Chinese writing was even forbidden. This has resulted in a younger generation not literate in Chinese. Indeed, in my visit to Surabaya in December 2002, I found that young Chinese (under 40 years old) generally speak Indonesian and Javanese rather than a Chinese language. However, there is also effort to revive the learning of Chinese. There are Chinese newspapers, and a temple in Marang that I visited has begun to promote the learning of Mandarin, albeit cautiously.

In Singapore, although predominantly Chinese in population, the government has been adopting a policy that emphasizes English education. It did not want Singapore to be seen as a third China in Southeast Asia. However, in recent years, the government has been concerned about too much westernization and the loss of Chinese ethics among the younger generation, hence the Mandarin campaign and the emphasis on Chinese studying Chinese as a second language. The language and education policies in Singapore are not as simple as they appear, for as shown by Selvan (1990), they are intertwined with the political calculations of the former Prime Minister, Lee Kuan Yew.

In North America where English is so dominant in all spheres of life, parents have difficulty getting children to study Chinese since almost everyone speaks English. The increasing recognition of multiculturalism has perhaps offered some opportunities to learn Chinese in schools, but the immediate problem is how to get children interested in studying Chinese seriously in an overwhelmingly English environment.

Thus, both government policies on language and education with regard to the studying of Chinese, as well as the internal dynamics of Chinese communities in response to the larger societies have consequences for Chinese identities. Other than Malaysia and Singapore, where the Chinese populations are relatively large, the social environments of the larger societies are generally not conducive to studying Chinese. In USA, for instance, Chinese children are so socialized in the dominant English-speaking environment that it takes considerable effort and determination to study Chinese.

In studying the assimilation of the Chinese in Thailand, Skinner (1964a: 86) stated that, 'The evidence is clear that a Chinese education retards whereas a Thai education accelerates assimilation, and that an absence of formal education is intermediate in its effects on assimilation'. This statement may be accepted if the word assimilation is replaced by 'acculturation', for we must distinguish between acculturation as cultural change and assimilation as change in subjective identification of ethnic identity. Anyway, the point is, literacy in Chinese has a significant impact on Chinese identities.

LANGUAGE, NATIONALITY AND IDENTITY

It is important not to confuse cultural identity with ethnic and national identification. Although the melting pot theory of America has become obsolete, many politicians and even scholars still hold some kind of 'melting pot' assumption with regard to the political attitudes and national loyalty of the people of Chinese descent.

It is often assumed that practicing more Chinese culture (such as being literate in Chinese) means being less integrated into the national society. It is also assumed that the greater the Chinese are acculturated by local communities, the more they are integrated into the national society. Based on this assumption, the Babas in Malaysia are seen as more integrated. The paradigm behind this reasoning is actually the melting pot paradigm. In actual fact, as a category of Chinese, the political sentiments of the Baba are similar to the non-Baba Chinese — they also perceive the Chinese as discriminated against in certain ways. The Baba may speak Malay, but we must remember that they identify themselves as Chinese and are accepted as such by the other ethnic groups, as well as by the state.

Similarly, it is wrong to assume that the Chinese-educated and those who campaign for Chinese education in Malaysia are less Malaysian. These Chinese may promote a literate Chinese cultural identity, but today they identify with Malaysia, and in fact they will feel quite offended if their loyalty to the country is questioned. If they express greater communal sentiment today, this is because they have identified fully (rather than less) with Malaysia, and therefore expect equality with the dominant ethnic group. They see themselves exerting their rights as citizens to promote their own culture and define Chinese identity in Malaysia. If in cultural matters, they seem more 'communal' than the Baba and most 'English-educated' Chinese, this is because the Chinese-educated emphasize Chinese identity differently and they feel that Chinese identity is threatened by government policies. Whether their actions are proper or not in a multi-ethnic country is another matter. The point is, their actions cannot be taken to mean less loyalty to Malaysia or that they are less Malaysian.

Many Chinese in Malaya before the Second World War might have been China-oriented, but with Independence in 1957 and the granting of citizenship, Chinese Malaysians today identify with the Malaysian nation. The 1992 Thomas Cup held in Kuala Lumpur was most illuminating. In the finals, Malaysia competed with China. The local crowd, whether Chinese or Malays or people of other ethnic origins, cheered for Malaysia. China was seen as another country and Chinese Malaysians like the other Malaysians wanted their own country to win.

Integration should be seen in terms of participation in the national society, not in terms of acculturation, assimilation or some notions of uniformity with the national culture as defined by the politically dominant group. Obviously, integration is very much a political question. It has to do with the acceptance of the minority by the national society and whether the minority has access to equal opportunities in the larger society. Bernard P. Wong (1979:171), for example, has observed that in the case of the Chinese in the United States of America, 'legal protection and open economic opportunity have precipitated the wider participation of the Chinese in contemporary American life.'

How then can we view the seemingly greater interest of the Chinese-educated in China and its publications? Here I should like to introduce the concept of cultural relevance (Tan 1989). China being the land of the ancestors of the people of Chinese descent and the original source of Chinese civilization has both historical and cultural relevance to the Chinese everywhere. This is more so for the Chinese-educated Chinese for their ability to read Chinese means that they can have access to and are in greater touch with the historical and cultural heritage of China.

When a Chinese-educated ethnic Chinese (not citizens of China) visits places in China, he or she sees these places differently from non-Chinese tourists. In the first place, the Chinese perceives China as the land of his ancestors and a land of his very civilization. Secondly, the Chinese-educated Chinese does not just do sightseeing. The historical places in China remind him of certain phases of Chinese history which he has read about. They may remind him of certain poets and their poems, or of certain heroes and sages which he has become familiar with through reading. In this respect, the Chinese-educated people of Chinese descent have certain cultural similarities with the citizens of China, but the similarities end there. Subjectively, the ethnic Chinese perceive themselves as people of different nationalities or as not belonging to China. There is a need to distinguish cultural identification from national identification and national loyalty. Among ethnic Chinese, the extent to which China is culturally relevant depends on their knowledge of Chinese history and the literature of China. For the illiterates, China is merely the land of their ancestors, and they may have historical memory of ancestral sites there or even be proud of their ancestral land. For those who are familiar with the historical and literary traditions of China, China of course means more. While those not literate in Chinese may have learnt about the history and even literature of China, the Chinese-educated generally know more and feel more intimate with the historical and literary traditions of China, hence their greater cultural identification with the overall civilization of China. There is a difference between one who merely admires the beauty of a historical site and one who thinks about certain Tang poems (for instance) upon seeing the sites or monuments. The cultural identities of the Chinese are very much influenced by their language of literacy.

The cultural relevance of China to the people of Chinese descent may in some ways be compared to the 'English-speaking' people's special interest in literature from Great Britain and the United States. An 'English-educated' Malaysian who identifies with the literary traditions of Great Britain is no less Malaysian in national identification. But China, of course, is also the land of civilization to the Chinese. This we may compare, in a limited way, to the relevance of the holy land in Arabia and, in fact, things Arabic (especially the Arabic language) to the Muslims outside Arabia.

The melting pot thinking as well as the confusion of the cultural relevance of China to Chinese with their national identification with China often results in ethnic Chinese, especially the Chinese-educated ones, being singled out unfairly by local politicians and even academicians as 'China-oriented' or not identifying with their country of residence. The fallacy is due to the failure to take into consideration the consciousness and the subjective experience of the ethnic Chinese.

The failure of the people of China to take into consideration the local consciousness of people of Chinese descent has also contributed to the inaccurate image of these people with regards to their political attitudes. For example, there are people in China who still describe a visit to China by Chinese from overseas as *huiguo guanguang* (return to the country to tour) while the reality is that these Chinese are simply visiting, and not returning to China. In the past, Chinese overseas who invested in China were seen as people that *aiguo* (love their country). There are people who argue that the 'Chinese abroad' can help to develop China's economy. In actual fact, investment by Chinese overseas in China is ultimately based on economic grounds — the desire to make a profit. Of course, in deciding to invest in China, ethnic Chinese may have the advantage of knowing the language and can mobilize their cultural resources and even kinship links if necessary. Here again, we stress the importance of distinguishing culture from national identification. In any case, as pointed out by Li Guoliang (1991), while a lot of investments in China have come from Hong Kong and Macao, investments by the Chinese from Southeast Asia or elsewhere account for very little.[3] Although China has recognized the Chinese overseas as citizens of their respective countries, the failure to take into consideration the local consciousness of the ethnic Chinese persists. This is due to the failure to keep up-to-date with changes since the Second World War, as well as the bias caused by a China-centric consciousness. This China-centric view can be so persistent that when a Chinese poet from Malaysia writes about his love for the motherland, he may be praised by writers in China for loving China whereas the poet actually refers to Malaysia as his motherland![4]

A TRANSNATIONAL CHINESE IDENTITY?

Literacy in Chinese allows Chinese from all over the world to have a common Chinese language. English as the global common language is and will continue to be the medium of communication for most Chinese transnationally, but for the Chinese-educated Chinese, the proper common language for the Chinese is Mandarin, referred to as *guoyu* (national language) or *putonghua* (common language) in China but as *huayu* (Chinese language) by the Chinese in Southeast Asia. There have been a number of conferences on the Chinese overseas. At those conferences organized by the Chinese and attended mainly by Chinese participants from different countries, English and Mandarin were used, and I used to hear Chinese-educated Chinese comment that it was a pity (some said it was a shame) that when Chinese met they still had to use English! In August 1991, the first Chinese International Entrepreneurship Convention was held in Singapore. The Chinese newspapers in Malaysia carried quite a number of criticisms against the organizer for using English rather than Chinese as the official conference language. As mentioned earlier, the Chinese-educated Chinese see Chinese identity in terms of the ability to speak Chinese, and evidently there is some 'racial' sentiment here. However, the fact is that English is still the most convenient common language transnationally for the Chinese worldwide, followed by Mandarin.

Nevertheless, Mandarin has, and will become more important for the Chinese globally. Following the end of the Cold War, there have been more contacts between the Chinese of all countries and of all ideologies. Transnational meetings between Chinese-educated Chinese will no doubt promote the use of Mandarin in the international arena. The expansion of the transnational investments of Taiwan and Mainland China and the opportunity for business and investment in China will no doubt enhance the status of Mandarin. After all, economic status reinforces the use of a language.

The publication of the Hong Kong-based *Yazhou Zhoukan* as a global Chinese magazine helps to promote Mandarin and to keep Chinese readers worldwide informed of issues that are of particular interest to the Chinese, irrespective of nationalities.[5] The use of a common computer system further enhances the status of Mandarin as a common Chinese language worldwide. It eases as well as improves the Chinese mass media. The use of satellites enables the Chinese of one country to have access to Chinese television programs in other countries, although access is still restricted by government policies.

The improvement and global expansion of the Chinese mass media brings the Chinese reading public closer culturally. This promotes greater sharing of cultural interest on things Chinese. At the same time, the diversity of Chinese communities worldwide becomes more clearly understood. *Yazhou Zhoukan* publishes for readers worldwide. As such, it has to be conscious of the diversity in certain Mandarin usages in different countries. This question of unity and diversity in Chinese language worldwide was regularly discussed in the early 1990s in its 'To The Readers' column — I found this column most interesting.

Nevertheless, there is no single united transnational Chinese identity. Only the more chauvinistic or 'racial' Chinese would be of the view that Chinese everywhere form some kind of a 'race' so to speak, and a great one at that. All Chinese are described as 'descendants of the dragon'. While these 'racial' Chinese see literacy in Chinese as necessary for Chinese identity, they are none the less ever ready to perceive any person of Chinese descent with an outstanding achievement as giving glory to all Chinese, even though the person concerned merely sees himself or herself as a Chinese American or an Indonesian of Chinese descent.

In this respect, as a global Chinese publication, *Yazhou Zhoukan* has also either consciously or unconsciously portrayed the Chinese everywhere as if they are one people. The achievements of Chinese anywhere in the world are reported as the achievement of Chinese worldwide. For example, the 26 August 1992 issue reports on the achievement of Chinese competitors at the Olympic games in Barcelona. But do badminton heroes like Alan Budi Kusuma and Susi Susanti of Indonesia see themselves as belonging to a transnational pan-Chinese community? Interestingly enough, the Chinese press and magazines always use the original Chinese names of these Chinese Indonesians (i.e. Wei Renfang and Wang Lianxiang) who have adopted Indonesian names. Similarly, does the tennis player Michael Chang of the United States see himself as belonging to a transnational Chinese identity beyond his Chinese American identity? The Chinese mass media have described him (Zhang Depei) as *huaren zhi guang*, the pride of Chinese globally.

The belief in some kind of a Chinese 'race' is based on ethnocentrism rather than social reality, for in the transnational context, Chinese interact as people of different nationalities. The increase in communication and interaction among the Chinese of different nations actually makes the

Chinese more conscious of their separate identities, and allows them to recognize the need to respect each other's distinct identities. To be sure, Chinese of different nationalities may stress amity by saying that 'we are all Chinese'. Even then, this phrase is expressed differently. Chinese from China may say 'we are all *zhongguoren*', while the Chinese from Southeast Asia prefer to say 'we are all *huaren*'. In this context, both terms mean Chinese irrespective of nationalities but the Chinese in Southeast Asia prefer to avoid the term Zhongguoren, which can also mean Chinese nationality.

In saying the phrase 'we are all Chinese', the Chinese of different nationalities actually stress the label component of identity. Chinese everywhere share the label 'Chinese'. But this similarity is superficial for identity as a whole is also and more importantly based on subjective identification and the use of cultural features as symbols of identity. The use of the phrase 'we are all Chinese' actually shows the existence of diversities, hence the use of a metaphor to stress amity situationally.

Ethnicity can be situational. Under certain situations one may be able or even forced to change ethnic identity or even national identity. In this situation, the common recognition of the label 'Chinese', though conceived differently, does provide the basis for claiming Chinese nationality, if so allowed. For example, in the 1950s and early 1960s, some 60,000 Chinese students from Indonesia 'returned' to China (Godley and Coppel 1990b). Obviously, they switched their national identification to China, and this was facilitated by their identification as 'Chinese'. In actual fact, they were not fully accepted as Chinese by the people in China. Not all of them could adjust to life in China and many left for Hong Kong. Godley and Coppel report that in some cases more than 40 years after leaving for China, many former students now living in Hong Kong still speak Indonesian or Javanese dialects!

Today, ethnic Chinese have a better understanding of their own distinct identities and may be proud of their respective national identities. China has officially recognized Chinese who are citizens of different countries as nationals of those countries. In fact, occasional ignorant comments by some politicians, officials and scholars from China that Chinese in Southeast Asia should be loyal to their countries or should contribute economically to their respective countries are taken as insults by people of Chinese descent who have identified with their respective societies.[6] Even Taiwan which has not yet officially renounced the *jus sanguinis* principle with regard to all persons of Chinese parentage, has in fact controlled the movement of non-Taiwanese Chinese into Taiwan, and it has taken strict measures to prevent the influx of 'illegal' non-Taiwanese Chinese labor into its territory.

In summary, Chinese everywhere do not form a 'race', and transnationally, they relate to each other as Chinese of different nationalities or as simply Chinese. Ultimately, identity is a matter of subjective identification that is shaped by the experience of living in a national society. Even the Chinese in Southeast Asia do not form a single entity despite so much that has been written about them.

CONCLUSION

This chapter shows that as far as ethnic identity is concerned, the persistence of Chinese ethnic identification does not depend on the persistence of the use of any Chinese language. There is thus a need to distinguish between cultural identity and ethnic identification. Anthropologists today are quite aware of this, especially since Barth's seminal work (1969a). A comparative study of Chinese communities worldwide serves to confirm this point. Even Chinese who do not speak any Chinese language can continue to identify as being Chinese.

However, culture — especially the language component — serves to portray the type of identity, and different levels of acculturation give rise to different perceptions of Chinese identity. There are different models of Chinese culture and there are different Chinese identities. For those literate in Chinese, the ability to speak and write Mandarin is seen as crucial to the persistence of both Chinese cultural and ethnic identities.

Table 5.1 Language and Chinese Identities

Type of Chinese	Language	Description
A	Speak at least a Chinese language and are literate in Chinese. LOI is usually a Chinese language. LOL is Chinese, and possibly other languages too. Preferred IGL is Chinese (Mandarin or other Chinese languages).	Because of common literacy in Chinese, Type A Chinese everywhere share certain similar interests in Chinese language, Chinese literature and Chinese arts. They generally have more knowledge and interest in Chinese history, philosophy and civilization than other categories of Chinese.
B	Speak at least a Chinese language, but do not read and write Chinese. LOI is usually a Chinese language. LOL (if any) is non-Chinese. Preferred IGL is usually Chinese and/or non-Chinese.	These include (a) Chinese who are illiterate but can speak at least one Chinese language and (b) Chinese who can speak a Chinese language but for whom the language of literacy is not Chinese.
C	Do not speak any Chinese language nor write Chinese. LOI is non-Chinese. LOL (if any) is non-Chinese. Preferred IGL is the same as LOI and LOL	These are 'acculturated' Chinese. The Baba of Melaka are a good example. They speak one or more non-Chinese languages (Baba Malay and English in the case of the Baba), and if literate, the language of literacy is also not Chinese (English and/or Malay in the case of the Baba).
D	LOI is a localized Chinese language and one or more non-Chinese languages. LOL (if any) is usually non-Chinese. Preferred IGL is the same as the LOI.	These are also acculturated Chinese but unlike Type C, they still speak an acculturated Chinese language. An example would be the Peranakan-type Chinese in Northeast Kelantan, who speak an acculturated version of Hokkien, Kelantan Malay dialect, many of whom also speak the local Thai dialect.

Note: LOI: Language of Intimacy   LOL: Language of Literacy
          IGL: Intra-Group Language

Our discussion on language in relation to Chinese identities may be summarized in Table 5.1. In the table, A and B types of Chinese see themselves as 'pure Chinese' in relation to Types C and D who may be referred to as 'Baba' — Baba in the descriptive sense and not as a sub-ethnic category of identification as in the case of the Baba of Melaka. It is the contrast between the less acculturated and the more acculturated. In Southeast Asia, the latter are usually referred to in Chinese writing as *tusheng huaren* (literally 'local-born Chinese'). This is, of course, not a proper term since most people of Chinese descent today, at least in Southeast Asia, are local-born. In Malaysia, the 'pure Chinese' popularly use 'Baba' to refer not only to the Baba of Melaka, but also to the more acculturated Chinese in general, especially those who speak Malay among themselves and wear some features of Malay dress. In Indonesia, there are the Totok Chinese ('pure Chinese') versus the Peranakan Chinese (the Baba), but in most countries there is no specific term for the so-called 'pure Chinese'. This is understandable since the 'pure Chinese' see themselves as Chinese and regard the acculturated Chinese as not quite Chinese, hence the use of usually derogatory labels for these Chinese.

Language of Intimacy (LOI) is the language regularly used at home. It is also the preferred language used for intra-group communication (IGL), that is, the language used among fellow Chinese. However, not all Chinese speak the same language, so Type A Chinese, for example, may have to use a language such as English as a medium of communication with, say, the Baba Chinese (Type C). Nevertheless, the preferred IGL for the Type A Chinese is either Mandarin or one of the other Chinese languages. In fact, in a predominantly English-speaking environment like the USA or Australia, the Type A Chinese may even have to compromise and speak English to their children, although their preferred LOI is a Chinese language.

The above classification of Chinese in relation to language may be applied to Chinese of all nationalities, although not all categories may appear in a country. In the case of Malaysia, the majority of the Chinese are Type A and Type B Chinese, with the former corresponding to the Chinese-educated Chinese. The Baba of Melaka as well as the English-speaking Chinese who do not speak a Chinese language belong to Type C, while the Peranakan-type Chinese in Kelantan belong to Type D. Penang Chinese, although speaking a localized version of Hokkien (but not as acculturated as the Peranakan-type Chinese) do not use Malay for communication among fellow Chinese, and so they are more appropriately classified as Type B 'pure Chinese'. The Peranakan-type Chinese of Kelantan, however, are comfortable speaking their localized Hokkien and the Kelantan Malay dialect at home. In the case of Malaysia, English is accepted as one of the languages for communication among Chinese, as is true of most other ethnic groups. Thus, the Chinese can be contrasted with the other groups based on the extent to which they use Malay as an IGL. Only the 'Babas' (Type C and Type D Chinese) accept Malay dialects as an IGL.

If we take the case of the United States, there are at least Type A Chinese and Type B Chinese too. There are also Baba Chinese (Type C), that is, Chinese Americans who speak, read and write English and do not know any Chinese language. I do not know if there are Type D Chinese Americans. Unlike countries like Malaysia and Indonesia, the US allows immigrants from China and elsewhere to enter, many of whom are members of the Chinese intelligentsia (Wang L. Ling-chi 1991). These form the less locally rooted Type A Chinese in contrast to the more rooted ones, and provide some dynamics in Chinese writing and cultural activities relative to the Type A Chinese.

Chinese can claim to be descendants of a civilization — the Chinese civilization. In literacy, they are 'united' by the common use of Chinese writing, and today, Mandarin is the common Chinese language for those who are literate in Chinese. As the Chinese language is closely linked to Chinese civilization, and the Chinese-educated Chinese are generally the dominant definers of Chinese identity, there has been and will continue to be psychological pressure on the non-Chinese-educated to learn some Chinese to be 'more Chinese' culturally. This also means that there is more need for the more acculturated Chinese to negotiate their identity, to come to term with their Chineseness. The alternative is to claim not to be Chinese, but as Ang (1993), has described, this is not easy when others still expect a Chinese-looking person to be Chinese. The Babas in Melaka generally avoid the identity problem by feeling proud of their Baba-ness, and situationally masking their Baba identity outside of Melaka by speaking English, an acceptable non-ethnic common language in Malaysia. There is still a need for the Babas to ignore the derogatory attitude of the mainstream Chinese, unless they are directly challenged about their Chinese identity. During the fieldwork I had often seen Baba individuals retorted, in Baba Malay, their non-Baba Chinese friends who teased them as not real Chinese.

The identities of ethnic Chinese are shaped by their experience of living in the respective national societies. The subjective experience of Chinese Malaysians is obviously different from the Chinese Americans in San Francisco. The increase in contact between Chinese of different countries actually highlights the diversities and the need to respect these diversities. Even the Chinese-educated Chinese Malaysians who may share many similar literary interests with people in China or with 'Chinese-educated' Chinese in the Philippines, may have different subjective experiences of being Chinese. For a Chinese Malaysian, his experience is shaped by his experience as a Malaysian. Similarly, a Chinese American is shaped by his experience of being an American.

This chapter stresses the need to distinguish culture from ethnicity, and it is also important to distinguish the cultural identification of the Chinese from national identification. A Chinese Malaysian who speaks Mandarin and likes Chinese literature cannot be considered as less Malaysian than a Baba who speaks Malay and likes some Malay folk songs, and they are both as Malaysian as other Malaysians of other ethnic origins. Ethnic and national identification are subjective and they cannot be measured by a list of cultural criteria.

Likewise, an ethnic Chinese who likes Chinese poems and publications from China should not be seen as identifying with China. Failure to understand the distinct national identities of the people of Chinese descent and the issue of China's cultural relevance leads to the belief that the people of Chinese descent comprise a potential fifth column which can be used by China, as was propagated during the Cold War. Now that the Cold War is over, the fifth column argument is by no means fully buried. As China emerges as a greater regional power in Asia, politicians, journalists and scholars who see China as a threat may still invoke this and other similar ideologies. This is especially so if China refuses to fit itself into the scheme of world domination envisioned by the industrial powers of the West. Events since the end of the Cold War (especially given the double standards of the US with regards to the South) have shown that the major Western powers — especially the US — do not tolerate the growth of regional powers which are independent of their control or influence. The case of Iraq is a good example; its invasion of Kuwait gave the West the excuse to finish it off.

We should also note that all the major international agencies of the mass media are from the West and represent the interests of the industrial powers. The way such media printed propaganda in favor of the United States and its allies during the Gulf War shows this bias very clearly. It is easy for this same media to propagate certain modes of thinking about Chinese overseas in relation to China — thinking which will serve the interests of the industrial powers in the North. Already, *The Economist* in its 18 July 1992 issue carried an article entitled 'Overseas Chinese: A Driving Force' (on pages 21 to 22, and on page 24). The article analyses the economic strength and roles of the 'overseas Chinese'. The analysis seems sociological but the underlying message is mischievous and, in fact, racist in so far as it is against the interest of the people of Chinese descent. It implies that the 'overseas Chinese' will serve China's interests. The sub-heading of the article reads: 'The 55 million overseas Chinese are one of the world's great economic engines. They will become greater still as they pull forward China itself'. In the opening paragraph, the article mentions that 'China is a giant that could dominate the 20th century'. It then comments that, 'If so, the overseas Chinese — ethnic Chinese living outside China — will have a big hand in the proceedings'. The article concludes with this remark: 'If the recent enthusiasm of the overseas

Chinese is anything to go by, the transnational Chinese economy, which in some ways already rivals Japan as a business influence in Asia, is poised for a great leap forward.'

In the first place, it is most misleading to lump the Chinese outside the 'Chinese land' with the Chinese in Taiwan and Hong Kong as 'overseas Chinese'. We have already seen that the Chinese overseas identify with their respective nationalities and relate to the Chinese of other states in this manner too. There is really no common transnational Chinese identity, nor transnational Chinese economy. To group the economic interests of ethnic Chinese worldwide and represent them as a transnational Chinese economy that will serve the interest of China is misleading.

The fate of ethnic Chinese is yet to be free of the politicking of major world powers or from the convoluted wrangling of regional politics. The international policies of China may make things difficult too. The declaration by China regarding her claim over the Spratly and Paracel Archipelagoes in the South China Sea has revived concern about the hegemony of China. Whatever the attitude of China towards the people of Chinese descent, the time when China can use them for its alleged hegemony is over. In fact, in the case of the Chinese in Southeast Asia, Professor Wang Gungwu had aptly pointed out that, 'Whatever China's ultimate intentions, the Southeast Asian Chinese are mostly irrelevant and no asset to China. On the contrary, there is evidence to suggest that they might be, if they have not already been, a considerable liability' (1979, see 1981: 283). Even in economic matters, if China can be successful in getting the rich Chinese outside China to invest in China, it is because these people of Chinese descent see the business opportunities there, as do non-Chinese investors (such as the Koreans and Japanese), and not because they are politically China-oriented or because they have primordial sentiments as Chinese.

Overall, the comparative study of Chinese communities worldwide in relation to language, nationality and identity helps us to understand the similarities and diversities of Chinese cultures and identities. There is a need for concerned scholars to make their findings and analyses widely available in order to correct the distorted representation of Chinese ethnicity, especially in relation to China.

6

Ethnic Chinese and Ethnic Relations: Some Economic Explanations

INTRODUCTION

Ethnic Chinese in different parts of the world have to adjust to living in different ecological and political conditions. They have to adjust to living with people of other ethnic origins, especially those who are politically dominant. Thus the study of ethnic relations between ethnic Chinese and the indigenous/majority people[1] will throw light on the dynamics of group relations. In other words, comparison of ethnic Chinese experiences in the Chinese ethnological field can tell us much more about ethnic relations involving different types of Chinese than studying the ethnic relations in one country only. In fact, in many places, especially in Southeast Asia, the citizens of Chinese origin are often still seen as 'immigrants', 'of immigrant origin', a 'trading minority', and so on.

There are a number of important studies on ethnic relations that are based on the experiences of the Chinese in their relations with the indigenous or majority people. In this chapter, I examine the nature of ethnic group relations between the people of Chinese descent and the indigenous or majority people, by discussing some of the theoretical works that provide economic explanations of ethnic relations. In particular I discuss the main arguments of W.F. Wertheim (1964), Edna Bonacich (1972, 1973, 1979) and Alvin Rabushka (1974). I also discuss the significance of class in ethnic relations, and in the conclusion I use the rational choice theory to interpret Chinese adjustments to the varying nature of ethnic relations in different societies. Throughout the chapter, I focus on the Chinese in Southeast Asia, especially Malaysia, with whom I am more familiar.

The chapter is comparative, so various examples from a number of countries are cited. Readers who are only interested in the result of this comparative study and discussion of 'theories' may go directly to the last two sections, the ethnic relations model and the conclusion. The conclusion summarizes the main features of relations between the Chinese and the indigenous/dominant groups; the section preceding it provides a general model for the study of ethnic relations.

ECONOMIC COMPETITION

In the study of relations between ethnic Chinese and indigenous people, it should be noted that cultural differences by themselves do not cause tensions in the relations between ethnic groups. In Southeast Asia, for example, the Chinese have lived there for a long time with very little cultural conflict with the local people. It is only when cultural differences are politicized that tensions occur.

In fact, where the Chinese are few in number, they have become fairly acculturated by the majority people, as in the Peranakan-type Chinese[2] in northeast Kelantan, Malaysia. Since the population in Kelantan is predominantly Malays who are Muslims, the Chinese there have even avoided selling and buying pork in public. I have shown elsewhere (Tan 1979) that in a multi-ethnic situation, certain norms are formed and observed for smooth interaction among members of different ethnic groups. This serves to filter out potential cultural conflict among groups.

In Malaysia, not offering pork or food containing pork or lard to the Malays is an important general norm in the context of Chinese-Malay interaction. Whereas in Kelantan the Chinese have to adjust socially more to the Malays as shown in their manner of selling and buying pork in the private Chinese domain, in Kuala Lumpur where the Chinese are numerous, they do not have to 'concede' so much socio-cultural adjustment to the Malays. In Kuala Lumpur, the Chinese can sell and buy pork freely in the markets and the peddlers can even sell pork from house-to-house using motorbikes or vans. In this situation, the Malays have adjusted to the cultural needs of the Chinese. This form of ethnic relations functions well, as long as the Chinese observe the general norm of not insulting the Malays with pork (such as throwing pieces of pork or pig's bones around the compound of Malay houses or teasing the Malays to buy pork), and Muslim politicians do not turn this aspect of cultural diversity into a political issue.

If cultural diversity by itself does not cause strain in the relations between the Chinese and other peoples (especially the indigenous majority people), then the attention is naturally focused on the nature of economic relations, since many ethnic Chinese are engaged in the commercial sectors. Economic competition is said to be the underlying cause of tensions between the Chinese and the indigenous people. In Southeast Asia, W.F. Wertheim has argued this most forcefully. In his article, 'The Trading Minorities in Southeast Asia', he argues that, 'it is not plurality which accounts for increasing tension, but the ability to compete in the economic and political field' (1964, 70). He presents his economic competition theory clearly as follows: It is economic competition between adjoining social groups which lies at the root of the tensions, as they present themselves in the actual phase of world history (1964, 76).

The economic competition approach is adopted by various scholars, such as Willmott (1967, 96-8) and The (1966), in their study of relations between the Chinese and the indigenous peoples in Southeast Asia. In fact, in almost all writings on the Chinese and the indigenous people, where there is tension, economic competition is identified as the underlying structural factor. In Mexico, for example, Jacques (1981) reports that by the late 19th century, the Chinese in Sonora had begun to consolidate their hold on the retail and wholesale grocery business as well as shoe factories. By 1910, there were 4500 Chinese in Sonora, and they competed with both the domestic labor and business people;

hence both the labor and the middle-class business people resented them. In fact, shortly before the Mexican Revolution of 1910, there was an epigram that said, 'The Americans do all the big business, the Chinese do all the little business, and we Mexicans hold office and shout VIVA' (Jacques 1981, 15). This epigram tells much about the nature of conflict between the Chinese and the indigenous people. As most Chinese are involved in the commercial sectors, they form a visible 'trading minority'. Furthermore, unlike the big Western capitalists, the Chinese business people have direct interaction with the local people, so they bear the brunt of any indigenous attack against economic exploiters, capitalists or 'aliens' who control the national economy.

The competition argument is important in most theories on ethnic relations. Robert Ezra Park of the ecological school, for example, holds competition as crucial to his argument on ethnic relations. In his analysis of 'race relations' and world economy, he argues that, 'the competition of goods, which is an effect of foreign trade, tends inevitably to bring about a competition of persons, which is an effect of immigration'. In his opinion, 'both the movements of goods and of populations seem to be merely aspects of a general tendency to redress the economic balance and to restore the equilibrium between population and food supply, labor and capital, in a world economy' (Park 1950, 143). One may not agree with his approach to ethnic relations, but the idea of economic competition is important. In fact, Park does not restrict competition to just economic competition. For him competition is 'the struggle for existence of races and people' (1950, 159). It is in this sense that we understand his argument that 'racial competition leads easily, and more or less inevitably to racial conflict' (1950, 60).

The economic competition argument is particularly relevant to the study of ethnic relations in Southeast Asia, mainly because the economic influence of the Chinese is more dominant and widespread, and the indigenous people continue to see the people of Chinese descent as controlling the national economy and hindering their economic progress. Using the economic competition argument, the tensions between the Chinese and the indigenous people following the independence of various Southeast Asian countries may be said to be due to the increasing involvement of the indigenous people in the commercial sectors, as well as their wish to eventually dominate the national economy. During the colonial era, as in Malaya, indigenous people such as the Malays were encouraged to remain in the rural subsistence sector, whereas the Chinese were allowed to concentrate their economic involvement in the mining, commercial and financial sectors. The British remained the overall controller of the economy. This segregation of ethnic groups by economic functions was economically sound and politically safe for the colonial regime. However, this led to a highly lopsided economic development in which the gap between the rural and the urban and between the Malays and the Chinese became wider.

By the time of independence, the commercial and industrial sectors as well as the financial institutions were dominated by foreign capitalists and the local Chinese business class, but it was the local Chinese who became a convenient target of criticism. Their critics were Malays who wanted to let off their frustrations arising from economic backwardness. The economic visibility is reinforced by geographical visibility (concentration in urban centers) and cultural visibility (as evident in the Chineseness of urban centers). Thus, the particular effect of historical development, economic competition, and the multiple visibility of the Chinese not only makes them an 'identifiable' target of attack but also scapegoats for economic crises and failures in socio-economic development.

With independence, the indigenous élites gained political power, and one of their early tasks was to push for economic nationalism, which aimed at restricting the economic influence of the Chinese in commerce, especially the retail and wholesale trades. This was in the class interest of the political élites. At the same time, it was politically advantageous, since the policy was promoted in the name of protecting the interests of the indigenous people. In overall economic development, it was of course unwise to suppress Chinese capital and their commercial and financial experience as well as their effective exchange network. In fact, Indonesia and the Philippines, which expressed severe economic nationalism against the Chinese, have since relaxed their oppressive policies.

Even in Thailand, which had not been colonized, economic nationalist policies were introduced in the 1930s (cf. Heidhues 1974, 20–7). This is not surprising, since trade in Thailand was traditionally controlled by the royal family that, in its own interest, had allowed the expansion of Chinese business. Thus by the 20th century, when nationalism was on the rise all over Asia, the Thai found the Chinese business class a formidable force in Thai economy. A consequence of the economic nationalism policy was the emergence of joint ventures between the Chinese and the indigenous élites. In Malaysia, the Ali-Baba phenomenon has become widespread. This is the practice of a Chinese business person paying a Malay 'sleeping partner' in return for using his or her name to apply for a business permit or license. Viewed another way, it is also the practice of a Malay business person or politician sub-contracting a contract to the Chinese who have the capital and experience to run a business or industry, thereby making profit without having to contribute any capital.

In Malaysia, the economic competition argument remains influential in the interpretation of Chinese-Malay relations. It is in fact an important justification of the Malay-dominated government to implement affirmative action programs for the Malays and other indigenous people. The justification is that although Malays are the majority people, they have been historically rendered in a weak position to compete with the Chinese without any affirmative action. Dr Mahathir (who later became the prime minister) explains the problem of competition as follows: 'Chinese business methods and the extent of their control of the economy of the country is such that competition between their community and other communities is quite impossible' (1970, 56).

In fact, the government regards the underlying cause of the worst race riots in 1969 a result of both the frustration of the Malays about their own socio-economic position *vis-à-vis* the Chinese and the political agitation of the Chinese. The government report on the 1969 riots had the following to say in response to the accusation that Malays enjoyed special privileges and that the non-Malays were discriminated against.

The Malays who already felt excluded in the country's economic life, now began to feel a threat to their place in the public service. No mention was ever made by non-Malay politicians of the almost closed-door attitude to the Malays by non-Malays in large sections of the private sector in this country (NOC 1969, 23–4).

There are now various reports on the 1969 race riots (see for example NOC 1969; Slimming 1969; Tunku Abdul Rahman 1969; Gagliano 1970; Goh 1971; McTaggart 1971; Comber 1983). I do not deal with the details of the riots, but by all accounts, it was not due to cultural confrontation. It was political. At the same time, the underlying economic causes are important, too.

The most important development in economic policy following the 1969 riots was the introduction of the New Economic Policy (NEP), which was to have major consequences on Chinese-Malay relations. The policy incorporated the thinking that had emerged from the first and second Bumiputra Economic Congress (1965 and 1968), that is, the call for government intervention to promote Malay economic interests. The NEP was introduced under the Second Malaysia Plan (1971–75). It 'seeks to eradicate poverty among all Malaysians and to restructure Malaysian society so that the identification of race with economic function and geographical location is reduced and eventually eliminated' (Malaysia Plan 1976, 7). It set as its targets 'the ownership and management by Malays and other indigenous people of at least 30% of commercial and industrial activities in the economy and an employment structure at all levels of operation and management that reflects the racial composition of the nation by 1990' (Malaysia Plan 1976, 30).[3]

To ensure greater *bumiputera* (indigenous people) share in the economy, the government controlled quotas and licenses as well as set up economic and financial institutions mainly in the interests of the Malays. The Chinese were not excluded from business, but more and more they had to compete with the state capital and deal with certain economic regulations which were aimed at increasing Malay share in the economy. However, the NEP emphasized the distinction between *bumiputera* and *non-bumiputera*. This resulted in much communal politics, which had serious consequences on Malay-Chinese relations. It caused more inter-ethnic rivalry and hence more ethnic tensions.

The political dominance of the Malay political élite had assured the success of the NEP, especially in creating a capitalist class of Malays. By 1990, Chinese and Malay politicians as well as the economists of the two camps disagreed with one another on the statistics of the *bumiputera* and *non-bumiputera* share of the economy. While the Chinese complained of discrepancies in the implementation of the NEP, the lower-class Malays were also unhappy about their economic status. The expansion and consolidation of Malay middle and upper classes (including the business class) did not solve the problem of poverty among the Malays. At the same time, poverty among non-Malays could not be ignored.

The NEP assumed that the economic cake would expand so that no one would be deprived, but the recession in the late 1980s, one can argue, had led to increased inter-ethnic competition for economic and social resources. In fact, in adopting the racial approach rather than the universal principle of social justice to correct what was perceived as ethnic imbalances, the NEP had heightened ethnic competition in all spheres. This is still true in the post-NEP period (after 1990), for the main policies of NEP remain in force. Students, for example, experience ethnic competition as they move up the educational level. After basic secondary education, they have to compete along racial lines, because of the ethnic quota system, to gain a place in the pre-university classes (Form Six). After that, they compete for a place in one of the local universities and government colleges; when they seek jobs, they feel the competition, too. Such competition as well as the communal thinking that the young people acquire from their socialization tends to lead to ethnic polarization. Perhaps this polarization is more serious than that experienced by the older generation. It is a cause of concern in national unity.

What I have described so far shows that it is more useful, in the study of ethnic relations, to examine not just economic competition but competition for both economic and social resources as an underlying structural cause of ethnic tensions. This is especially so in the modern nation-state, in which individuals and groups are integrated or forced to be integrated into the national economic, political and social institutions, that is, into a common economic niche. In an ethnically stratified society, this means competition along ethnic lines for both economic and socio-cultural opportunities.

However, the economic competition theory neglects the motivating force of ideology, and the economic determinist approach tends to undermine political factors. In fact, Mackie (1976) has criticized both Wertheim and The Siauw Giap for not paying sufficient attention to socio-cultural factors and especially political factors. An important contribution of Mackie's analysis of the anti-Chinese outbreaks in Indonesia is his analysis of how anti-Chinese sentiment was manipulated 'as part of the struggle for power between the right- and the left-wing forces in Indonesian politics' (1976, 98). He identifies various factors that account for the outbreak of anti-Chinese violence and groups them into three categories, which he calls predisposing factors, restraining factors and precipitating factors. The (1980), in his review article, replies to Mackie by using historical materials at his disposal, to show a pattern of economic competition in Chinese-Indonesian relations. He shows that a cultural factor like religion by itself does not lead to inter-ethnic tensions. Anti-Chinese riots were not for safeguarding Islam that was never endangered by the Chinese. I agree with this view, except that I will examine not only economic factors but also political factors, not just merely as factors intertwined with the economic factors but also as independent factors.

To be sure, Wertheim and The Siauw Giap did not altogether neglect socio-cultural and political factors that they touch on in their analysis of economic competition. The main weakness is that when the economic argument becomes determinist, major political factors may be ignored. Mackie, in contrast, stresses political and socio-cultural factors over economic factors. In my opinion, both socio-economic competition and the politics of ethnicity are crucial factors that cause ethnic tensions. Indeed, inter-ethnic competition provides the crucial base for political mobilization along ethnic lines and thus either creates or intensifies ethnic tension.[4] At the same time, as Mackie has shown, certain political factors may directly cause ethnic tensions.

It is also necessary to examine ideologies as a motivating force in the economic and political structures and thereby causing ethnic tensions. Surely the economic nationalism in Southeast Asia cannot be explained merely by the economic argument. I have analyzed elsewhere that in post-independent Southeast Asian states, the dominant indigenous groups seek to create a nation which is meaningful in the context of their indigenous past (Tan 1987, 103). Thus in Malaysia, Malay 'nationalism' (which really is Malay communalism in post-independent Malaysia) provides an ideological force in nation building, and the non-Malays, notably the Chinese (the second largest ethnic group after the Malays), are worried that their interests and identity will be undermined. The political will of the Malay élites to decolonize and indigenize according to the Malay perspective is not new. By the first few decades of the 20th century, Malay nationalism was not just against colonial domination but also very much against the increasing economic domination of the Malays by the Chinese.[5] For the Malay communalists, decolonization and indigenization mean acquiring Malay dominance in all spheres, and this is a strong motivating force.

Thus the indigenous communal ideology and the politics of it is a crucial factor which affects the relations between the Chinese and the majority indigenous group.[6] Communal nationalism provides the indigenous ruling élites a way of 'imagining'[7] the new nation-state which includes the people of Chinese descent as citizens. In Malaysia, where the Chinese population is quite big (28.1% compared to 50.0% Malays, according to the 1991 census), there is much communal politics; indeed, there are both more radical Malay communalists and Chinese communalists who even communalize non-communal issues. In Indonesia, the Suharto government adopted an assimilationist policy that aimed to integrate the Chinese through assimilation. In Thailand, the Thai national identity is established, and the Chinese there are easily accepted as Thai as long as they speak Thai and identify themselves as Thai. There is, however, also some official Thaification of the Chinese, as seen in the closing of Chinese schools and integration of the study of Chinese in the Thai system. In the Philippines, despite the presence of some economic restrictions, the Chinese minority has been left alone culturally. Having been heavily influenced by the Spanish culture and the English language, the identity of the Philippines has been evolving without as much politics of indigenization as in Malaysia and Indonesia. It was only during President Corazon Aquino's term that the Tagalog-based 'Filipino' was officially identified as the national language.

The communal ideology of nation building in Southeast Asia affects the political sentiments of the Chinese and the indigenous groups about one another. Another ideology that affects the 'Sino-native' relations is radical communism. This is evident in the case of the Chinese in Cambodia and Vietnam. Willmott (1967) had reported about the good relations between the Chinese and the Cambodians, but under the pro-China Pol Pot regime, about half (about 200,000 or more) died in less than four years, from 1975 to 1978 (Kiernan 1986, 18, 27). Many fled the country by boat and became refugees. Yet it was the Khmer Rouge's communist ideology of oppressing capitalists and urban dwellers rather than a distinct racist policy that caused the Chinese to be executed or to perish as a result of starvation or disease after being removed from Phnom Penh and sent to the countryside. Nevertheless, in such a campaign against urban dwellers and 'capitalists', prejudice against the Chinese was inevitable, due to the concentration of the Chinese in Phnom Penh and their involvement in the commercial sectors. Yet, as Kiernan (1986, 27) points out, 'it is difficult to choose between their fate and that of the tens of thousands of Chams and Vietnamese and hundreds of thousands of Khmers, such as the Eastern Zone peasantry, who were targeted for execution even though they were undoubtedly of poor social origins'.

We are also familiar with the exodus of the Chinese from Vietnam to China and by boat to Southeast Asia since 1978. Although there had been Vietnamese resentment against the Hoa (people of Chinese descent), the exodus was due to a number of factors, especially the Sino-Vietnam conflict. The campaign to eliminate the merchant class in South Vietnam after liberation inevitably resulted in the Chinese being persecuted. This was worsened by the Sino-Vietnam conflict that followed. As Porter (1980, 59) points out:

> The Hoa were clearly the victims of the restructuring of the Vietnamese economy they had long dominated. But they were even more victimized by the conflict between Vietnam and China, which both provoked the Hoa exodus and was spurred by the Vietnamese reaction to that exodus.

Thus ideology is a force itself. Although communal ideology may be said to arise out of the economic and political structures, and it may be created or perpetuated by the élite of an ethnic group to compete more successfully with that of another, it is undoubtedly also necessary to consider it as an independent factor influencing ethnic relations.

From the discussion on economic competition as the underlying factor of ethnic tensions, we now arrive at a general model of explaining ethnic relations; that is, ethnic relations can be explained by studying the nature and intensity of competition for socio-economic resources between ethnic groups as well as the ideologies and the political factors which influence ethnic relations. In other words, the study of ethnic relations is basically a study of economic and political relations between ethnic groups and between the 'minorities' and the state and how ideologies are mobilized in the economic and political relations that are significant to the relations between ethnic groups.

CLASS ANALYSIS

The theoretical analysis that is of special significance to the competition model of ethnic relations is class analysis. In ethnic studies, the first scholar who seriously used class in his analysis of ethnic relations was Oliver C. Cox (1948). I do not deal with his work here.[8] Instead, I show the need to pay attention to the question of class in the competition model.

In the context of Chinese-Malay relations in Malaysia, it is inadequate to talk of competition between Malays and Chinese as if they are homogeneous racial blocks. Each ethnic group has its classes, but in a pluralistic society like Malaysia, social classes are also polarized along ethnic lines.[9] We should also note the influential roles played by the élites. One can argue that it is the Malay and non-Malay political élites supported by the economic élites and segments of the respective intelligentsia that are the champions of communalism. The Malay élites in their own political and economic interests project themselves as the guardian of Malay interests against what they portray as the economic domination and political challenge of the Chinese. The Chinese élites, in contrast, seek to unite the Chinese masses in the name of protecting Chinese interest against Malay dominance. We should note that although the middle and upper class Malays compete with the similar classes among the Chinese, there is also much cooperation among the upper classes of the two ethnic groups, for mutual class interests.

Indeed, it is necessary to understand the class factor in ethnic competition and the mobilization of communal politics. This will also enable us to understand the differential ethnic expression by different intra-group classes. Lim Mah-hui (1983, 311) for example, in his study of ownership and control of large corporations in Malaysia, concludes that:

> The New Economic Policy has brought about increasing partnership between state, foreign and local Chinese capital. Among the large corporations, the consequences of this policy have not been as problematic as it has been for the small firms. Hence the protest from big Chinese and foreign capital has been less strident compared to that from middle-level Chinese businesses.

In other words, there is more ethnic dissatisfaction among the middle-level Chinese business people than among the big Chinese capitalists. We can also argue that the Malay and Chinese middle classes have more need to compete with one another whether in businesses or in job promotion or other opportunities, so they are the more communal (racial) classes.

In the analysis of the 1969 race riots in Malaysia, Stenson (1976) and Lim (1980), who use class analysis, are able to highlight the class factors behind inter-ethnic competition. For Lim (1980, 149), the 1969 riots 'represented discontent expressed by different classes within the Malay community'; the riots were a response to the non-Malay threats and they led to the overthrow of *laissez-faire* capitalism and laid the foundation for state capitalism. For Stenson (1976, 48) the riots arose from 'a form of transferred frustration having its roots in intra-Malay class conflicts'. Although one may not agree to the specific argument of Stenson, his analysis of intra-Malay class conflict in the context of inter-ethnic rivalry is important.

The tensions between the Chinese and the dominant indigenous groups in Southeast Asia are perpetuated by the myth of Chinese as the class of 'the haves', in contrast to the indigenous groups as 'the have-nots'. The heterogeneity of class within each ethnic community is ignored. This is the problem of treating a whole ethnic group as a 'class'. As Weightman (1986, 93–4) has described in the Philippines,

> Increasingly Filipinos perceived Chinese to be rich exploiters. They were totally unaware that most Philippine Chinese were concentrated in the working classes.

This is a common problem encountered by people of Chinese descent throughout Southeast Asia. It is so in Malaysia and even in Indonesia, where the Chinese form less than three percent of the total population. We have seen that during the anti-capitalist campaign, the Chinese had the problem of convincing Khmer Rouge and Vietnamese soldiers that they were of lower class origin, for the soldiers' stereotype was that the Chinese belonged to the 'haves' class.

In an ethnically stratified society, intra-ethnic class competition and power relations are easily projected into inter-ethnic relations. Lower class frustration is expressed mainly at the other ethnic group that is perceived as a rival to one's 'race' or as exploiter/oppressor of one's other ethnic members. Ethnic competition and discrimination may be actually experienced or merely perceived, but this is sufficient to make one feel that one's group is threatened by the ethnic group in question. Even the competition and/or discrimination experienced by another class is seen as the problem or fate of the whole 'race' and therefore is relevant to an individual. Such is the expression of ethnicity.

The class approach orients us to the class basis of ethnic relations, which is often neglected if the focus is purely on the racial nature of ethic relations. In his study of Monterey Park in California, where Asians form the majority of the city's population, Fong (1998) points out that in the 1950s and 1960s when middle-class Chinese and Japanese moved in, they were welcomed. But from the 1970s when affluent Chinese moved in, with their investments, ethnic tension began to rise. Fong (1998, 168) is of the opinion that racial conflict in Monterey Park is 'very much a class conflict between residents and developer interests struggling over control'.

Thus in our inter-ethnic competition model, it is important to pay attention to the question of class. However, we should avoid any determinist approach like reducing everything to class relations. Instead of reducing all ethnic phenomena to class relations, it is better to view the broader inter-ethnic competition as the basis of conflicting ethnic relations and see how class plays a role in this context of inter-ethnic rivalry. Class may be seen as a principle of mobilization, and in present-day Malaysia, there is not much mobilization along the class lines. The main principle of mobilization is ethnicity.

THE SPLIT LABOR MARKET THEORY

If we move from Southeast Asia to North America, the nature of ethnic relations differs. In the past (the 19th century), Chinese laborers in the United States were highly discriminated against. In Southeast Asia, the Chinese immigrants and the indigenous people were by and large involved in different economic sectors. The Chinese immigrants either involved themselves in business or worked as laborers, especially in the tin mines. Most of the indigenous people were still confined to the subsistence sector, and few were willing to work as hard laborers who were poorly paid. In the United States, where the Chinese laborers displaced the higher paid white laborers, there was much antagonism against them.

This leads us to Edna Bonacich's split labor market hypothesis, which is as follows:

> The central hypothesis is that ethnic antagonism first germinates in a labor market split along ethnic lines. To be split, a labor market must contain at least two groups of workers whose price of labor differs for the same work, or would differ if they did the same work. (1972, 549)

The split labor market hypothesis is also an economic explanation of ethnic relations. Competition is important in the explanation of ethnic relations, but the focus of the hypothesis is on the difference in the price of labor as the underlying cause of ethnic antagonism. It emphasizes class struggle. Bonacich (1979, 20) explains that in white and non-white relations, 'the real division is not between white and non-white, but between high-priced and cheap labor'. Thus the theory is rather deterministic in that it sees ethnic division as really not ethnic but economic, arising out of the difference in labor price.

However, the presence of the split labor market by itself need not necessarily lead to ethnic antagonism. Hilton (1979), who finds the split labor market hypothesis useful for his study of Chinese immigration to the United States, points out that although white labor resented the cheaper Chinese labor force, their antagonism was not consistent. In certain industries, widespread employment of Chinese labor did not lead to any significant protest. He explains that antagonism need not arise if an economy can expand fast enough to absorb cheaper immigrant labor without displacing native labor. 'Contractions, on the other hand, intensify the competition for each job, making antagonisms all the more fierce' (106).

In Malaysia there are various situations of a split labor market that do not manifest ethnic antagonism. Indian housemaids, for example, are paid less than Chinese maids. The Chinese employers usually explain that Chinese maids are more hardworking and the Indian maids are less efficient; also, they do not speak any Chinese language. The communication between the Chinese employers and the Indian maids is in Malay, since the former do not understand any Indian language. In fact, the Chinese maids have more job options in the urban private sector, which is predominantly Chinese. Unless they are paid reasonably well, Chinese women prefer other jobs to housemaids. The Indian maids who are often recruited from Indian settlements in the rubber estates have few, if any, other job choices. Furthermore, the demand for housemaids in Kuala Lumpur is high, and even maids from the Philippines are recruited. In this situation, the poorer section of the urban Chinese does not resent the presence of lower priced Indian maids.

The illegal Indonesian immigrants, to give another example, provide cheaper labor for the estates in Malaysia. Chinese antagonism towards these immigrants, by and large, is not due to the split labor market. Rather, it is the fear that these immigrants will eventually be given citizenship and thus increase the population of Malays. It is a communal and political issue. There is a shortage of plantation labor, as the local 'laborers' prefer to go to cities like Kuala Lumpur and Singapore to be employed as urban laborers or factory workers. The Indonesian immigrants, like the early Chinese settlers, are willing to take up low-priced job — they have no choice.

Azizah Kassim (1987, 271), in her analysis of Malaysian public response to Indonesian immigrants, mentions that the public response is influenced by class and ethnicity. Certain segments of the Malaysian population, such as plantation owners and housing developers and contractors, welcome the immigrants, whom they pay low wages. Contrary to the Chinese perception, the lower class Malays in Azizah's study do not welcome Indonesian immigrants. The middle-class Malays 'welcome some of them' (277). We can say that both the Malay and Chinese middle classes generally have little to gain or to lose economically from Indonesian immigrants; hence their view towards the Indonesian immigrants is the most ethnically polarized. The Chinese have a strong resentment because of the ethnic consideration mentioned above, whereas the Malays have nothing to lose as far as 'race' is concerned. The opposition of the lower-class Malays is due to competition for socio-economic resources and jobs. It is the overall competition for resources and jobs rather than merely the split labor market that causes the antagonism towards the Indonesian immigrants.

Supporters of the split labor market theory may protest that the above Malaysian examples are not suitable, for the theory emphasizes class struggle. In split labor markets, conflict develops among three key classes: business, higher paid labor, and cheaper labor (Bonacich 1972, 553). The theory is used 'to show that the race' question is really a class question, in that racially oppressed groups typically mark 'cheap labor' (Bonacich 1979, 34). Thus, the theory seems to work well in societies where class is a major principle of social mobilization and where workers are organized. The Malaysian examples above do not fit neatly into such a framework. But here lies the limitation of the split labor market theory. How can it explain ethnic problems in the many societies where classes in the Marxian sense (not mere social strata, cf. Dahrendorf 1959, 75–6) are not politically significant? We should also note that cheap labor groups, such as the Indonesian immigrants in Malaysia, are not necessary *racially* oppressed groups, although they are discriminated against economically by employers of all ethnic groups.

The split labor market theory is an economic 'theory' of ethnic antagonism, which emphasizes a particular kind of competition, that is, 'competition which arises from a price differential' (Bonacich 1972, 534). It has its merits, especially in directing our attention to the idea of a split labor market, the situation which gives rise to it, and the consequences. But it is certain situations giving rise to competition for jobs which account for ethnic antagonism; the split labor market is just one aspect of it. It is therefore more useful to view competition for social and economic resources as a source of ethnic tensions rather than to focus specifically on the split-labor market.[10] Furthermore, the split labor market argument is rather deterministic by reducing all ethnic relations to the question of the price of labor (class question) only and ignoring the force of 'racial' ideology and the wider politics of 'race' as well as the power relations between ethnic groups. It is an *a priori* explanation of ethnic relations by treating it as merely a phenomenon of class struggle. It ignores the fact that ethnicity can be a principle of mobilization by itself, which may be influenced by social strata and class but not necessary defined by class struggle.

MIDDLEMAN MINORITY AND ETHNIC ENCLAVE

Ethnic Chinese have often been described as a middleman minority.[11] For example, Furnivall in describing the Chinese in the Indies (now Indonesia) wrote that, 'The Chinese, like the Indian in Burma, acts as a middleman between European and native, tending to be a focus for the animosity of both, and yet at the same time a buffer, averting the direct collision of their conflicting interests' (1948, 232). Various scholars have not only referred to Chinese communities as middleman minorities but also talked of a theory of middleman minorities. This is especially so with Bonacich (1973, 1980; Turner and Bonacich 1980). The so-called theory outlines the characteristics of middleman minorities, largely based on the experiences of Chinese communities and other 'foreign' minorities. Although the labels 'middleman minority', 'trading minority', etc. are convenient, they give the impression that the Chinese as middleman minorities are all traders. This is not true, although the indigenous people in Southeast Asia and various writers have characterized them to be so.

The middleman minority concept is not only inaccurate, it also, as far as ethnic relations are concerned, focuses on the so-called middleman minority instead of the government (such as the colonial government) and the socio-economic and political forces of the larger society.[12] In Southeast Asia, it was colonialism which set the stage for the Chinese to be described as a middleman minority. The colonial government portrayed the Chinese as the middleman between the colonial élite and the indigenous people, and as exploiters of the latter, thus masking colonial exploitation while at the same time portraying the colonial master as the protector of the indigenous people. The middleman minority concept was in fact a product of the ideology of divide and rule.

The Chinese had traded with the Southeast Asian people long before the arrival of Western powers. Chinese communities were established before the Western colonialization of Southeast Asia. In Malaya (now Malaysia), the British commercial interests depended very much on the local Chinese merchants, who had good distribution networks. The Western firms also appointed local merchants as compradors. The Chinese were thus described as a middleman minority, but this was actually a concept seen from the perspective of the colonial élites. Seen from the perspective of the Chinese merchants then, the European merchants in colonial Southeast Asia might also be regarded as influential 'middlemen' between them and the Western markets. Wong (1985) has correctly criticized the application of 'middleman minority theory' to Chinese Americans, Japanese Americans, and Korean Americans. He observes that as the Chinese communities today cannot be placed neatly as a segment in a 'tridically structured inter-group configuration', the 'middleman minority theory' now revolves around a description of group characteristics rather than a demonstration of group function (61). He asks, 'between whom are the Chinese and Japanese Americans middlemen?' (62). The 'theory' functions to single out Asian Americans (but not white American groups) as separate. It has the effect of treating the middleman minority as a 'collective sojourner' and perpetuates the sojourner image. Indeed, even in 19th-century Southeast Asia, this portrayal of middleman minority as sojourners is not accurate. In the Straits Settlements comprising Penang, Melaka (both in Malaysia now) and Singapore, successful Chinese merchants in the 19th century were largely local-born Straits Chinese who identified very strongly with the Straits Settlements rather than with China. They were not sojourners.

In fact, a few writers who have identified with the middleman minority 'theory' could have left out this 'theory' in their analysis without weakening their analysis of 'trading minorities' and commerce or minorities and ethnic relations. For example, Hamilton's (1978) analysis of minority capitalism would have been better without linking his analysis to the concept of 'middleman minority', especially in the conclusion. Despite the awkward term 'pariah capitalism', his analysis of political power in relation to minority capitalism is important, especially his discussion on the ethnicization of certain roles in the occupational structure. Similarly, the middleman minority concept really explains nothing in the paper by Zenner (1987), which analyzes very well the competition of Christians and Jews as well as ethnic relations in Late Ottoman Syria.

It is also not really accurate to say that 'middleman minorities are noteworthy for the acute hostility they have faced' (Bonacich 1973, 589), for as we have seen, this depends on the nature of economic and political relations. For example, there was little expressed hostility towards the Chinese in Southeast Asia during the colonial era, due to the nature of the colonial economy and the politics that I have described above. There is also little hostility between Chinese traders and subsistence peasants, since they do not compete in production.

Overall, the 'theory' of middleman minorities should not be regarded as a theory at all. The usefulness of having one is doubtful, for even the term 'middleman minority' is problematic. I should like to add that in North America, the Chinese have been 'complimented' as model minority. This is a result of the perception of Chinese success in education and in getting into professional occupations. However, this is actually a misrepresentation, as many Chinese, especially new immigrants, are still struggling hard for a good living; Asian Americans still face obstacles in reaching the upper levels of administration and management (Ling 1998, 168–9). Furthermore, the 'compliment' has the effect of pitching the Chinese against other minorities. Like the 'middleman minority' stereotype, it also serves to keep the Chinese as 'alien' communities within the US and Canada.

Related to the middleman minority concept is the concept of 'ethnic enclave'. It is often used in the description of Chinese communities in the West, although it is also used in the description of other 'migrant' communities [see for example Cobas's (1987) description of Cuban exiles in Puerto Rico]. The most interesting debate to date is that between Sanders and Nee (1987a, 1987b) and Portes and Jensen (1987). Portes and others advance the 'enclave-economy hypothesis'. They emphasize the salience of ethnic solidarity and suggest that there is no cost to segregation, despite the social isolation of the enclave (cf. Sanders and Nee 1987, 746). Sanders and Nee stress the need to discuss immigrant workers and immigrant bosses in an enclave economy. Using Cuban enclaves in the Florida cities of Miami and Hialeah, and Chinese enclaves in San Francisco, Sanders and Nee show that the ethnic enclave is not a protected sector of the US economy. They point out that their findings conform to assimilation theory in that '(1) an inverse relationship exists between immigrants' socio-economic achievements and their spatial concentration in ethnic enclaves; and (2) lower levels of cultural assimilation are related to lower socio-economic achievement' (1987, 765–6). Various studies have in fact shown that the phenomenon of the 'ethnic enclave' is actually a product of minority adjustment to the larger society. In his study of New York's Chinatown, Wong (1979, 172) mentions that, 'its economic activities and social relations are adaptations shaped by the forces of racism and exclusion from the larger society'. In his study on Chinatown in London, Watson (1975, 127) shows that the restaurant niche is where 'the emigrants can interact with the alien outside world on their own terms'. Thus, where there is an ethnic enclave or 'enclave economy', it is necessary to take this into account in the study of the relations between ethnic Chinese and the larger society. The nature of the relations, however, is to be seen in the context of the larger economic and political structures, as is obvious in Wong's comment above.

THE FREE MARKET

Another economic theory of ethnic relations of concern here is that of Alvin Rabushka, who draws his experience mainly from his research on the relations between the Malays and the Chinese in Malaysia. He provides a theory of ethnic harmony and asserts that, 'racial tensions and conflict are kept to a minimum under conditions of voluntary exchange in free markets' (1974, 69).

The Chinese in Southeast Asia will undoubtedly find Rabushka's argument very agreeable, since they have been more established than the indigenous people in the capitalist economy. Under conditions of voluntary exchange in free markets, the Chinese will maintain an upper hand in the competition for resources. This is where Rabushka's argument is not realistic. It fails to take into account the aspirations and attitudes of the indigenous people who had been left behind economically by the very nature of the colonial economy. It is because the indigenous people want to have a greater share in the commercial and industrial sectors that tensions arise between the indigenous people and the Chinese. Given this situation, it is difficult to see how racial tensions and conflict can be kept to a minimum under conditions of voluntary exchange.

The free market argument is in favor of the strong against the weak, and given the increasing political consciousness of the indigenous people, the free market cannot ensure racial harmony; it may actually increase racial tensions. The theory ignores the competition along ethnic lines as an important source of ethnic tensions.

Rabushka argues that ethnic relations were better during the colonial period than after the countries concerned had achieved independence (1974, 74–82). This is misleading, as he ignores the structure of the colonial power and economy. In Malaya, the segregation of economic functions by 'race' and the political power of the colonial government ensured that there would be little or no ethnic confrontation. The 'free market' was in favor of the colonial governments and the commercial class of immigrants (mainly Chinese) who formed a class crucial to the colonial exploitation of the local economy. It became necessary for the indigenous people to free themselves from the shackles of colonialism in order to attain political and economic liberation.

The nationalist movements of the 20th century and the defeat of the colonial powers by Japan during the Second World War eventually led to the end of colonialism. But indigenous nationalism has continued in the form of communal ideology to check the 'economic power' of the Chinese. Thus, the ethnic tensions in Southeast Asia have to be seen in the larger context of the colonial past. The tensions are not just a post-colonial development; they are also a legacy of colonialism. Furthermore, in Malaysia, it is not after independence that pro-Malay policies were introduced; the British had already introduced their pro-Malay policies to keep the Malays content. They had also played off the Malays against the non-Malays (cf. Abraham 1983, 28). In colonial Malaya, as explained by Lim (1980, 142), 'the primary relations between the Malays and the non-Malays occurred not at the level of production but at the level of exchange'; hence there was little ethnic conflict. This is important, but we should add that this is so to the extent that the peasants are not deprived of their main subsistence and forced to rely on traders for even their basic food supply.

Now, given a free market, will the Chinese business class help the indigenous people to establish themselves in commerce and industries? This is unlikely, for the Chinese are worried about eventual competition from the indigenous people, especially after independence, when the Malay élites are politically dominant. Ironically, cooperation among the Chinese business classes and the Malay economic and political élites came about as a result of policies which seek to curb the economic power of the Chinese business class, making it advantageous for Chinese business people to have joint-ventures with indigenous politicians and business people. Obviously, the communal approach of the indigenous élites in dealing with the people of Chinese descent, and vice versa, increases ethnic tensions. If the 'free market' cannot bring about ethnic harmony, what is the alternative? It seems to me that the only alternative is for the government to adopt a non-racial approach in socio-economic policies while at the same time efforts are made to help the poor and the disadvantaged in general. In fact, ethnic relations are largely socio-economic and political. In Malaysia, for example, the view that Malays are economically more backward than the Chinese is an ethnic representation of social reality. The lopsided development between the urban and the rural is cast racially, for more Malays are in the rural sector and most Chinese are in the urban areas.

If development policies are based on the actual socio-economic needs of the people rather than on ethnicity, they will help to reduce ethnic tensions. The quota system is a convenient way of allocating resources along ethnic lines, but it will not help to reduce ethnic tensions and will create more ethnic polarization. In fact, the racial approach through the quota system, say in education, can be avoided if special consideration can be made for those students who are disadvantaged because of poor education facilities in the rural areas or because of poverty. This is particularly relevant in Malaysia, where those from the rural areas are predominantly Malays and other indigenous groups. Here the consideration is based on socio-economic needs and not on 'race'.[13]

ETHNIC RELATIONS MODEL

I have so far discussed the structural relations between the Chinese and the indigenous or majority people, that is, relations at the group level. As mentioned earlier, even when ethnic polarization exists, interpersonal interaction across ethnic groups need not necessarily manifest conflict. Although there is much talk of ethnic polarization in Malaysia, interpersonal interaction between the Chinese and Malays does not appear conflictual, and in certain places like Terengganu and Kelantan, Chinese-Malay interaction appears to be fairly intimate. Nevertheless, Chinese individuals, including fairly acculturated ones like the Baba in Melaka and the Peranakan-type Chinese in Kelantan, do hold certain negative views of Malays as a group, as do the Malays about the Chinese. Although acculturation may facilitate greater inter-ethnic interaction, the acculturated Chinese individuals in Malaysia share certain political sentiments with other Chinese about discrimination. The relations between the Chinese and the majority indigenous people may still be characterized as 'one of uneasiness, or even latent hostility', as Mely G. Tan (1987, 75) has pointed out in the case of Indonesia, where people of Chinese descent have moved away from 'Chineseness'.

In this chapter, I have focused my discussion on economic competition. I suggest that this be broadened as competition for social and economic resources. Competition for resources is a common and important source of conflict between ethnic groups, whether between 'tribal' groups or between technologically more advanced groups. I have also suggested that it is necessary to look at the ideological and political aspects of ethnic group relations. In Southeast Asia, communal ideology in nation building is an important source of tensions between the indigenous groups and the so-called non-indigenous groups. Even in countries like Australia, the US and Britain, white racial ideology remains a factor in relations between whites and non-whites. Thus, ideologies should not merely be seen as offshoots of the socio-economic and political structures or as a legitimizing factor; they can be a motivating force.

In modern nation-states, the roles of the government and party politics greatly affect ethnic group relations. In Malaysia, for example, communal politics arising out of both communal 'ideology' and social inequality identified with ethnicity is a major contributory factor to ethnic polarization. Even the extent of group tensions arising out of competition for resources is very much determined by the nature of political mobilization along ethnic lines. An examination of political mobilization also directs our attention to other non-economic factors like religion and language, which may be mobilized for inter-group rivalry or for consolidating intra-group solidarity and identity. The study of ethnic relations should be placed in historical and international contexts. It is in the historical context that we can understand the colonial effect on ethnic group relations, why the Chinese in Southeast Asia have become the scapegoats for economic backwardness of the indigenous people, and why the people of Chinese descent are still treated by the indigenous people as somewhat alien.

The international context is important, since the modern nation-states are open to global economy and affected by international politics. Recession in industrialized countries like the US and Japan can affect the economy in Malaysia, which in turn may affect Chinese-Malay relations because of the increase in the inter-ethnic competition for resources and opportunities. International religious resurgence, for example Islamic resurgence, has affected Malaysia, too. In relations between the people of Chinese descent and the indigenous majority groups, the China factor remains important. We are familiar with the anti-Chinese riots following the abortive coup in Indonesia in 1965 (cf. Coppel 1983, 52–72). The anti-communist campaign and the accusation of the involvement of China in the coup, as well as the words of war between China and Indonesia, were important factors that caused the anti-Chinese riots. Nevertheless, one should note that the riots were aimed at the so-called left, not just at Chinese, and the majority of the victims were in fact indigenous Indonesians (Heidhues 1974, 83).

International conflict between China and another country may result in the people of Chinese descent being discriminated against, many of whom have lived in the country for many generations. In India, for example, the small number of Chinese there was discriminated against following the Sino-India War in 1962 (Schermerhorn 1978). In Vietnam, we have seen that the exodus of Chinese since 1978 was the result of persecution against urban dwellers and capitalists, who were also victims of Sino-Vietnam conflict. The Vietnamese case also shows the danger of not having a clear agreement with China on the nationality question. As Porter (1980, 55) has pointed out, 'Vietnamese control over the Hoa was a sensitive issue between the Democratic Republic of Vietnam and the People's Republic of China even when relations between the two states were closest'. The nationality question became an issue of conflict when, in 1977, China protested against Vietnam's registration of the people of Chinese descent (Porter 1980, 56), and the relations of the two countries worsened.

Even in Burma, where relations between the Chinese minority and the Burmese have been good, there were anti-Chinese riots in Rangoon in 1967 as a result of deteriorating relations between Burma and China. This was partly due to the 'spillover effect' of China's cultural revolution (Mya Than 1997, 133; Win Shein 1982, 183). The Burmese case is interesting. As in Thailand, the Burmese are Theravada Buddhists; the Chinese who are Mahayana Buddhists and followers of traditional

Chinese beliefs and practices are able to establish social links with the Burmese by participating in temple rituals and feasts as well as sponsoring the temple activities. There is considerable inter-marriage, too. Furthermore, the Burmese competed more with the Indian business class, and as in Cambodia up to the 1960s when the Cambodian hostility was directed at the Vietnamese rather than the Chinese (Willmott 1967, 40), in Burma the Burmese hostility was directed at the Indians. But with independence and the promotion of 'patriotic' ideology, the presence of the Chinese became very visible. The negative attitudes towards the Chinese were intensified 'when the Chinese out-distanced the Indians economically' (Win Shein 1982, 182).

From our above discussion of the relations between the people of Chinese descent and the indigenous or majority people, we can propose that the study of ethnic relations should involve examining the competition for resources and the politics of ethnicity which arises out of inter-ethnic rivalry for socio-economic opportunities and/or domestic rivalry between political forces, as well as the politics of cultural domination. It is basically a study of ethnicity and political economy.

The ethnic group relations model may be summarized as follows:

1. Ethnic relations can be explained by the nature and intensity of socio-economic competition between ethnic groups.

2. In addition to competition for resources, political factors are crucial for the understanding of ethnic relations, especially the communal political process, that is, how socio-economic inequalities and cultural phenomena are mobilized along ethnic lines, as well as how ethnicity is mobilized in political competition.

3. Other than economic and political factors, ethnic relations are affected by ideologies that may be studied as part of the political process, of how they are mobilized in ways that affect the status and the fate of one or more ethnic groups.

4. Ethnic relations should be related to the class factor in the expression and perpetuation of inter-ethnic rivalry.

5. Ethnic relations should be seen in the historical context, in order to understand how the developments in the past influence the present ethnic relations.
6. Ethnic relations should also be seen in the context of global economy and international politics.

In this model, which deals with structural ethnic relations, ethnic tensions are economically and politically caused; they are not culturally caused. The general model is preferred as ethnic relations cannot be explained merely by a specific theory. At the same time, the model avoids determinist approaches. In fact, specific 'theories' such as the split labor market argument can be taken into account within this general model.

It should be pointed out that the general model assumes that one has already taken note of the larger social environment of an ethnic group, especially the general characteristics of the national society, such as the political system, the economic system, the population sizes of the various ethnic groups, as well as the political and economic roles and status of the ethnic groups in a country. The population size affects an ethnic group's political and economic strength and, hence, its political relations with the other ethnic groups. Overall, it is mainly the political and economic factors that cause tensions between ethnic groups rather than merely the difference in population size. In other words, we have to see the question of ethnic relations from the perspective of the above model, which outlines the factors that should be considered in any study of ethnic relations. Which factor is more important depends on the larger society and its historical background.

In addition, although we have said that ethnic tensions are not due to cultural differences, this does not mean that cultural factors are not important. Cultural differences, in the context of inter-ethnic competition and antagonism, are crucial for ethnic mobilization. They can be used for political manipulation as well as for reinforcing ethnic identification and drawing boundaries between ethnic groups. Cultural factors become important in the competition and conflict between ethnic groups when the political élites of the dominant groups impose cultural oppression on another ethnic group. But we must stress again that cultural differences by themselves do not cause ethnic tensions. As a result of ethnic differentiation, cultural differences can be used to mobilize and reinforce the identity and differentiation of each ethnic group. Of course we should distinguish cultural differences and ethnic identity from cultural differences and ethnic relations. The two are really different issues, although interrelated.

CONCLUSION

Ethnic Chinese in different countries experience different types of ethnic relations, depending on their number and the nature of politics. Where their number is small, their interests depend very much on the policies of the government dominated by the dominant group. Their course of action depends very much on the degree of democratic space. Where there is little democratic space, as in Indonesia under the Suharto government that adopted an assimilation policy on the Chinese, Chinese citizens have to adjust to the various policies of cultural oppression.

In North America, the Chinese pioneers 'suffered from blatant white racism in the form of anti-oriental riots, discriminatory legislation, and socio-economic restrictions' (Ban 1976, 348). Today, the governments of the United States and Canada espouse the policy of multiculturalism. Chinese Americans and Chinese Canadians make full use of their access to socio-economic and especially educational opportunities for upward mobility and finding a place in the white-dominated economy. With greater acceptance from the larger society, the Chinese become more integrated into the national society. This is well argued by Bernard Wong (1979, 171) as follows:

> Legal and economic discrimination against the Chinese have generated the defensive response of the Chinese. Conversely, legal protection and open economic opportunity have precipitated the wider participation of the Chinese in contemporary American life.

This does not mean that there is no longer any white prejudice against the Chinese in countries like the US, Canada, Great Britain, Australia and New Zealand. White prejudice against Asians and Blacks persists, and it emerges now and then in subtle ways. It is interesting to note the survey carried out by the Political and Economic Planning (PEP) Institute (now the Policy Studies Institute) of Great Britain in 1966–67 (Banton 1988, 98). An Englishman, a Hungarian, and a West Indian were employed as testers. They applied for jobs, for housing, for car insurance and certain other services. The Englishman consistently got the most offers, but the West Indian got the least and was even asked to pay higher rent for accommodation. In the United States, in comparing whether the Chinese, Japanese and Filipino have 'made it' in reaching earnings parity with Anglos, Morrison Wong (1982, 73) concludes that economic discrimination against the Chinese was still substantial. He points out that 'an individual Chinese-American male cannot expect to earn as much as an Anglo male with the same generation status, number of years of completed education, and general level of employment' (76).

Nevertheless, today there is not much group antagonism against the Chinese in these countries. But visible success may also bring about the jealousy and racial sentiment of the whites, as in the overwhelming success of Chinese students in certain élite schools, seen as causing the displacement of the less successful white students. This is highlighted by Peter Li (1998, 154) in his study of the Chinese in Canada: 'Racial tensions have surfaced in urban centers where Chinese Canadians have grown in number and outperformed other groups in terms of business success, financial security, and educational and occupational achievements'. Another researcher, Li Zong (1998, 453) describes the situation thus, 'While Canadians generally support the values of equality and democracy, many have exhibited a remarkable degree of intolerance towards the increased presence of a visible minority in Canadian society'. In Australia, Crissman, Beattie and Selby (1998, 103) report that most Brisbane Chinese find most Australians friendly towards them, but many are ambivalent and thought many Australians were not disposed to be friendly towards them.

Acceptance by the majority group and fair treatment thus help to integrate the Chinese into the national society and reduce ethnic polarization. In Southeast Asia, this is evident in Thailand. Generally, the Thai accept the Chinese as any other Thai, as long as they identify with the Thai national culture and society. We find that the Chinese in Thailand integrate themselves into Thai society. Although the closeness of religions promotes social interaction, it is the structural factors in the economic and political sectors that affect group relations and integration.

By contrast, the Chinese in countries like Indonesia and Malaysia are regarded as somewhat alien even though they are citizens, and their political loyalty may even at times be questioned. This is not just due to cultural diversity expressed as Muslims versus non-Muslims. It is actually the drawing of boundaries due to inter-ethnic competition. It also justifies discrimination or the exclusion of the Chinese in certain areas of national life. In the Philippines, the Chinese are also regarded as aliens by more chauvinistic people, although now the more subtle way of saying this is 'those not national-born Filipinos' (Weightman 1986, 103). The most glaring expression of this attitude was the call by certain elements in the parliament in 1982 to impeach Justice Claudio Teehankee on the ground that he was not 'a natural-born Filipino', although the effort was to embarrass President Marcos (Weightman 1986, 103).

By continuing to treat people of Chinese descent as somewhat alien, albeit informally, the boundary between the 'indigenous' and the descendants of immigrants ('aliens') is kept rigid. This, together with the communal approach to nation building, does not facilitate the unity of the Chinese and the dominant majority group.

The ethnic Chinese make their choice of adjustment according to the situation. If we bring in the rational choice argument in ethnic relations (cf. Barth 1969b; Banton 1983),[14] we can say that the people of Chinese descent make their 'rational' choice according to their numerical strength and political power/influence versus the political power of the dominant group and depending on the scope of democratic space. But we must see 'rational' from the point of view of the people concerned rather than any objective criterion of maximum gain. In each country, diverse choices are represented by various groups of people of Chinese descent, depending on their calculation of socio-economic interests versus the perpetuation of cultural and ethnic identities. For example in Indonesia, there has been a section of Chinese who opt for full assimilation and drop their Chinese identity. Others want to make a socio-cultural adjustment without losing their Chinese identity.

Giving up an ethnic identity in favor of another in return for maximum economic and social gain as reported by Barth (1969b) happens only under special circumstances. Indeed, rational choice is most relevant in the context of extreme situations that force choice for survival. Giving up one's Chinese identity to become Indonesian happens in the context of the assimilation policy of the Indonesian government. Most Chinese in Southeast Asia make their choice within the context of retaining their Chinese identity. Where the Chinese are numerous and have considerable political power, as in Malaysia, the views towards adjustment range from considerable accommodation to Malay culture to finding all means to retain all aspects of Chinese culture. The Chinese racialists (who think of a larger Chinese 'race') find it rational not to compromise on cultural issues, in order to retain a 'pure' Chinese culture and identity, even though such action may lead to stronger Malay communalism that is not in the interest of the Chinese.

The political strategy of the Chinese in Southeast Asia in relation to the majority groups has been largely based on short-term defensive strategy. In Malaysia, there is no long-term strategy to adjust to the increasing political consciousness of the indigenous peoples and the communalism of the Malay élites. Unlike in business, where Chinese traders try to cultivate long-term relationships with customers for maximum gain, in politics the Chinese have largely been rather short-term in response and rather sectarian too, that is, concerned with Chinese interests only, even to the extent of indifference to the problems encountered by other ethnic groups. For these Chinese, the sectarian approach is a 'rational' response to Malay communalism. Yet from another point of view, this approach is not 'rational', since the long-term interests of the Chinese cannot be divorced from the interests of the other communities in a common nation-state in which the Chinese have to deal with the political dominance of the non-Chinese élites.

All in all, we can draw from the above analysis the major features of ethnic group relations between the people of Chinese descent and the indigenous people/dominant ethnic group.

1. The population of the people of Chinese descent varies from country to country. Although the population size may affect the political and economic power of the Chinese as well as the nature of their adaptation to the majority ethnic group, it is the political and economic factors that really account for the nature of ethnic relations between the people of Chinese descent and the other ethnic groups.

2. Where there is no direct socio-economic competition and political agitation, group relations are fairly harmonious.

3. Tension has existed between the Chinese and the dominant indigenous groups in Southeast Asia since independence. This is different from certain Western countries like Great Britain, Canada and the United States, where there was severe discrimination and persecution against the Chinese in the 19th century but today the group relations have been fairly good and the Chinese as a group are not oppressed. Individual experiences of subtle prejudice, however, persist.

4. Ethnic tensions between the Chinese and the indigenous people/ majority people do not arise out of cultural differences but out of socio-economic competition and political factors, especially the process of communal politics.

5. Acculturation may increase interpersonal interaction between the Chinese and the indigenous people or majority people, but it does not necessarily lead to good group relations. Where discriminatory policies exist, the acculturated Chinese feel discriminated against, too, and share similar political sentiments against the dominant group.

6. Certain ideologies like 'communal ideology' and radical communism are also responsible for ethnic tensions or hinder harmonious relations between the Chinese and the majority group.

7. Class is an important factor in the functioning and development of ethnic relations between the Chinese and the indigenous people or majority people.

8. Conflict between a country and China can cause anti-Chinese sentiments in the country and/or the oppression of people of Chinese descent.

9. Anti-Chinese riots are generally political, although they usually have a socio-economic base.

10. Chinese in Southeast Asia are mostly involved in the urban and commercial sectors and are regarded by the indigenous people as controlling the national economy, even in countries where they are only a small minority. Cast in the role of economic exploiters, the Chinese have become a convenient and visible scapegoat for the economic underdevelopment of the indigenous people or for economic crises in the country.

11. Due to various contradictions in the relations between the Chinese and the indigenous people in Southeast Asia, Chinese citizens are still regarded as somewhat alien, in one form or another. This has the effect of justifying some forms of exclusion as manifested in socio-economic and cultural policies as well as in the implementation of policies.

12. Where Chinese citizens are accepted as equal citizens without being cast as 'somewhat alien' and are allowed to have fair access to socio-economic opportunities, they tend to be integrated smoothly into the national society.

13. The people of Chinese descent adjust to varying situations of ethnic relations by making choices which are rational from the point of view of maximum socio-economic gain or from the point of view of maximum gain in the maintenance of cultural and ethnic identity, or a balance of the two perspectives.

It is obvious from our model of ethnic relations that where there is competition and political agitation along the boundary of Chinese and the majority people, there is ethnic tension. The more intense the competition and the politics of ethnicity, the more there is ethnic tension. We can also say that where socio-economic inequalities are seen ethnically, there is a feeling of antagonism against the Chinese. The greater the inequalities, the greater the feeling of antagonism. I have thus argued that ethnic tensions can be reduced, especially in Southeast Asia, through the application of social justice in government policies and their implementation, in order to redress socio-economic inequalities. There should be no racial approach in socio-economic planning; neither should there be uncontrolled capitalism that works against the interest of the poor and the weak.

Our comparative study also shows two common themes, which highlight human attitudes towards others. Where the Chinese population is very small and not perceived as a threat, they may be regarded as tolerable 'aliens among us'. Even though there is no ethnic tension, Chinese individuals may be seen as of lower status and teased. The incident of the Black basketball player Shaquille O'Neal teasing his Chinese rival, Yao Ming, 'ching chong yang wah ah soh' is most likely due to this condescending attitude towards the Chinese rather than a hatred of the Chinese. Given the racism that the Chinese in the US had experienced from the larger society, it was not surprising that the Organization of Chinese Americans decided to protest against O'Neal (*South China Morning Post*, 18 January 2003, 22), even though Yao Ming is a player imported from China. An example from Sri Lanka is even more appropriate. Rodrigo (1998, 234) reports that the Chinese 'were looked down upon as an alien, unimportant group of people by the majority'. Chinese students in school were laughed at 'for their narrow eyes and flat noses' (Rodrigo 1998, 235). The Sri Lankans were not hostile to the rather small Chinese minority, and Rodrigo (1998, 235) mentions that the only time they were hostile was during the Sino-Indian border war. This reflects a negative side of human nature, of treating minority 'aliens' who are of no threat: looking down on or teasing them. In

Malaysia and in Hong Kong, where people of South Asian origin are in the minority, the Chinese tend to regard them as of lower ethnic status; some even describe them as 'smelly'.

The other common theme is that ethnic Chinese are often treated as somewhat alien even though they are citizens in a country or have a fairly long history of settlement there. From the white majority societies in the West to the Malay majority societies in Southeast Asia, we find this to be so, more in some than in other places. In Indonesia and Malaysia, the idea of Chinese as aliens is even incorporated into the implementation of policies and so is more obvious. In North America and Australia, the adoption of multiculturalism in place of assimilation is an improvement in the treatment of non-whites, but this does not necessarily mean Asians are treated as full-fledged equal citizens. In fact, non-whites as others may be reinforced in multiculturalism; only multiculturalism, if it succeeds, teaches respect of others.

Because Chinese remain distinct as others, if they become visible in number or in socio-economic success, the attitude of the majority becomes hostile, fearing competition, or that successful 'aliens' will threaten their interest. We find that human beings are the same in this regard. In Malaysia, the Malays fear Chinese economic dominance. In the West, as we have seen, where the Chinese have become visibly successful, some members of the majority population become unfriendly towards them. This visibility theory is important in understanding ethnic relations between the majority and the minority. Fear of competition is the crucial factor, and this competition may not be really economic; it may be merely perceived, even irrationally.

What all this means is that ethnic relations are not to be understood by economic factors alone, even though these are important. Ultimately, it requires humans to learn to accept people of other ethnic backgrounds as truly equal, to be free of fear of others. What this paper has shown is that reducing economic factors that cause ethnic tension is an essential first step towards reducing the fear of others.

7

Culture and Economic Performance with Special Reference to the Chinese in Southeast Asia

INTRODUCTION

The achievement of the Chinese in Southeast Asia in commerce has led to the stereotype that all Chinese are good in business. The economic achievement of the four newly industrialized countries — South Korea, Taiwan, Hong Kong and Singapore (known as the four little dragons) — has also led to the myth that Confucianism has something to do with good economic performance. This myth is popular especially among the Chinese, for it is pointed out that Japan (which has had remarkable economic achievement since the Second World War), like Korea, also has Confucian influence. What is Confucian in relation to economic achievement is not clear, although such values as hard work and frugality are often mentioned. In mainland China, however, Confucianism has been blamed on and off for hindering modernization.[1]

Various writers (Wu 1977; Lee 1978, 19, 23; Linda Lim 1983; Yoshihara 1987) have discussed the economic performance of Chinese overseas. Of these, Linda Lim (1983) has given a fairly comprehensive discussion on Chinese economic monopolies. She points out that 'Chinese kin and social networks clearly give them (Chinese) one important economic advantage over other ethnic groups, in access to labor, credit, information, market outlets and security'. However, Lim (4–7) points out that the large-scale Chinese immigration to Southeast Asia coincided with the growth of commercial opportunities, 'especially as middlemen and intermediaries'; and 'the Chinese had both the motivation and the wherewithal to enter business and trade'.

In this chapter, I discuss the relationship between Chinese 'culture' and Chinese economic performance, 'Chinese culture' being used loosely to refer to not just the value system but also the institutions and ways of life that may be said to be Chinese. In reality, there is no one Chinese culture but different models of Chinese culture (Tan 1983, 71). By exploring the aspects of 'Chinese culture' that are relevant to economic activities, I shall show the relevance of culture to economic achievement. In so doing, I hope it will be obvious that it is misleading to think of the relevance of Chinese culture to economic activities according to rather vague 'Confucianism', although Confucianism as a value system and ideology has had tremendous influence on traditional Chinese culture.

The analysis naturally leads us to a discussion on the Weberian thesis, and I intentionally do not want to begin this chapter with such a discussion. The discussion on culture and economic performance of the Chinese in Southeast Asia will enable us to have a wider perspective on the modernization of China as well as on the need for more rationalization in the economic organization of ethnic Chinese. The economic achievement of the Chinese in Southeast Asia is a result of the ability of the Chinese to draw upon the strength of their internal socio-cultural resources and to adapt to the ever-changing political and economic conditions of their respective national societies as well as the global political economy. For ethnic Chinese, there is a continuous need to ensure good relations with the majority people.

ECONOMIC DIMENSIONS IN CHINESE CULTURE

We should first note that the Chinese who migrated to Southeast Asia came from a society that had a long history of using and handling money. Money in the form of coins was used in China as early as the fourth and third centuries BCE (Xiao 1987; Yang 1952), and paper money was circulated from the 11th century on (Yang 1952, 2). Furthermore, pre-modern China already had an elaborate network of marketing structure comprising market towns with permanent facilities and periodic rural markets (Skinner 1964b, 1965a, 1965b). Thus, most of the emigrants from China might be peasants but they were familiar with monetary economy and commercial activities, especially the itinerary trade that characterized the periodic rural markets. The migrants to Southeast Asia were able to use their familiarity with money and market systems to take up the expanding commercial opportunities in Southeast Asia. Many Chinese pioneer traders in Southeast Asia were in fact itinerary traders who penetrated even the most remote part of Southeast Asia, thus enabling the Chinese trading community as a whole to reach the remote villages in Southeast Asia on the one hand, and international markets on the other hand.

Although the credit system was not well developed in traditional China, the immigrants in Southeast Asia and elsewhere were able to adapt the traditional credit society into one for raising the necessary capital for investment. Generally known as *hui*, the credit society of the Chinese originated in China (Yang 1952, 75–8). Judging from the writings of early writers and anthropologists on China (Smith 1899; Kulp II 1925; Fei 1939; Gamble 1954), it was quite widely practiced even in rural China.

The Chinese credit society has a number of variants and is known by a number of specific names (that is, specific types of *hui*). The three major types are *lunhui* or 'rotating society' in which the order of rotation is fixed by agreement, *yaohui* or 'dice-shaking society' in which the person to collect the fund is decided by lot or by casting dice, and *biaohui* or 'auction society' in which the one who offers the highest interest rate gets to use the fund (Fei 1939, 267–74). In English, *hui* has been translated as 'cooperative loan society' (Smith 1899), 'mutual aid club' (Kulp II 1925), 'loan society' (Freedman 1959; Jacques 1931), 'rotating credit association' (Wu 1974), and others.

Fei (1939, 267–8) describes the traditional credit society as follows:

The financial aid society is a mechanism for collective saving and lending. It consists of a number of members and lasts for a number of years. The members meet several times a year. At each meeting, each subscribes a share. The total subscription of the members is collected by one of the members who can thus use the money to finance his activities. Each member in turn collects the sum. The first collector is the organizer. From the very beginning, he is a debtor to the society. He repays his loan bit by bit during the whole course with a certain amount of interest. The last collector is a depositor. He collects at the end the sum of his deposit and its interest. Other members change from depositors to debtors as they collect the sum. The order of collection is determined either by contract, by lot, or by auction.

The system obviously evolved out of the need for mutual aid in the agrarian Chinese society. It requires trust and so, as Fei points out, 'the nucleus of such a group is always the kinship group', and default is prevented 'not by legal sanction but by the acknowledged social obligations between relatives'. Fei (268–9) reports that the usual purpose of organizing a *hui* in his area of study is to finance marriage ceremonies; relatives are therefore obliged to help.

The credit societies were 'particularly popular in the Ching period' especially for people of the middle and lower classes to raise liquid funds (Yang 1952, 75). Most of the Chinese who migrated from China did so in the 19th century and carried with them the institution of the credit society. However, the immigrant business people turned this system into one for raising crucial capital for business ventures, especially at a time when banking was not yet well developed.

David Wu (1974), who did his research on the Chinese in New Guinea from 1971 to 1974, provides us with the best description of the credit society of Chinese overseas. He shows how the Chinese business people there used the simple traditional rotating credit society 'to create extremely active and complicated financial networks' for loans, savings and finance. In New Guinea, there are usually 24 to 36 members in a rotating credit society. The operation is as follows:

> If the members, say thirty-six of them, including the head of a *Hui*, agree to subscribe $100 a month, its head would initially collect the

sum of $3,500 at the first meeting on the first month. In the following thirty-five months, the head has to pay back $100 each month to the *Hui*, while the other members bid against each other in order to draw the fund. The one who bids the highest amount, i.e. the one who is willing to pay the highest interest, will draw the fund on that particular month. Given the highest bid of 15 percent interest ($15) on the second month, the members will each pay the bidder $85 (i. e. $l00-$15), except the head, who has already drawn, should pay $100. The bidder would thus draw $2,990 ($100 from the head plus $85 from each of the other thirty-four members). In the next month, if the highest bid is still 15 percent interest, the bidder would draw $3,005 (i.e. $100 each from the head and the first drawer plus $85 from each of the other 33 members). By the end of the entire *Hui* cycle, the last to collect the fund from the *Hui* would get the full amount of $100 from everyone and thus collecting $3,500. We realize that he has paid $100 on the first month and $90 or less, depending on the bid in each month, from the second month to the thirty-fifth month. (Wu 1974, 573–4)

There is an agreed upon minimum interest rate of ten percent among the Chinese in New Guinea, and the last collector is exempt from any interest. Wu shows that a big businessman (such as a wholesale dealer) is able to organize several *hui*, thus raising huge capital; at the same time he may be a subscriber in a number of other *hui*. In fact, he may also use his wife's name and his company's name to subscribe two or more shares in any one *hui*. In this way he can accumulate a huge capital of 'up to several hundred thousand dollars in a single month'. Wu also points out that there is an interlocking relationship among the organizers of the rotating credit associations. He concludes, 'whether or not the rotating credit association is adaptive to economic development depends on the way it is operated, not on the nature and quality of its structure' (582).

The use of the traditional credit association to raise quick capital for business ventures has been important throughout Southeast Asia. To this day, there are still Chinese who organize *hui*, indicating that the institution has remained functional for those who need quick capital or who do not have sufficient security to borrow money from the banks. In the case of the *hui* discussed here, the security needed is 'trust' (*xinyong*; more discussions on *xinyong* follow) arising out of kin relations or friendship. The presence of *hui* in present-day Malaysia comes to light occasionally when an organizer defaults, and the protest of the subscribers is reported in the local newspapers.[2]

'Shrewdness in handling money' (including the handling of debt and credit) is the major thesis of Freedman (1959) on the economic sophistication of 'Overseas Chinese'. This, with the experience of the traditional market systems, certainly gave the Chinese immigrants in Southeast Asia an advantage over a majority of the natives who still largely lived in a subsistence economy. Today, in the remote parts of Sarawak, we can still witness this advantage of Chinese business people over the indigenous rural peasants, who are just beginning to experience the full effect of monetization over their traditional economy.

In addition, the Chinese in Southeast Asia have developed an elaborate system of credit linking the smallest business people in the rural areas to the major import/export business people in the major cities. T'ien is the first to give us a detailed analysis of this system of credit relations. At the lowest level, it involves the credit relation between Chinese shopkeepers and farmers. T'ien (1953, 37) writes, 'the shopkeepers, owning some capital, act as loan-making capitalists and bankers; while the planters (farmers), having none, constitute a labor force in his employ'. At the level of rural shopkeepers and peasants, the credit system mainly involves the shopkeepers advancing goods on credit to the peasants in return for their promise to sell their agricultural produce (such as rubber) to the shopkeeper. When the peasants sell their rubber, they settle only a portion of their outstanding debt, and in this way a regular client is able to get more provisions from the shopkeepers on credit.

Although T'ien writes about the credit relations between the shopkeepers and Chinese 'planters', the Chinese shopkeepers also deal with the indigenous peasants in this manner.[3] The rural shopkeepers in turn get their goods on credit from a bigger business person in town, and the system may be traced from one level to another (i.e., small business people getting credit or even loans from bigger business people who may be able to borrow money from banks or even bigger business people). Eventually, one can find a chain of credit relations from the rural shopkeepers to the business people in town and, in Sarawak, to the large Chinese firms in Kuching; these major business people in Kuching are eventually linked to the large firms in Singapore. To this day, the commercial farmers in Malaysia get their loans from the business people in town, who in turn get to buy the produce from the farmers at a rate favorable to the business people.

The access to a wide network of trade and credit relations among Chinese business people at different levels and in different localities plays a crucial part in the Chinese operation of business in Southeast Asia. In fact, early Chinese traders in Southeast Asia already had contact between the major colonial bases, which the Chinese business people made as their own business bases, too.

Of these, Singapore, which was developed by the British in 1819, was the most important. Traders from Kuching, Java, for example, were all linked to Singapore. Earl (1837) reports that in his voyage from Java to Singapore, there was a Java-born Chinese on board, carrying with him goods worth £1000 to Singapore. He also mentions that after they entered the Straits of Banca, a Chinese junk passed by and the crew hailed the Chinese passenger to enquire about the state of the markets. This shows that the network of relations among the Chinese of different trading centers allowed them not only mutual access to capital and business but also to market information. The Chinese in Southeast Asia needed a center and this, as Wang Gungwu (1959: 19) puts it, 'Stamford Raffles had found and established for them', and Singapore became 'the headquarters of Chinese commercial activity in the Western Nanyang'. When the British established Hong Kong as their other commercial base, this not only formed a new base for Chinese emigration to Southeast Asia, it also became part of a large 'network of relations' between business people in Southeast Asia and Hong Kong, and therefore China (Wang 1959, 19, 23). This is still true today.

The theoretical interest in globalization and transnationalism today, as well as the emergence of China as an economic power in Asia, has led to an interest in studying economic networks among Chinese overseas and the significance of ethnic Chinese in creating a strong 'Greater China' (cf. Chan 2000; East Asia Analytical Unit 1995; Golberg 1985; Weidenbaum and Hughes 1996; Yeung and Old 2000). In fact, the transnational network among Chinese overseas and between them and China, both individual network and network through associations, is not new. It is more visible and intensive now, made possible by the advance of technology that makes it easy to transfer capital and establish networks across state boundaries.

So far, we have seen that the monetary orientation of the Chinese, the adaptation of the traditional credit association for creating capital for business, and the development of a wide network of business relations among the Chinese in Southeast Asia have contributed to the success of the Chinese in business. There is also an ideological orientation that favors commercial development. Unlike the indigenous people then, the Chinese who came to Southeast Asia already had a clear distinction of business value from kinship value, best expressed by remarks which indicate that 'business is business' when say, a friend initially declines accepting the return of a small amount of money (like one or two dollars only) — such an initial decline is usually a polite gesture in view of the friendship or kin relations, and it is important that the debtor insist on returning the money (if it is borrowed in the first place) rather than accept the declination. Freedman, in his study of the lineage organization in Southeastern China, noted this 'business is business' attitude of the Chinese. According to him, 'economic relations between households were regulated in fact or might in principle be regulated by the free play of the market'. He writes:

> The high price of credit might be paid by neighbor to neighbor and kinsman to kinsman. The structure of the economic relations among kith and kin was certainly often at variance with the ideals of cooperative ties between relatives and neighbors. (1965, 18)

The clear distinction or separation between economic principle and kinship principle is good for the development of business, as kinship consideration does not hinder economic relations between relatives. In fact, it allows the Chinese to mobilize relatives for economic purposes and makes it acceptable to charge relatives interest. This point can be clarified by the explanation of my Malay informants in Bukit Ramai, Melaka, where in 1977 I did my fieldwork on the Baba who lived in this village comprising Malay and Chinese villagers. I was told that there was a Malay shop in the fifth to the sixth mile section of the village. Asked why it closed, the most striking answer was that many Malay relatives wanted to buy things on credit and the shopkeeper found it embarrassing to pressure them to pay their debts. Here is an example of kinship principle dominating economic principle, or to put it another way, economic relation was subordinated to kinship relations. David Wu (1982, 106) also reports bankruptcy among native storekeepers being caused by relatives not repaying their debts.

Among the Chinese, a business transaction is a business transaction; it cannot be subordinated to kinship considerations. At most, a shopkeeper can charge a lower price if he thinks fit. At the same time, he could pressure his kin to repay the debt and the latter is obliged to do so, more rather than less so because of kin relations! Furthermore, a Chinese shopkeeper has easier access to his or her creditors in town.

Chinese economic relations are also guided by *xinyong*, or 'trust'. This 'trust' is crucial to credit relations and overall business relations. It underlies the Chinese economic dealings by verbal agreement. Even the use of post-dated cheques, which is practiced both in Southeast Asia (Chia 1987) and Taiwan (DeGlopper 1972, 308), relies on *xinyong*. *Xinyong* is not just trust in the social sense. It refers to a person's reliability in economic relations. DeGlopper (304) describes it very well: *xinyong* 'refers to an individual's or a firm's reputation, reliability, credit rating'. As a general principle, *xinyong* seems to be universal, but its practice, as manifested by how Chinese business people deal with one another, like doing business by verbal agreement or the reliance on economic standing and kin relations as 'security' in the operation of credit associations, is quite Chinese. Thus *xinyong* underlies the economic relations between Chinese business people.[4]

Chinese business people in Southeast Asia have also evolved their own business strategies and methods of management. Various scholars have commented on Chinese strategies of business, but it is Limlingan who has made this the focus of study. He describes the Chinese business as based on a 'low margin/high volume strategy aimed at capturing market share'. In other words, by offering a lower price and therefore having a smaller profit margin, a Chinese businessman is able to sell faster (Limlingan 1986, 88, 92). Another economic rationality of the Chinese is the concern with long-term economic relations. This is most obvious in rural Southeast Asia and smaller towns where Chinese shopkeepers seek to establish long-term relations with clients; these relations are, as we have seen, intertwined with the complicated network of credit relations. The low-margin strategy helps here in ensuring long-term trade relations. This concern with long-term relationship is common with Chinese business people. Silin (1972), for example, reports that, 'market people among themselves were clearly concerned with long-term trading relationships and reputation'. Silin studied marketing and credit in a Hong Kong wholesale market. His comment that 'only when one moves outside the field of people one knows well, where social sanctions are less binding, does short-term maximization at the potential expense of business reputation occur' (352) is generally valid and helps to clear away the stereotype that Chinese business people are ruthlessly exploitative.

As for business management, the Chinese immigrants had the abacus and the Chinese system of bookkeeping. Again, this shows that the traditional Chinese culture already contained elements favorable for business ventures in Southeast Asia. Today, large Chinese firms use computers and the Western system of accounting. Although calculators and cash machines are widely used now, some shopkeepers still use the abacus.[5] Even the Chinese accounting system is still used by many shopkeepers for internal purposes, although for official purposes, the business people in Malaysia, for example, have to provide the standard Western system in a language (English) understood by non-Chinese.

Chinese business is family-based. Even the management system of large Chinese firms of today is still largely family-centered but uses professionals. This is well described by Limlingan (1986, 150); that is, the structure of the Chinese managerial system consists of:

(a) An entrepreneurial group consisting of the family;

(b) A professional management group consisting primarily of professional managers; and

(c) A custodial group which performs the control function for the entrepreneurial group over the professional management group and which consists primarily of family members and trusted retainers.

This section shows that the historical and cultural background (economic dimension) of the Chinese in Southeast Asia gave them an edge over the indigenous peoples. The ability to adapt traditional values and institutions to new or changing environments allows Chinese business people to continue to do well. The management system of the large Chinese firms just described above is an example of adapting the traditional style of managing small family businesses to the need of managing large firms. The question facing Chinese business people today is how they can adjust to the competition of multinationals and state-sponsored enterprises of the indigenous people.

SOCIAL STRUCTURE

Chinese form voluntary associations wherever they go. Associations called *huiguan* or *gongsuo* had a long history in China where people of the same territorial origin (such as districts and provinces) or similar occupations formed such associations in the cities to cater to the members' interests (Cihai 1979). In Southeast Asia, Chinese voluntary associations are formed on the basis of various principles: territorial origin in China and 'dialect' groups, kinship (such as clan associations), occupation and trade, cultural and recreational, as well as athletic and alumni activities, mutual aid, and religion (Cheng 1985; Cui 1990; Hsieh

1978). The associations function as institutions that meet the socio-cultural, economic and political needs of the Chinese and are crucial to the adaptation of the people of Chinese descent everywhere to their national societies. Even in 'Chinese land', associations have been important. Yin (1981), for instance, reports on the rural migrants from Penghu islands to Kaohsiung in Taiwan forming voluntary associations to help them to adapt to the new environment, including coping with business competition with Kaohsiung natives and migrants from other parts of Taiwan.

In Malaysia, there are many Chinese voluntary associations in both big and small towns. Li Yih-Yuan (1970, 86), for example, found that in a medium-sized town like Muar in Johor, there were 72 Chinese voluntary associations in 1966 for a Chinese population of around 35,000. These range from the specific trade associations such as the Fish-sellers Association to the influential Chinese Chamber of Commerce. In most towns, the Chinese Chamber of Commerce, led by the most prominent business people in town, is the most important association of business people. In fact, business people dominate all associations, irrespective of whether they are commerce-based or not. Furthermore, as pointed out by Skinner (1958), in Thailand, there is an interlocking relationship between the associations' leaders, and the most prominent business people lead a number of associations.

Even public temples and major religious organizations in Malaysia are led by business people. The public temples of the Chinese in each town in Malaysia function as the communal centers of the local Chinese community, and the committee members elected are largely, if not all, business people. The committee in charge of specific religious 'cults' (such as the committee in charge of the Ghost Festival Celebration) is also usually headed by a business person. The syncretic 'sect' of Chinese religion in Malaysia and Singapore, called *Dejiao* ('Teaching/Religion of Virtue'), which I studied, was established by Teochiu businessmen. To this day, the *Dejiao* associations throughout Malaysia are dominated by business people who contribute much, at least to the material success of the associations, as can be seen in their modern buildings. The involvement of business people in *Dejiao* gives them direct and indirect socio-economic advantages (Tan 1985, 62), although in so saying I do not of course question their religious sincerity. For example, existing business links are reinforced and new contacts established, while business leaders of a religious organization or temple gain status among the Chinese community. In fact, the religious participation of business leaders has positive influence on their business activities.

Associations, where they are established, have been useful for Chinese business people to establish links, exchange information, consolidate business interests, and to protect their overall commercial interests. Even a trade association in a small town may be linked up with relevant associations in the cities. For example, Kapit is a small town in the hinterland of Sarawak, with a Chinese population of only about 3,000 people. The Kapit Coffee Merchants and Restaurant Proprietors' Association may appear an insignificant local association, but it is affiliated with Federation of Coffee Merchants and Restaurants Association Sarawak. This allows it to have access to all member associations in the Sarawak state. The Kapit association is also affiliated to the Malaysia Singapore Coffee Shop Proprietors' General Association, which has its headquarters in Kuala Lumpur, the capital of Malaysia (Tan 1995b, 33). Networking is not necessarily confined to within a country. Liu (1999), for example, in his study of the Chinese Chamber of Commerce and Industry, has shown the significance of a Chinese association in promoting organized Chinese transnationalism and the institutionalization of business networks.

Prominent business people may even raise capital from association members for the companies they control. The collapse of a number of Chinese cooperatives in Malaysia in the 1980s highlighted this. Tan Koon Swan, for example, was a prominent businessman sent to jail in Singapore and Malaysia for criminal breach of trust. As he was a prominent Hainanese leader with influence over Hainanese organizations, many Hainanese bought shares in his companies and his collapse was painful to many Chinese investors, especially the Hainanese. The relevance of associations to Chinese business is more significant in Southeast Asia than in North America, mainly because there are more Chinese and more Chinese associations in Southeast Asia, where many Chinese are involved in the commercial sector. Nevertheless, in North America and Europe, Chinese associations still perform useful roles, including regional and transnational networking, even though young local-born Chinese have established new associations that are more relevant to them (cf. Lai 1998; Ng 1998; Ng 1999, 31–9; Li Minghuan 1998).

Business people are intimately linked with the communal affairs of the ethnic Chinese. The Chinese community in the past and in the present needs the donation of business people to sponsor communal activities, be they education, charity, health or others. In return, the business people gain prestige and influence, which in turn have positive influences on business (cf. Chia 1990). Thus, economic success is closely linked to communal participation and vice versa, and economic status and social status are interrelated.

Indeed, for Chinese business people, economic relations and social relations are intertwined. This has to do with the nature of the Chinese social fabric that focuses on the ego. Fei (1985) explains that Chinese social relations are egoistic, and one builds up a network of social relations with others with reference to the degree of intimacy with oneself. The Chinese social world is oriented toward the ego rather than toward a well-defined group. I am not concerned with the effect on selfishness here. In the context of business, building up the right relationship is important. The Hokkien in Southeast Asia often talk of *au piah soâ* (lit. 'mountain behind'), meaning that there is someone who can help one financially or ensure one's business success. Stories of successful business people in Southeast Asia often mention how a poor immigrant finally got the help of a relative or friend and how this eventually led to an opportunity for becoming rich. The Chinese social world is a network of *guanxi* or personal relations bound by differential degree of *ganqing* (intimacy of relations) or *renqing* (observation of obligation between relatives and friends).[6] Business people are especially conscious of building up economically advantageous relations. And as one gains more wealth, one is able to put more people under obligation, as well as have access to a wider and more influential network of relations.

The family orientation of Chinese business (cf. Redding 1993) is the result of the Chinese system of social relations. In one's network of relations, family members are the closest and can be trusted most. Confucian influence is strong here. Confucianism views human relations as extending from family to society, but the ego orientation of human relations in practice means emphasizing the self and family members. The family forms the convenient and reliable unit for running business. This style of running business has served Chinese business people well in the past, but today multinational businesses are forcing Chinese capitalists to reform their style of ownership and management.

MOTIVATION AND VALUES

Most Chinese immigrants left China in poverty, hoping to seek wealth in Southeast Asia, and then returned to China. There was a strong motivation to endure hardship, to work hard, and to gain wealth. There was what Syed Husin Alatas (1983) calls 'emigrant spirit'. To work hard to gain wealth for the sake of the family in China was a 'calling'. We can say that there was a pioneer spirit, too. The 'calling' and the pioneer spirit accounted for how Chinese itinerary traders could endure not only hardship but also risked their life to go to the remotest part of Southeast Asia; they no doubt contributed much to the Chinese dominance in the retail trade throughout Southeast Asia. In Sarawak, for example, Chinese traders ventured into the interior at a time when there was still head-hunting.[7]

A businessman in Trusan, Sarawak, Malaysia, told me about how his father traded with the indigenous people. Although the Chinese in Trusan are predominantly Hokkien, this businessman, Mr Sim, is a Teochiu. His father emigrated from Swatow (Shandou) toward the end of the 19th century and went to Thailand before going to Brunei. From Brunei where he lived, Mr Sim senior traded with the Lun Bawang as

far as the upper Trusan River. The boat was built in such a way that
only one native at a time could enter to examine the goods — this was
necessary as a precaution against the Lun Bawang (then called Muruts)
taking his head! Mr Sim senior carried a shotgun, which could be used
to disperse the 'Muruts' if they attempted to swim toward the boat at
night. He sold iron, cloth, salt, dry foodstuff and other items in exchange
for local produce like rattan, bird's nests and other jungle products. Mr
Sim senior had a wife in China, but he also married a Lun Bawang in
Trusan. Thus, Mr Sim the son (born in 1915) now has many Lun Bawang
relatives, and this is good for his grocery business.[8]

The Chinese immigrants thus had the spirit of what the Hokkien
call *piā* or *pin* in Mandarin. It means 'work hard and struggle to succeed'.
This spirit of *piā* is today popularized in a Taiwanese pop song (in the
Minnan language, called Hokkien in Southeast Asia), which says *ai piā
chai e nya*, meaning one should *piā*, only then will one succeed. This
spirit of *pin* is related to another value, that of competition. Competition
for achievement is well established in Chinese culture. In fact, Hsu has
argued that ancestral authority shapes the personality of the Chinese,
and competition is an important feature of Chinese culture, which
emphasizes ancestor worship.[9] This point is seldom noted by scholars
on Chinese society, and is worth quoting, as follows:

> Between those whose relation with one another is marked by the
> authority-submission pattern there cannot be competition. But
> between those whose relation with one another is marked by equality,
> there can and is bound to be competition. In a family organization
> which prescribes that all sons, regardless of age, have equal claims
> to the ancestral inheritance, that all sons have opportunities to head
> independent family units, and that every son may become the favorite
> son of parents and ancestors because of personal achievements, this
> drive for competition tends to receive additional encouragement. It
> is responsible for the struggle for more wealth, for large family homes,
> for more 'advantageous' graveyards, for bigger clan temples, for
> costlier ceremonials, and for a host of other measures which are

calculated to increase the welfare and prestige of the living and of the dead. It is also responsible for the weak position of the clan… The individual family cohesion is so strong that even the joint household has difficulty in maintaining its existence (Hsu 1949, 243).

Ethnic Chinese emphasize competition and struggle to succeed. Whereas the 'Chinese-educated' Chinese still talk of *guangzong yaozu*, or 'performing well to bring honor to one's ancestors', the people of Chinese descent are not so much under the ancestors' shadow now. If clanship in China was weakened by family cohesion, it was less significant in Southeast Asia because, except for a few exceptions, not enough members of the same lineage in China migrated to the same locality. Despite the existence of 'clan associations', most of which are based on the principle of same surname rather than on actual relationship within a lineage or a clan, Chinese ancestor worship in Southeast Asia is generally not an affair of a corporate group of worshippers. Many people of Chinese descent have also embraced other religions, especially Christianity. We can say that the family was the basic unit of Chinese economic organization. It was, and is even more so in Southeast Asia, where lineage organization has become insignificant. The family orientation of the Chinese in Southeast Asia emphasizes the present and the future; given the weakening of the ancestral authority, and many have ceased worshipping ancestors regularly or even totally. There is much emphasis on the success of the future generation, often much more than on one's own success in the present. This is a manifestation of both the continuity and transformation of traditional Chinese culture which focused on ancestor worship and which linked the past generations to the present and the future generations. The present concern with the future generation is a motivation for economic achievement, just as the traditional concern with glorifying the ancestors was an incentive for success.

The concern for future generations is expressed in the Chinese parents' push for their children's success in education, which is crucial for mobility and achievement. One often hears Chinese who re-migrate (cf. Wang 1991a) say that they do so for their children's education and implicitly their future. This is not merely an excuse to migrate because of the ethnic quota system of admission to the local universities. In Malaysia, for instance, many Chinese parents worry that their children might not get into the local universities or to the course they want to pursue (such as medicine), because of keen competition. For those who can afford to migrate, places like Australia and Canada are preferred for the better educational opportunities and future professional careers offered.

Although the Chinese immigrants and their descendants had established Chinese schools, many of them did not hesitate to send their children to study in a non-Chinese-medium (English) school that had economic value. The concern for mobility and economic success precedes the similar important concern for cultural identity.[10] The Chinese in Singapore provide a good example. The government emphasis on English as the most important official language and as the major language of commerce led to the Chinese in Singapore sending their children to English-medium schools, so much so that eventually the Chinese-medium schools disappeared. Singapore is now promoting the study of Mandarin, but English remains the most economically valuable language. In Malaysia, Chinese parents send their children to either Malay-medium or Chinese-medium primary schools, but only a small minority send their children to the private secondary Chinese-medium schools, which are considered not as good for upward mobility in Malaysia. Linguistically, the Chinese in Malaysia have a dilemma, for their children have to learn not only Malay, the national and official language, but also English, which has remained an important language of commerce in Malaysia and is the international language. On top of that, the Chinese want to retain Chinese (Mandarin) for cultural identity and increasingly for its economic value, as not only has Taiwan become a newly industrialized country, but mainland China has emerged as a vast nation of high economic growth and there is increasing direct business between Malaysia and mainland China.

We should also note that Chinese of all classes value education highly. This is evident in the building of Chinese schools wherever the Chinese settled. In traditional China, education was the way to reach officialdom, and scholars had high social status and influence. Although in Southeast Asia it has been the business people that have influence and economic power, education remains highly valued. It is crucial for mobility and success. The general good performance of Chinese students, whether in Southeast Asia or in North America, is linked to this cultural emphasis on education. In Malaysia, for example, Chinese are mostly urban dwellers, and the good educational facilities in the towns and cities compared to the rural areas partly account for the general good educational performance of the Chinese students. But the cultural value on education, as well as the cultural emphasis on competition, gives the Chinese an edge over students from cultures which do not place as much emphasis on education. With the quota system in the universities, this edge is not so obvious, except in science wherein Chinese students still do better. Given free competition, Chinese students have the edge until other ethnic groups also place similar value and emphasis on education and competition. Chinese students are still considered good in mathematics. They are not born to be good in this subject; the urban environment and the cultural orientation explain their performance. In addition, Chinese students from business families will have been exposed to the practical value of mathematics at a very young age. Furthermore, among ethnic Chinese, the family provides strong support for children's education: parents are actively involved in children's homework and educational achievement (cf. Caplan, Choy and Whitmore 1992; Zhou 1992, 227).

The Chinese pattern of socialization reinforces the emphasis on self-reliance as well as competition and struggle to succeed.[11] This is conducive to Chinese performing well in free competition in the context of Southeast Asia, that is, if there is free competition. The punishment and reward method emphasizes competitiveness and merit. Children who do well in school are rewarded in one way or another, but they are always reminded to do even better. If they fail to maintain the standard once achieved, they are criticized by the parents even though their marks may indicate that their performance is still fairly good. In present-day Malaysia and Singapore, the pressure on children to do well is so strong that they are sent for tuition after school. The performance of children in school is linked to the prestige of the parents and the family as a whole. Siblings compete to do well and are so encouraged by parents. This reminds us of Hsu's argument about competition under the ancestors' shadow.

For the Chinese in Southeast Asia, the struggle to succeed is linked to the crucial value of wealth. Chinese societies in Southeast Asia originated from immigrants who came to seek wealth to better their livelihood. Businesses provided the successful ones the opportunities to attain wealth. Thus it is not surprising that wealth has become the crucial value of the Chinese, and business is favored as an occupation. It is also no wonder that business people dominate Chinese society — they, rather than scholars, form the 'élite' of the Chinese community. Scholars are respected but it is wealth that determines leadership. *Shang* (business people) thus occupy a higher stratum than *shi* (scholars), for unlike the *shi* in traditional China, the 'scholars' in Southeast Asia have no power. Power is in the hands of the business people who have wealth, and who can be counted to sponsor communal activities.

Wealth is therefore a central value, and a motivation for success. As Ryan (1961) has reported of the Chinese in Modjokuto in central Java, other values like work, self-reliance, frugality etc. are in fact linked to the focal value of wealth. One works hard and is thrifty in order to accumulate wealth which will offer one material needs and in turn create more opportunities. In Southeast Asia, this value on wealth orientates the Chinese to pursue business and motivates them to strive for success through business. The preference for the private sector is related to this, since government servants have regular income but not enough for gaining wealth. Success is still evaluated by the wealth one can attain. My relatives often asked about my salary when I taught at the University of Malaya in the 1980s. The usual comment was that it was lower than what they thought, but they were quick to add politely: 'but you have regular income'. During an interview with a well-known businessman (since deceased) when I did my research on *Dejiao* associations in 1981, the businessman asked about my salary. When told, he blatantly asked me to work for him, as he could offer higher pay. At first I felt insulted, but I realized quickly that that was how the ethnic Chinese measure 'success'.

The early exposure of children to their family businesses helps orient them toward preference for business. These children are exposed to Chinese business culture at an early age. They help to sell in the shops or stalls. They learn how to do business and to handle money. Parents and relatives who are business people teach the children about business strategies and how to handle credit as well as to judge people's *xinyong*.

Contrary to the indigenous people's stereotype, Chinese business people are guided by business ethics. They gain profit through well-calculated business strategies, not through crude exploitation. In fact, there are various Chinese sayings about doing business. Lee S.M. (1986, 249) lists some of these, such as: 'a man without a smiling face must not open a shop'; 'if a little cash does not go, much cash will not come'; 'a good customer will not change his shop in three years, and a good shop does not lose its customers in three years' (this emphasizes enduring relationships with customers).

In some Chinese shops in Malaysia, one can see maxims of business management hung on the wall. These are attributed to Tao Zhugong of the third century BC. Lee S.M. (250) has translated some of the maxims as follows:

In business, there must be hard work and a sense of urgency.

Economize expenditure.

Be affable in dealing with people.

Buying and selling must follow the times.

Negotiated prices must be clearly stated and agreed upon.

Give credit to people you know.

Accounts must be inspected and audited.

Good and bad must be clearly distinguished.

Goods must be orderly arranged.

Use upright people.
Be careful in receipts and payments.
Goods must be examined.
Payments on installments must be fixed by agreement.
Money and property must be accurate.
Manage with responsibility.
Be calm in making decisions.

There is yet no study on the effect of these teachings, but the common exhibition of maxims attributed to Tao Zhugong in the Chinese shops in Malaysia indicates that Chinese business people value them. They must have the effect of reminding the business people about business ethics and about the need to have good business strategies and management.

THE LARGER SOCIETY

The expanding colonial economies that offered opportunities for Chinese business people accounted for much of their success. They formed the intermediaries between the indigenous people and the Western firms. Many became compradors, the intermediaries of Western firms. The more stable political condition was favorable to commercial development. The end of headhunting in Sarawak, for example, facilitated even more Chinese ventures into the interior. The introduction of Western laws and bureaucracy was conducive to commerce. Western banks allowed major Chinese merchants access to more credit, which enhanced their own financial situation and commercial activities within the Chinese community. By the 1930s, the Chinese began to break into the Western-dominated financial sector by setting up a large number of their own banks.[12] This further consolidated the development of Chinese commerce.

The development of infrastructure in colonial Southeast Asia benefited not only Western firms but also Chinese business people. Chinese entrepreneurs also contributed to the development of transportation, as is still evident in the Chinese dominance in the transport business up the major rivers of Sarawak. The expansion of colonial economies also caused more demand for cheap labor, and a large number of Chinese migrated to Southeast Asia in the 19th and the early 20th centuries. In fact, the Chinese contributed much to the economic development of Southeast Asia, not only commercial and industrial development but also urbanization. The development of towns in Malaysia, for example, was closely linked to the settlement and commercial activities of the Chinese.

The Chinese, who had traded with Southeast Asia long before the Western powers did, at first had the upper hand in commercial development, especially in mining and commercial agriculture. However, by the early 20th century, when Western monopolies began to use modern technology and management, Chinese capital was pushed to the background (Simoniya 1961, 48). The Chinese were involved early in the development of commercial agriculture in Malaya. Guided by the getting-quick-returns orientation, they invested in the planting of gambier, pepper and tapioca, using shifting cultivation to plant commercial crops, what Jackson (1968) calls 'shifting commercial agriculture'. Both the Chinese and European planters also practiced sedentary agriculture, especially in planting sugar cane.

It should be noted that the emergence of an influential Chinese business class in the 19th and 20th centuries was closely linked to the presence of some successful Chinese business people in Southeast Asia even before British, Dutch, Spanish and French colonization there. In Malaya, the Baba (Straits-born Chinese) in the Straits Settlements played a crucial role in the development of the colonial economy. The successful business people in Melaka, for example, financed tapioca planting in Melaka and Negri Sembilan.

Furthermore, the prominent economic presence of the Chinese in Southeast Asia owed much to the fact that the immigrants were a very diverse lot, who among them had a wide range of occupational skills. Thus, they were able to be involved in all kinds of economic activity in Southeast Asia, providing all kinds of business and service. Vaughan

(1879) therefore wrote that 'the Chinese are everything' and gave a long list of all kinds of occupation in which they were engaged in 19th-century Straits Settlements.

British colonization in Malaya provided the existing Chinese shopkeepers and other successful business people more commercial opportunities. Early major merchants owed their success to the various monopolies that they obtained from the colonial governments or local rulers. Securing the right to an opium farm (the franchise to sell opium), for instance, opened up the road to richness or more richness.[13] Indeed as Trocki (1999, 139) points out, the opium farmers in Southeast Asia 'were invariably Chinese'. Even the one who became a *kangchu* (Chinese headman of a river valley, whose right to the valley was granted by the Malay ruler) held a monopoly over the goods moving into and out of his territory (Jackson 1968, 18). The *kangchu* in Johor also had access to credit from the merchants in Singapore. Thus, the system allowed the *kangchu* to become rich. This is not just a matter of a few Chinese becoming rich. The monopoly system provided capital for investment. Trocki (1999, 156) was of the opinion that the opium farming system was 'the primary vehicle of capital accumulation for Chinese during a large part of the nineteenth century'. He even compares the revenue farms to bamboo scaffolding used in the construction of modern skyscrapers in Hong Kong and Singapore (Trocki 1999, 158).

Despite the stereotype that links Chinese in Southeast Asia with business, most Chinese immigrants did not become business people. In fact, the richness gained by both Chinese and Western merchants was based on the colonial economy that allowed the exploitation of cheap labor. Chinese merchants were in a good position to use Chinese laborers, many of whom were indentured. Called *zhuzai* or 'piglings', these laborers were immigrants who were passed by the agents to employers. The 'piglings' had to work for the employers to pay off the debt, usually for at least a year (Jackson 1968, 4; Yang 1986, 21–58). The laborers were highly exploited and worked in extreme hardship in the mines or plantations. Thus, in discussing the achievements of Chinese 'capitalists' in colonial Southeast Asia, one should not forget their exploitation of Chinese labor.[14]

Overall, the larger economic and political systems either favored or constrained Chinese economic development. The largely *laissez-faire* policy of the British was conducive to the economic performance of the Chinese, especially the business class. Of course, colonial policies were geared toward the domination of the colonial government and Western firms. In the Philippines and the Dutch East Indies, the colonial governments even introduced policies to restrict the movements of the Chinese, to control their commercial activities (Diaz-Trechuelo 1969; The 1989, 160).

Chinese business people in different societies have to adjust to the larger economic and political systems. They have to adopt strategies to adapt to the external conditions. Getting close to or gaining the support of the ruling élite was, and still is, an important strategy of Chinese capitalists. Even in Thailand, which was not colonized, political patronage was an important factor of commercial success, a notable example being the success of Khaw Sim Bee, who served the Thai court and whose family's business network spread to Malaya and the Dutch East Indies (Cushman 1986). The royal family encouraged Chinese immigration to Siam (Skinner 1957, 25), which helped the Chinese involvement in business.

The role of the larger society becomes clear when we compare the Southeast Asian context to that in North America. In North America, the Whites dominated both the political and economic systems. Unlike in Southeast Asia, where Chinese business people did not have to compete with any significant indigenous business class (although they faced the competition of Western firms), the Chinese in North America who wanted to venture into business had to face White domination and exclusion in almost all economic spheres. Hence, Chinese who ventured into business ended up largely in the laundry business in which the Whites were not keen, and in the Chinese restaurant business in which the Chinese could do without White competition. The history of the Chinese immigrants in North America was a bitter one, as the coolies (Chinese laborers) were not only more terribly exploited and ill treated, but the Chinese as a whole encountered White racism and exclusion (Chen 1981).

Bernard Wong (1979, 172), in concluding his study of New York's Chinatown, mentions very correctly that, 'its economic activities and social relations are adaptations shaped by the forces of racism and exclusion from the larger society'. Thus, in North America, Chinatowns had become an economic and social niche for the Chinese. To this day, the Chinese in North America find it difficult to break into the White domains of business. However, the younger generation has done well in education; they have better success as professionals, even though they experience discrimination, too (Chen 1992, 142; Ling 1998, 141). Similarly in Canada, Peter Li (1998, 117) reports that with educational achievement and improved attitudes towards them, Chinese Canadians have moved to middle-class white neighborhoods, and Chinatowns have become mainly commercial and tourist areas. Zhou (1992, 227), however, reminds us that leaving Chinatowns to live in the suburbs does not mean cutting off from the Chinatowns, as some continue to work there.

In South America, the experiences of the Chinese indentured laborers were especially bad. In Cuba and Brazil, for example, the coolies were imported to work in the sugar cane plantations and were treated more or less as slaves (Hu-DeHart 1998, 81). The exploitation and control was so severe that many committed suicide, and many died (Fraginals 1981; Wu Jianxiong 1988, 417–76). In Peru, Chinese coolies who were sent to the Chincha Islands to extract guano encountered a similar fate and led miserable lives as slaves (de Azua 1981). Despite the initial extreme hardship, once the Chinese were free of indentured labor and left the farm, many eventually set up businesses (Yuan 1988, 21).

Thus, the larger society shapes the adaptation of the Chinese. Nevertheless, it is misleading to be deterministic about this with regards to Chinese economic performance. This chapter has shown that the overall 'culture' of the Chinese does contain favorable factors for commercial achievement, and the Chinese have the values and motivation to acquire wealth. What is argued here is that the larger societies shape Chinese adaptation and the nature as well as the extent of their economic performance; but without the internal cultural resources analyzed above, they may not have been able to adapt to larger societies the way they have done and still attain a certain level of economic performance, even in hostile environments.

THE WEBERIAN THESIS

The discussion on culture (in the general sense) and economic performance obviously reminds us of Weber's thesis on capitalist spirit: it was the ethics of ascetic Protestantism which, among other things, accounted for the rise of modern capitalism in the West. Capitalism as perceived by Weber (1958, 17) 'is identical with the pursuit of profit, and forever renewed profit, by means of continuous, rational, capitalistic enterprise'. For Weber, the Protestant ethic, which regards work and the pursuit of wealth as God's calling, is a powerful motivating force that favors the development of modern capitalism. He writes, 'the religious valuation of restless, continuous, systematic work in a worldly calling, as the highest means to asceticism, and at the same time the surest and most evident proof of rebirth and genuine faith, must have been the most powerful conceivable lever for the expansion of that attitude toward life which we have called here the spirit of capitalism' (172). This 'calling' not only motivates economic pursuit but also legitimizes work and seeking wealth. Weber is of the opinion that the lack of a spirit equivalent to ascetic Protestantism in other parts of the world explains why modern capitalism emerged in the West and not elsewhere. In the case of China, he tries to illustrate his thesis in his *The Religion of China* (1951).

Our analysis, however, shows no lack of the idea of 'calling' and the positive values on work and economic pursuit, even in traditional China. In fact, the China case must have been a headache to Weber in his attempt to prove his thesis, for he found in Confucianism the this-worldly orientation that was favorable to economic pursuit. In the final analysis, however, he concludes that the failure of China to have modern capitalism is due to the lack of the 'capitalist spirit' characteristic of ascetic Protestantism. We do not know if his thesis pushed Weber in the direction he wanted, but he obviously did not have the advantage of reading the major publications on China that we have today, nor was he able to read Chinese works. As Yu (1987) has shown so clearly from Chinese materials, China did not lack the values listed by Weber necessary for capitalism; the crucial values of industry and frugality are not only important in Chinese culture but had been emphasized since ancient times. Yu (1987, 97–166) also describes the spirit and ethics of business people in China.

In his defense of Weber against critics like S.H. Alatas, who tries to show there is the spirit of capitalism in Asia, Buss (1986, 8) complains that the Weber thesis 'is treated in isolation and is not integrated into a sociology of rationalism, or into the global outlook which Weber himself gave to his studies on Asian religions'. As far as his writing on Chinese religion is concerned, Weber is himself to blame also, because his focus is on showing the lack of capitalist spirit in Chinese culture. The problem with China is not the lack of capitalist ethics; the failure to have modern capitalism lies with other structural factors.

Elvin (1973: 314) has shown that China in fact had a medieval economic and technological revolution but still failed to develop modern capitalism. He gives the 'high-level equilibrium trap' theory, which may be explained as follows:

> All that we have shown here is that in late traditional China, economic forces developed in such a way as to make profitable invention more and more difficult. With falling surplus in agriculture, and so falling per capita income and per capita demand, with cheapening labor but increasingly expensive resources and capital, with farming and transport technologies so good that no simple improvements could be made, rational strategy for peasants and merchants alike tended in the direction not so much of labor-saving machinery as of economizing on resources and fixed capital. Huge but nearly static markets created no bottlenecks in the production system that might have prompted creativity. When temporary shortages arose, mercantile versatility, based on cheap transport, was a faster and surer remedy than the contrivance of machines. This situation may be described as a 'high-level equilibrium trap.

Elvin's theory opens up a new dimension. Nevertheless, Weber's idea of rationality is still useful for us to understand the economic performance of the Chinese, in China and outside China. Weber focuses on the Chinese lack of a 'permanent intrinsic character of their religious beliefs', and I have shown that this is not accurate. The problem with traditional China, as well as modern China, is 'external historico-political situations' which Weber (1958, 40) sees as a factor, but he emphasizes the need to look at the intrinsic character of religious beliefs. The idea of rationality should be linked up with the historico-political factors, not just with value orientation.

Modern rational capitalism not only needs technology but also 'rational structures of law and administration' (Weber 1958, 25). Weber (1951) finds that China lacked a 'formally guaranteed law' and a 'rational administration and judiciary'. This is an important point. The administration was dominated by the Confucian élite, who manipulated 'Confucian ideology' to consolidate its dominance. This ideology may be called state Confucianism,[15] to distinguish it from the higher values (spiritual traditions) taught by Confucius and Mencius. State Confucianism was traditional in outlook, oriented toward the past, and legitimized the imperial structure as well as the political role of the Confucian élite. It emphasized, rather than changed, the status quo that would threaten the dominance of the Confucian literati. It is thus understandable why radical modern Chinese thinkers, notably Lu Xun, attacked Confucianism, which unfortunately was taken to mean anything Confucian. In fact, it was the particular kind of system (the 'Confucian' mandarinate) and the use of an ideology rather than the overall Confucian teaching that could be said to hinder change and development. The problem lay more on the structure of political relations.

The Confucian mandarinate was more concerned with upholding the feudal structure and the gentry class structure than with the rational economic organization of society. In fact, the Confucian mandarinate obstructed commercial enterprises by keeping merchants down (Wang 1991b, 195). In the traditional Chinese system of stratification, the

202 <i>Chinese Overseas</i>

merchant (*shang*) was placed last, after the gentry (*shi*), farmer (*nong*) and craftsperson (*gong*). The merchants were not only given negative stereotypes by the Confucian élite, they were indeed kept down. For a long time in Chinese history, the merchants were not allowed to sit for examinations to become officials, and they even had to wear distinct dress, which indicated their low status. This was in addition to the harassment to pay tax and the restrictions on their commercial activities (Eberhard 1962).

Thus, the Confucian structure of imperial China hampered commercial development and obviously could not encourage the rise of modern capitalism. The overall system of stratification that made gentry 'a privileged group before the law' (Chang 1955) certainly was not conducive to bringing about a more rational system of laws and administration. Furthermore, mobility was through identification with state Confucianism rather than through achievement in all fields, including science and technology.

Overall, one should be clear that it was not so much the lack of a certain mentality among the Chinese people that accounted for China not having modern capitalism. It was more the nature of the Chinese bureaucracy and the social structure that made the gentry a special class apart from the others. The state under the control of the Confucian mandarinate did not help to promote the interests of the merchants. On the contrary, it hampered their commercial pursuits. However, this should not be taken to mean also the lack of development in ethics that was good for commercial pursuit. In fact, Wang Gungwu (1991b) argues that because the merchants in China had to operate in the most difficult conditions, 'they became the most flexible and most skilled in learning how to grasp opportunities for profit-making'. This is in fact an important factor in Weber's conditions for modern capitalism.

Although communism did away with state Confucianism, the rational structures of law and administration still failed to develop in China. As far as economic development was concerned, the situation was worsened by the communist system, which took away the individual incentive and competition found in the traditional culture. In a sense, state Confucianism was merely replaced by communism as ideology, while the bureaucracy had become even more centralized, and capitalism officially condemned; however, since 1979 China has accommodated capitalism. It is obvious that China cannot fully modernize its economy and society without rationalizing the administration and judiciary; to do so, it has to drop its ideological control, be it state Confucianism in the past or communism in the present.

When we compare the economic development of China before 1979 with that of Hong Kong and Taiwan or with the Chinese-majority Singapore, the economic achievement of the Chinese outside mainland China is obvious. The attribution of success of the so-called 'four little dragons' to Confucianism is misleading. In the first place, what is Confucianism in relation to economic achievement is not clear. The frequent reference to industry and frugality in the context of the Chinese is best seen as part of an overall 'Chinese culture' rather than as Confucianism.

Confucianism was an important tradition that influenced the masses, but not every aspect of Chinese culture could be described as Confucianism. Ancestor worship may be supported and even propagated by Confucianists, but the worship of ancestors predated Confucius. It is also misleading to say that the Japanese and Koreans have industriousness and frugality because they have Confucian influences, as if without Confucianism the Japanese and Koreans today would not have industriousness and frugality as core values.

One should also note that traditional China did not have one single religion only. The Chinese masses observed the folk religion that had evolved from the ancient past and had incorporated various religious and philosophical teachings throughout the history of China. There is also the need to distinguish state Confucianism from Confucianism the spiritual tradition. State Confucianism may be condemned and thrown out, but the Chinese will still need spiritual values (such as those found in Confucianism and Daoism) to ensure that development is humane and in keeping with the harmony between people and nature.

When we compare the situation in China to that of the Chinese in

Southeast Asia, the picture becomes clearer. This chapter shows that traditional Chinese culture does contain the values favorable and even necessary for economic achievement. In fact, the values Weber says are necessary for capitalism are present in Chinese culture. Given the historico-political situations and opportunities in Southeast Asia, the Chinese have been able to attain significant economic success. They owe this to both the historico-political situations and to their own cultural resources and orientation, such as their familiarity with market economy, their ability to adapt traditional institutions such as the Chinese credit society to the situation in Southeast Asia, and not least to their values of industry, frugality and self-reliance.

In other words, a value system (and motivation) alone cannot bring about economic success. It is the interaction between the value system and favorable external conditions (such as rational legal and administration systems, the access to modern technology, etc.) which can account for economic success. Values and motivation can only be active in situations where there is room for expansion, not in static situations. Furthermore, where external conditions permit the values for economic success to be activated, the interaction can produce a push effect such that the values and motivation can be intensified, and this in turn further motivates economic performance.

We can say that Chinese values play a part in economic pursuit in Southeast Asia, and the situations in Southeast Asia further reinforce the motivation and values for economic success. If in traditional China the glorification of one's family and ancestors represented an incentive for success (a kind of calling), the immigrants' intensity of calling was even stronger because of their wish to bring money back to their families in China and to realize the dream of establishing oneself economically — the dream that motivated them to leave their homeland for other lands. Their local-born descendants continue the dream of seeking wealth. Wealth as a value was emphasized to the extent of becoming an end in itself. Economic pursuits are oriented toward getting wealth and more wealth. Today, 'wealth' has become a dominant value among the Chinese in Southeast Asia, and it defines status and leadership.

Similarly, the competition element in traditional Chinese culture has played a part in the economic achievement in Southeast Asia. In traditional China, competition was expressed not just in economic achievement but even more in ceremonialism. In Southeast Asia, the greater economic opportunities gear the competition more toward economic achievement, although ceremonialism is emphasized, too, in marriage and funerals. But ceremonialism in marriage (like the number of guests invited) and funerals for business people are in fact also geared toward promoting *guanxi* and exhibiting financial strength.

In the functioning of an economic institution like *hui*, we have seen that the Chinese in New Guinea have adapted the traditional institution into an important credit institution for business investment. In traditional China, hui was not just linked to business but also to, and in Fei's study more for, social functions like weddings and other ceremonies. Thus, the situation in societies outside China encourages action toward greater economic achievement; it encourages greater rationalizing toward attaining wealth.

In a sense, there is more orientation toward formal rationality of economic action rather than substantive rationality that may be oriented toward non-economic ends (Weber 1964). However, in Chinese economic action, there is no distinct boundary between formal rational economic action and substantive rationality. Chinese business people who lower prices to ensure long-term relationships may be formally rational in the long-term, but in the short-run this appears to be rather substantive in rationality.

What is argued here is that the same values and cultural principles that promote economic achievement can become oriented toward substantive rationality in the absence of opportunity for economic growth. They can even work in ways that hinder the development of more rational legal and administrative systems, hence hindering economic development. For example, the Chinese in Southeast Asia continue to organize their social relations under the principle of *guanxi*, but for business people, the networking of *guanxi* is geared toward the ultimate aim of achieving more commercial success. In mainland

China today, where bureaucracy is characterized by serious red tape and corruption, the *guanxi* principle has led to a bureaucracy that has declined in rationality and which hampers economic growth.

In these systems, things can only be done fast through the back door (King 1991, 70) whereas those without proper connections will have to suffer from the inefficiency of the bureaucracy.[16] Before 1979, this was worsened by the central planning system which took away individual incentive; civil servants tended to regard their jobs as rather unrelated to the self, creating a serious problem in a society whose principles of social relations focus on the ego, not on a larger whole. Thus, what is *gongjia* (public) is not so important.

Weber concludes his study of China by saying that 'the varied conditions which externally favored the origin of capitalism in China did not suffice to create it'. He mentions that in China 'all communal action there remained engulfed and conditioned by purely personal, above all, by kinship relations', and that 'the pervasive factors were tradition, local custom, and the concrete personal favor of the official' (Weber 1951, 241, 248). Weber is only partly right here, for I have shown that the study of culture in relation to economic performance must be linked to the overall situation of the economy as well as the legal and administrative systems. The comparison with Chinese 'societies' outside China shows this very clearly. Traditional Chinese culture, for example, does distinguish economic relation and kin relation, but it is outside China that the distinction is made manifest because of the business orientation of Chinese business people.

Compared to China, the conditions in Southeast Asia were more conducive for Chinese commercial activities, despite the various constraints imposed by the colonial governments. The Chinese abroad were free of the suffocating control of the mandarins, and the Westerners as well as the indigenous élites (such as the royal family in Thailand, or the Malay Sultan who granted a river valley to *kangchu* and collected tax) valued the trading ability of the Chinese and used them in their own pursuit of profit (Wang 1991b, 194). Even today, Western and Japanese firms prefer to collaborate with Chinese business people.

In other words, in China, the presence of motivation and values does not bring about better economic performance. This is due to an economic condition that does not offer sufficient economic opportunities, and here Elvin's 'high-level equilibrium trap' is helpful as an explanation. The legal and administrative systems also are not conducive to rational economic management and development. China needs revolutionary changes, not only in technology but also in the legal and administrative systems. There must be a rule of law and the bureaucracy has to be more rational. Weber is right that the varied conditions did not suffice to create modern capitalism, but the cause is not so much a lack of particular mentality as structured problems in the larger society.

CONCLUSION

This chapter shows the relationship between culture and economic performance of the Chinese, both with regards to small trade and capitalist business. It shows that traditional Chinese culture lacks neither motivation nor values for economic performance. The economic achievement of the Chinese in Southeast Asia, and of course Taiwan and Hong Kong, shows that motivation and values can activate the orientation toward economic success only in a larger society whose economic and administrative systems are rationally organized for economic achievement and where there is room for economic expansion. The ability to adapt to changing situations and to organize efficiently by drawing upon the strength of kinship, social organizations, and other forms of *guanxi* has been important for Chinese economic achievement.

The most significant influence of culture on Chinese business is the role of the family. Small Chinese businesses are owned and run by individual families. In large commercial enterprises in which a Chinese capitalist may own a number of firms, family ownership is still important, although the management is modified to bring in professional managers, as described by Limlingan. Familism has obviously played a crucial part in shaping Chinese business and in attaining commercial success.[17] Even in Hong Kong, Chinese familism has played an important role in commercial and industrial development (Huang 1991, 172–99).

However, Chinese capitalists find that they have to adapt to competition with Japanese and Western multinational companies. In consideration of this need to adapt to the changing international economy, analysts generally consider familism as a hindrance for further economic achievement. Omohundro (1981, 142), who has studied commerce and kin of Chinese merchants in Iloilo City in the Philippines, points out that trust and reliance upon only the inner circle of family members for major tasks inherently limits businesses. S.Y. Lee (1990), for example, says that the new generation of Chinese businessmen should discard their 'old family conception' in business and expand their business organization internationally, so that they can be more efficient and competitive.

In an interesting paper on Chinese business continuity and discontinuity, Yoshihara points out the factors favoring and hindering Chinese business continuity — his concern is with Chinese capitalist enterprises, not small businesses. Of Chinese culture, he points out that the equal inheritance of the Chinese is not good for the continuity of business, but this can be solved by appointing an heir to take over the business before the old man dies (Yoshihara 1987, 121). He also points out that banks tend to be more lasting and they are usually jointly owned and managed more professionally. He therefore thinks that for Chinese business to grow, there is a need to bring in more outside capital and there is a need for greater separation of management from ownership (Yoshihara 1987, 125).

The general consensus is that to break into the international multinational enterprises, the Chinese will have to de-emphasize family management and even family control, in order to have access to more capital and international markets as well as more professional management. There is also the need to use modern technology. Nevertheless, one should not write off familism in Chinese business at the level of national economy. At small- and medium-range businesses, Chinese family-style business does have its advantages, too. As Lee (1978, 40) himself has pointed out, family-type business can have more resilience in time of recession, as family members are more willing to work harder with less pay at such times.

In fact, it is how a family firm is run that determines its scope for expansion and continuity. A one-person show is fine for a small business, but it is limited in scope for expansion. Thus, even in the past, some Chinese capitalists incorporated Western methods of management into their family businesses. In Singapore, Lee Rubber of Lee Kong Chian is still a large enterprise today. Lee Kong Chian, who was active in the early 1950s, introduced Western management and delegated power to competent managers. In contrast, his contemporary Tan Lark Sye (1897–1972), also a rubber magnate, ran a one-person show and did not bother to incorporate modern methods of management. His Aik Hoe is no longer in existence (Lim 1990; Yoshihara 1987, 419).

In the prewar era, Oei Tiong Ham ran a very successful sugar-based conglomerate in the Dutch East Indies. His was a family business but he adopted Dutch business methods and employed professionals (Mackie 1991).[18] Today, Chinese capitalists have generally incorporated modern management into their family businesses. For example, the Kuok group, of the Malaysian-born commodities and property tycoon Robert Kuok, is a family company that uses a core of professionals. The Kuok group has firms not only in Asia (China, Hong Kong, Indonesia, Malaysia, Philippines, Singapore and Thailand) but also in Canada, Chile, France, Germany, Fiji and Mexico.[19]

Whatever it is, Chinese business people have adapted and will continue to adapt to changing situations and new challenges, relying on internal socio-cultural resources where possible and adopting new techniques where necessary. Competing with Western corporations is not something new. Even during the colonial past, the Chinese found it difficult to compete with large Western firms; now it is the multinationals of both the West and Japan that the Chinese have to deal with. Obviously, if Chinese capitalists do not just want to be compradors, then they will have to pull their resources together and find strategies to break into Western and Japanese domination in the international economy. In fact, Yoshihara has pointed out that Southeast Asian capitalists (largely Chinese) who have set up sophisticated industries are in fact Japanese compradors, especially as distributors of Japanese cars. He describes Southeast Asian capitalism (including Singapore) as dependent on foreign capital and technology and its industrialization as industrialism without development. He describes this kind of dependent capitalism as ersatz capitalism. Yoshihara concludes by saying that the three problems facing the capitalism of Southeast Asia are technological backwardness, low quality of government intervention, and discrimination against Chinese (Yoshihara 1988, 111–2, 131). However, Yoshihara (1995, 83) himself concedes that not all Southeast Asian capitalists can be described as 'ersatz'.

Chinese economic performance in Southeast Asia is shaped by the nature of the national society and the opportunities available. In the post-independence period, Chinese business people in Southeast Asia have to cope with varying degrees of economic nationalism which discriminates against them, especially in the Philippines, Indonesia and Malaysia (Somers Heidhues 1974, 20–7). Ironically, the safeguard for Chinese business people is their strong presence in the economy, which is what the policies of economic nationalism seek to curb in the first place to help bring about a competitive indigenous business élite. Chinese capital, entrepreneurship and a wide distribution network are too important to national economic development to be curbed severely. Even in Indonesia, where there was both economic nationalism and an official policy of assimilating the Chinese and where there had been a number of racial riots against the Chinese because of their strong presence in the economy, President Suharto used Chinese capital and entrepreneurship in his attempt to rehabilitate the Indonesian economy (Mely Tan 1987, 69).

However, in Southeast Asian countries like Indonesia and Malaysia, ethnicity will continue to be a major factor in economic planning, as long as there is perceived Chinese dominance in the economy and as long as Chinese are still regarded by the indigenous people as somewhat alien, even though they may be citizens. Neither the indigenous political élite nor the Chinese can ignore the aspiration of the indigenous masses to see that the indigenous élite is also well represented in commerce and industries. The Chinese, of course, respond according to what they see is worthwhile from their business point of view. Jesudason has shown that in Malaysia, the New Economic Policy, which aimed to restructure the economy to enable more *bumiputra* participation, caused Chinese business people to comply (especially the larger firms, which can meet the state's requirement), or to refrain from investment, or to invest and buy companies abroad, particularly in Singapore, Hong Kong, Australia and North America. The Malaysian government has relied more, and in fact still does, on foreigners than on the Chinese to re-crank the economy (Jesudason 1989, 195, 198).

The policies of economic nationalism in Southeast Asia have further encouraged Chinese business people to continue to emphasize a get-rich-quick attitude and to be speculative rather than make long-term rational economic plans. In the 19th century, this was encouraged by the wish to get rich quickly and return to China. Furthermore, the feeling of insecurity both in the past and today tends to encourage speculation rather than long-term planning. The economic constraint on Chinese business has also encouraged prominent Chinese business people to be close to politically influential indigenous politicians from the lowest to the highest levels, such as the prime minister or the president. In fact, many prominent Chinese business people are close to indigenous politicians and have benefited from the relationship.[20] Yoshihara (1987) points out that this is bad for business continuity for, when the politicians fall, Chinese business is affected. Nevertheless, in the short run, this strategy offers a quick route to commercial success and richness. Related to this is the phenomenon of what is called Ali-Baba business in Malaysia and Indonesia, a kind of partnership between a Chinese entrepreneur and an indigenous sleeping partner or licensee. However, this will no doubt create resentment from the indigenous people, and there will be pressure to have genuine partnership. Economic nationalism also creates more opportunity for corruption, thereby weakening rational administration in the long run. In short, economic nationalism, if pursued seriously, will constrain not only Chinese business in the domestic sphere; it will also affect national economic development and ultimately will have a negative effect on the indigenous people.

Furthermore, it will make the country even more dependent on foreign investment and foreign technology.

Chinese business people in Southeast Asia have to cope with the reality of ethnicity and development. They can do their part to gain the confidence of and solidarity with the indigenous people by involving themselves in not just Chinese communal affairs but also in the concerns of the indigenous people. For example, they can contribute more directly to reduce poverty or provide financial assistance to both poor Chinese and indigenous students. This will help to correct the indigenous stereotype that the Chinese are exclusive. Ultimately, however, the indigenous people — in particular the indigenous political élite — have to accept the Chinese fully, without considering their ethnicity. This is, however, the most difficult part. In Indonesia, where the younger generation of Chinese has taken steps to acculturate even to the extent of adopting indigenous names, they are still regarded as separate (Mely Tan 1987, 75).

In August 1991, from the 10th to the 12th, the first international Chinese Entrepreneurs Convention was held in Singapore. More than 800 Chinese entrepreneurs from all over the world (30 countries) attended the conference.[21] Among the issues discussed were Chinese culture and economic development. This convention was a significant development in that for the first time, Chinese entrepreneurs from different parts of the world met to discuss their strengths and weaknesses as well as the challenges facing Chinese entrepreneurship. It paved the way to more dialogue and cooperation among Chinese entrepreneurs. Since then, the convention has been held biennially in different cities. The second convention, for example, was held in Hong Kong in 1993.

Overall, this chapter shows that the economic achievement of the Chinese in Southeast Asia is influenced by both culture and larger societies that offer opportunities for economic development. The use of internal socio-cultural resources for economic achievement, the ability to adapt traditional Chinese institutions and Western technology for economic goals, the ability to take advantage of opportunities for profit-making, the strong work ethic, frugality and self-reliance all contribute to the success in economic enterprises. The comparison of Southeast Asia with traditional and modern China highlights the need to examine both the cultural and structural factors of the larger society in order to understand economic achievement. Cultural factors alone cannot explain economic achievement, but external material and institutional factors are also insufficient as driving forces; access to cultural and social resources does influence economic achievement.

We have examined the aspects of Chinese culture that are relevant to economic performance. In doing so, it has been shown that Chinese culture cannot be reduced to Confucianism, no matter how influential it was. In fact, although state Confucianism hampered the interests of the merchants, this did not mean that ethics favorable for commerce did not exist. In a favorable larger society, Chinese (as in Southeast Asia) have been able to adapt their traditional culture for economic achievement.

Weber is correct about the role of culture in economic development. Cultures that do not have the core values for commercial development will have to acquire them. Human beings are adaptive and can always emphasize the relevant values (and de-emphasize the negative ones) in their cultural system if external conditions for commercial development are conducive and if there is a will to develop. In China, it was not the lack of ethics necessary for capitalism that accounted for the failure to have modern capitalism. It was, and still is, the problem arising from 'temporary external historico-political situations'.

However, Weber's economic rationality is more useful. In this respect, Chinese capitalism in Southeast Asia is still not as rationally organized as Western capitalism. Chinese capitalism is still characterized by speculation, calculation for quick wealth, and relying too much on Western and Japanese capital and technology. This is not so much due to cultural limitation as to external factors, such as the economic nationalism in Southeast Asia and especially the domination of Western and Japanese capitalists in the international market and economy.

In Weber's study, capitalism is identical with the pursuit of unlimited profit. For the Chinese and for the countries in the South, the Western form of unlimited profit-making capitalism need not be ideal for them, and they need not seek to attain the full Western form of capitalism. The evil of unlimited capitalism is obvious — its consequences on the poor and on the environment are examples. China is a big country with a huge population; it cannot afford to develop at the expense of the masses in favor of a minority of capitalists, nor can the Chinese capitalists in Southeast Asia be indifferent to communal affairs and the plight of the majority, who are not well off. There is room and, in fact, necessity for spiritual values in economic development to make development more humane. Confucianism (the higher values in Confucian teaching) as well as Daoist and other Chinese teachings are after all both relevant and necessary for modernization. From this perspective, it is a blessing if the capitalism of China and other developing countries is guided by a mentality (not lack of mentality) different from that which Weber says promoted occidental capitalism.

Lastly, it is hoped that this chapter shows the need and advantages of doing comparative studies of Chinese societies. The different experiences of the Chinese in different parts of the world, when compared, can show us more clearly the nature of Chinese 'culture', the continuity and transformation of cultural principles and institutions, the process of adaptation and its consequences, and many other themes. The study of the people of Chinese descent should not be regarded as merely marginal to the study of the Chinese land. It is a study in its own right. Ultimately, it can also enlighten us about the question of culture and development in China itself. The anthropology of Chinese societies has much to contribute to the study of Chinese ethnicity, culture and societies, as well as to social science in general.

Notes

Chapter 1

1. A number of anthropologists have discussed the unity of Chinese culture. Ward's (1965, 1985, 41–60) discussion of varieties of the conscious model is well known. This approach has, for example, influenced Li Yih-yuan (1970, 245–6; Tan 2000, 26–7). Watson has explored the unity of Chinese culture through his analysis of 'standardizing the gods' (1985). He also argues that 'orthopraxy (correct practice) reigned over orthodoxy (correct belief) as the principal means of attaining and maintaining cultural unity' in late imperial China (1993, 84).

Chapter 2

1. In the languages of the various speech-groups originally from southern China, the historical label 'People of Tang' is still commonly used. For instance, in *Minnanhua* or the Hokkien speech in use in Malaysia and Singapore, the term for Chinese is *Teng-lang*. In Cantonese, it is *Tohngyahn*.
2. For a description of intermarriage and the formation of Chinese Peranakan identity, see Tan (1988a).
3. For a discussion on the identification of the acculturated Chinese in Kelantan, see my article (Tan 1982, 28–31) and Teo (2003). See Tan (2002a) for a description of the Peranakan-type Chinese in Terengganu.
4. In the case of the Chinese in Cambodia, Willmott (1967, 43) mentions that 'intermarriage has led to assimilation either to Khmer or to Chinese society and nowhere has a separate Sino-Khmer community emerged'.
5. This is reflected in Violet L. Lai's book (1985, 37):

    Emma was the envy of her girl friends who were adjusting her new wedding *holoku* (a princess-style gown with a ruffled train). 'You are so smart to marry a *Pake* (Chinese) who works and brings home *kala* (money) for you to spend.' Someone made a remark about the stinginess of the *Pakes*, and agreed that the Hawaiian husband was more generous, but he only had land (sometimes) and little money.

6. For a discussion of missionary activities and the acculturation of the Chinese in 19th-century California, see Barth (1964, 157–73).

7. In her account of Aloiau (Wang Lo Yau), a Chinese immigrant to Hawaii, Violet L. Lai (1985) deals with this attitude of ensuring that Chinese remain Chinese. The following description of Lai (1985, 48) is illuminating:

    Although outwardly happy, Emma confided in 1910 when Rose was married to En Sue Kong, a Chinese, that she had hoped at least one daughter would have married a Hawaiian. Aloiau thought differently. He urged his daughters to marry their own kind — Chinese. When they pointed out that he had married Emma, a Hawaiian-German, he explained, 'That's different. When Emma married me, she took my name and became Chinese. Now, when you girls marry foreign devil, you take his name and become a foreign devil, yourself.'

    A story is told of Aloiau's pacing up and down the living room when one of Rose's part-Hawaiian suitors came calling all the way from Hilo. To her embarrassment, Aloiau kept saying in Chinese, 'When is he going home, anyway?'

    While he disapproved of interracial marriages for his children, he reacted favorably to his Hakka sons-in-law, although he was a Punti because they were at least Chinese.

8. Stewart (1951, 129, 225) also mentions marriage between Chinese coolies and Peruvian women.

9. *Tok* is a Malay word, and *Pek* (i.e., *peh* or *a-peh*) is a Hokkien term that literally means 'father's elder brother'. Both are terms of address for old people or people (male) of one's father's generation. Historically, the local people (both the Malays and the local-born Chinese) used *Pek* or *A-Pek* to address the older immigrants. In time, this term came to imply not only inferior immigrant status but also behavior associated with immigrants who had not yet culturally adjusted to the local environment.

10. For a discussion on the terms *Cina* and *Tionghoa* in Indonesia, see Coppel and Suryadinata (1978).

11. There are also Chinese who now migrate 'back' to the 'Chinese land', especially to the more prosperous Taiwan in the 1980s [cf. 'Migration: Taiwan's Open Door', *Far Eastern Economic Review* 28 (April 1988): 22] and to the economically stronger mainland China since the late 1990s (cf. 'Opportunities in China Entice Overseas Chinese Tech Professionals Returning to China', *The San Francisco Chronicle*, Wednesday, 2 January 2002).

12. The Chinese in India are distributed mainly in West Bengal and Maharashtra (Oxfeld 1993; Schermerhorn 1978, 292).

Chapter 3

1. For works on the Chinese Peranakan in Indonesia, see, for example, Oetomo (1984), Salmon (1981), Mely Tan (1963), Skinner (1960), Suryadinata (1976), and Willmott (1960).

2. For academic studies on the Baba of Singapore, see, for example, Clammer (1980), Pakir (1986), Rudolph (1998), and Tan (1993).

3. For works on the Baba of Penang, see, for example, Ho (1985), Ooi (1967), and Tan (1993).

4. In my first article on the Peranakan-type Chinese in Kelantan, I used the term Peranakan (Tan 1982). This influenced the local leaders who decided to use the label Peranakan to describe their own community, and their association formed in 1987 was called Persatuan Peranakan Cina Kelantan. Before the formal establishment of the association, the first president discussed with me the use of the term 'Peranakan'.

Chapter 5

1. Here, I am concerned with the Baba of Melaka only. Many Babas from Melaka went to Singapore in the 19th and early 20th centuries and contributed to the emergence of the Baba community there. The Babas also call themselves 'Peranakan', which in Malay means 'local-born'. In Indonesia, the Chinese Peranakans prefer to be called 'Peranakan' although the label 'Baba' is used too.

2. The Chinese in Malaysia had also launched a similar campaign. The slogan was '*duojiang Huayu, shaoshuo fangyan*' or 'speak more Mandarin, less *fangyan*'. *Fangyan* refers to Chinese languages other than the standard Mandarin, such as Hokkien, Cantonese, Hakka and others. The campaign may be seen as an attempt by the Chinese-educated Chinese to define the changing Chinese identity.

3. I have discussed Li Guoliang's paper in Tan (1992).

4. *Tudi de Nahan* (Voice of the Earth) by Jiang Tian (Goh Then Chye) was published in China in 1989. A number of poets and other writers in and out of China have reviewed favorably this collection of poems by a Chinese Malaysian. There is a clear difference between reviewers who review from the perspective of 'China consciousness', and those who review from the perspective of the poet's local consciousness. For the China-centric reviewers, any suggestion of the motherland in the poems is interpreted as the Chinese poet's love of or yearning for China whereas in actual fact, for the poet, his motherland is Malaysia.

5. While there are monthly Chinese publications that provide coverage on Chinese overseas, these cannot match the frequency, coverage and distribution of *Yazhou Zhoukan*. Of the monthly, the Hong Kong based *Depingxian Monthly (Dipingxian Yuekan)* has a regular section that provides analysis of

themes on Chinese overseas, especially Chinese in Indonesia and North America.

6. In 1990, Premier Li Peng of China, while visiting Malaysia, called upon Chinese Malaysians to be good citizens of Malaysia and contribute to the development of the country. This comment would have been appropriate in the 1950s when there were many Chinese who were still China-oriented, but today the Chinese in Malaysia have identified fully with Malaysia. No wonder Chinese Malaysians protested against the Chinese Premier's uncalled-for comment. Consequently, Li Peng made some clarification before leaving Kuala Lumpur (*Yazhou Zhoukan*, 30 December 1990, p.19). In April 1992, at the World Chinese Conference in Mauritius, China's Deputy Minister of Culture was reported to have remarked that the Chinese in Malaysia should be loyal to Malaysia. Again, Chinese Malaysians were angry at this remark (*Xingzhou Ribao*, 28 April 1992, p. 3). Obviously, China's leaders have to learn more about the people of Chinese descent, and to be more sensitive to their feelings, especially on the question of identity and loyalty.

Chapter 6

1. In Southeast Asia, the distinction of the Chinese from the indigenous people is still maintained, although they are both citizens of the same country. For convenience of discussion, I keep this distinction.

2. These are Chinese who have acquired certain Malay cultural characteristics. For example, the young people prefer to speak to each other in the Malay of the Kelantan dialect. Unlike the Baba or Chinese Peranakan in Melaka, the Peranakan-type Chinese in Kelantan still speak a somewhat acculturated Hokkien (southern Fujian) dialect, and many speak the local Thai, too. For a brief description of the Peranakan-type Chinese in Kelantan, see Tan (1982).

3. For an analytical description of the affirmative action policy in Malaysia, see Lim (1985).

4. Because of the 'special position' of the Chinese as a visible minority or 'non-indigenous' group disliked and envied, they can become not only scapegoats for economic problems but also scapegoats in the political competition between different domestic political forces, as shown in the description of Mackie. To give another example, the Liberals and the Conservatives in Western Canada before the 1920s used the Chinese as scapegoats in their competition for votes (cf. Ban 1976, 348).

5. For a description of Sino-Malay relations in Peninsular Malaysia before 1942, see Khoo (1981).

6. See Lee (1990) for a discussion on the role of racial ideologies in colonial Malaya and in present-day Malaysia.

7. I borrow the concept of imagination from Benedict Anderson's 'imagined political community' (Anderson 1983, 15).

8. For a critique of Cox's theory, see Miles (1980).

9. Here I use 'classes' in a very loose sense to refer to social strata, too. Although inaccurate from the strictly Marxian perspective, it eases discussion of a multi-ethnic society like Malaysia, where mobilization along the class line is not distinct.

10. Although Makabe (1981) supports the split labor market theory in her comparison of the Japanese experience in Brazil and Canada, she actually emphasizes general economic competition. The thesis which she arrives at is: 'If there is no economic competition between ethnic groups, no antagonism arises between them, nor does one group move to exclude others' (Makabe 1981, 804).

11. Although the term 'intermediary' is often used nowadays, anthropologists and sociologists still use 'middleman'. I have therefore kept this term in this chapter.

12. This paper was originally written in 1989. Since then, I have read a good paper by Chun (1989). Although not rejecting the 'middleman minority' concept, Chun stresses the need to look at the 'social relations of production'. Although the Chinese 'middleman economy' in Malaya was characterized by liquidity and ephemerality, Chun (1989, 254) writes, 'these characteristics were representative only of its material forces of production, to use the Marxist term, and overlooked the social relations of production underlying its mode of operation, which could not be explained in terms of a theory of the middleman minority economy'. Chun's paper highlights the roles of the established Chinese merchants, the secret societies, the credit system, and the cheap labor; in other words, he highlights the institutional linkages both within and between the various Chinese enterprises in Malaya.

13. Other scholars like Chandra Muzaffar (1987) and Sanusi Osman (1983, 20) have also suggested this approach. This will help to reduce and avoid ethnic tensions. A racial approach to socio-economic policies or the allocation of resources will only create more ethnic polarization. Social justice is the key to reducing ethnic tensions, not free market nor restructuring of society along racial lines.

14. I do not discuss the exchange theory of Barth and the rational choice theory of Banton here. Those who are interested in the rational choice theory may want to see the articles in *Ethnic and Racial Studies*, 8 (4) October 1985 for critiques on the theory.

Chapter 7

1. For a good discussion on the debate on Confucianism in relation to the economic performance of the little dragons and Japan, see Wang Gungwu (1991b, 258–72).

2. For example, on 1 August 1985, *The Star's* headline was 'Tontine Swindle: organizers abscond with $1.4 million'. The report mentions that about 400 people in Bukit Mertajam (Penang State) were cheated by a couple that fled with the tontine *(hui)* money. The report also mentioned another case in

Kuala Lumpur where a woman organizer of *hui* cheated 20 tontine members of about $200,000. She was reported to have fled to Hong Kong.

3. Chia (1987) reports on a system in Kelantan in which a Malay who sells rubber sheets and lumps to a Chinese dealer does not collect his money there. Instead, the Malay gets his groceries from a grocery shop that collects the payment from the rubber dealer. The limit on the amount of goods that the Malay can get is agreed on beforehand between the rubber dealer and the shopkeeper. Chia writes about *xinyong* (trust). The types of credit (including credit associations) among the Chinese business people in Kelantan also extend 'controlled' credit to Malay business people, but the credit extended is shorter and more expensive because of 'the relatively weak credit-rating of Malay businessmen'.

4. Other writers who have discussed *xinyong* include Robert H. Silin (1972), Clifton A. Barton (1983), and Thomas Menkhoff (1990).

5. In my village in Batu Pahat, Johor, Malaysia, a Malay shopkeeper of Javanese origin has learned to use the abacus, which he uses in his business.

6. Various writers have written about Chinese social relations; see for example, Fried (1953), Silin (1972), DeGlopper (1972), and King (1991).

7. There are numerous reports in the *Sarawak Gazette* about Chinese traders losing their heads. For example, C.A. Bampfylde (1895) reported that a Chinese called Ah Liang from Belaga in interior Sarawak lost his head to the Lepu Jingan people. Charles Hose (1897a, 74), a resident of Baram reported that a Chinese trader called Ah Pin who was killed at night in his boat at Long Lobang in the Tinjar. Hose (1897b, 147) also reported that another Chinese called Wang Ka who was murdered in Baloit and that his head was in a 'head feast' held in Upper Baloit. For a study on Chinese pioneers in Sarawak, see Daniel Chew (1990).

8. I interviewed Mr Sim Thoon Soon on 10 June 1989. He was the headman in Trusan.

9. Although Hsu studied the Minjia in Yunnan, who identify as Bai today (cf. Wu 1990), his argument was generally relevant to the Han Chinese.

10. Wickberg (1965, 16) reports that the Chinese in the Philippines during the Spanish period accepted baptism as a shrewd business move. The religious policy of the Spanish government encouraged conversion to the Roman Catholic faith, and a Chinese who converted got to enjoy a number of advantages: 'Besides reduced taxes, land grants and freedom to reside almost anywhere, one acquired a Spanish godparent, who could be counted upon as a bondsman, creditor, patron and protector in legal terms.'

11. For anthropological studies on Chinese socialization, see for example, Diamond (1969, 30–45), Ward (1970), and Wolf (1970, 37–62).

12. Chinese banks have appeared since the beginning of the 20th century. For example, Kwong Yik Bank, the first Chinese bank in Singapore, was established in 1903; see Song (1923, 353). In the Dutch East Indies, the legendary Oei Tiong Ham (1865–1924) established his Oei Tiong Ham Bank in 1906 (Suryadinata 1988, 263).

13. Both the Dutch and the British colonial governments practiced excise farming. In Malaya, the farming system covered opium, gambling, spirits, and pawn-broking. Well-known rich Chinese of the colonial period in Malaya like Khoo Thean Teik, Yap Ah Loy and Loke Yew all benefited from revenue farms (Khoo 1988). Chinese merchants who obtained monopoly farms from the Dutch government in Indonesia also grew rich (The 1989).

14. Most writers on Chinese economic performance in Southeast Asia tend to forget about the role of cheap labor. Chun (1989) is an exception. This factor is important, but it was not the only major factor. Furthermore, it could not explain the Chinese domination in retail trade.

15. In his paper, 'Little Dragons on the Confucian Periphery', Gungwu Wang (1991b) refers to this as state Confucianism, official Confucianism, and imperial Confucianism.

16. *The Malay Mail* (30 September 1991, 21), under the heading 'A lesson in Chinese bureaucracy', reports on the scenario of red tape and inefficiency of Chinese customs, which hinder international trade.

17. For ethnographic studies on kinship and commerce of the people of Chinese descent, see Omohundro (1981) and David Wu (1982, 87–106).

18. In addition, *Southeast Asian Studies*, vol. 27 no. 2 (Japan, September 1989) is on 'Oei Tiong Ham Concern: The First Business Empire of Southeast Asia'. The three major articles are by Yoshihara Kunio, Onghokham, and Charles A. Coppel.

19. *Far Eastern Economic Review*, 7 February 1991, 46–9. See also Sia (1993).

20. In Indonesia, Chinese business people who collaborate with members of the Indonesian power élite are called *cukong* (Hokkien for 'master'). A well-known example is Liem Sioe Liong, who was closely linked to President Suharto. He headed Indonesia's (and the world's) largest Chinese-owned conglomerate called Salim Group. However, since the fall of Suharto in 1998, Liem's business interest in Indonesia has been affected badly. *See Far Eastern Economic Review*, 14 March 1991, 46–52; MacKie (1991); and Suryadinata (1988).

21. *See Yazhou Zhoukan, Asiaweek* (Chinese version), 25 August 1991, 38–40; and *Nanyang Shangbao*, 13 August 1991, 1.

Bibliography

Abdullah, bin Abdul Kadir. 1970. *The Hikayat Abdullah*. Kuala Lumpur: Oxford University Press. Reprint of the annotated translation by A. H. Hills. In *Journal of the Malayan Branch of the Royal Asiatic Society*, 28(3), 1955. Original Malay work, 1849.

Abraham, Collin E.R. 1983. 'Racial and Ethnic Manipulation in Colonial Malaya.' *Ethnic and Racial Studies*, 6 (1): 18–32.

Ahern, Emily. 1973. *The Cult of the Dead in a Chinese Village*. Stanford, CA: Stanford University Press.

Alatas, S. H. 1963. 'The Weber Thesis and Southeast Asia.' *Sociologie des Religions*, Vol. 8, pp. 21–35.

——— . 1972. *Modernization and Social Change*. Sydney: Angus and Robertson.

Anderson, Benedict. 1983. *Imagined Communities: Reflections on the Origin and Spread of Nationalism*. London: Verso.

Ang, Ien. 1993. 'To Be or Not To Be Chinese: Diaspora, Culture and Postmodern Ethnicity.' *Southeast Asian Journal of Social Science*, 21(1): 1–17.

——— . 2000. 'Transforming Chinese Identities in Australia: Between Assimilation, Multiculturalism, and Diaspora.' In *Intercultural Relations, Cultural Transformation, and Identity: The Ethnic Chinese*, edited by Teresita Ang See, pp. 249–58. Manila: Kaisa Para Sa Kaunlaran, Inc.

————. 2001. *On Not Speaking Chinese: Living Between Asia and the West*. London: Routledge.

Asmah Haji Omar. 1987. *Perkamusan Melayu: Satu Penilaian* (Malay Lexicography: An Evaluation). Kuala Lumpur: Perpustakaan Universiti Malaya.

Azizah Kassim. 1987. 'The Unwelcome Guests: Indonesian Immigrants and Malaysian Public Responses.' *Southeast Asian Studies* (Tokyo), 25 (2): 265–78.

Bampfylde, C.A. 1895. 'Sibu: Monthly Report—January.' *The Sarawak Gazette*, 25 (351), 1 April.

Ban, Seng Hoe. 1976. *Structural Change of Two Chinese Communities in Alberta, Canada*. Ottawa: National Museum of Canada.

————. 1979. 'Relative Community Power and Degrees of Assimilation: Exploration of a Theoretical Synthesis of Chinese in Colonial Southeast Asia and in North America.' *In Poverty and Social Change in Southeast Asia*, edited by Ozay Mehmet, pp. 252–64. Ottawa: University of Ottawa Press.

Banton, Michael. 1983. *Racial and Ethnic Competition*. Cambridge: Cambridge University Press.

————. 1988. *Racial Consciousness*. London: Longman.

Bao, Jiemin. 1999. 'Chinese-Thai Transmigrants: Reworking Identities and Gender Relations in Thailand and the United States.' *Amerasia*, 25(2): 95–115.

Barth, Fredrik. 1969a. 'Introduction.' In *Ethnic Groups and Boundaries: The Social Organization of Cultural Difference*, edited by Fredrik Barth. London: George Allen & Unwin.

————. 1969b. 'Pathan Identity and Its Maintenance.' In *Ethnic Groups and Boundaries*, edited by Fredrik Barth, pp. 117–34. London: George Allen & Unwin.

————, ed. 1969c. *Ethnic Groups and Boundaries: The Social Organization of Cultural Difference*. London: George Allen & Unwin.

Barth, Gunther. 1964. *Bitter Strength: A History of the Chinese in the United States, 1850–1870*. Cambridge, MA: Harvard University Press.

Barton, Clifton A. 1983. 'Trust and Credit: Some Observations Regarding

Business Strategies of Overseas Chinese Traders in South Vietnam.'
In *The Chinese in Southeast Asia, Vol. 1: Ethnicity and Economic
Activity*, edited by Linda Y.C. Lim and L.A. Peter Gosling, pp. 46–64.
Singapore: Maruzen Asia.

Basham, Richard. 2001. 'Ethnicity and World View in Bangkok.' In
Alternate Identities: The Chinese of Contemporary Thailand, edited
by Tong Chee Kiong and Chan Kwok Bun, pp. 107–36. Singapore:
Times Academic Press.

Bentley, C. Carter. 1989. 'Ethnicity and Practice.' *Comparative Studies
in Society and History*, 29(1): 24–55.

Bonacich, Edna. 1972. 'A Theory of Ethnic Antagonism: The Split Labor
Market.' *American Sociological Review*, 37 (5): 547–59.

———. 1973. 'A Theory of Middleman Minorities.' *American Sociological
Review*, 38 (5): 583–94.

———. 1979. 'The Past, Present, and Future of Split Labor Market Theory.'
In *Research in Race and Ethnic Relations: A Research Annual*, Vol.
1, edited by Cora Bagley Marrett and Cheryl Leggon, pp.17-64.
Greenwich, CN: Jai Press.

———. 1980. 'Middleman Minorities and Advanced Capitalism.' *Ethnic
Groups*, 2 (3): 211–19.

Bourdieu, Pierre. 1977. *Outline of A Theory of Practice*, translated by
Richard Nice. Cambridge: Cambridge University Press.

Brown, Iem. 1990. 'Agama Buddha Maitreya: A Modern Buddhist Sect
in Indonesia.' In *The Preservation and Adaptation of Tradition:
Studies of Chinese Religious Expression in Southeast Asia*, edited by
Tan Chee-Beng, pp. 113–24. *Contributions to Southeast Asian
Ethnography*, No. 9.

Bruner, Edward M. 1974. 'The Expression of Ethnicity in Indonesia.' In
Urban Ethnicity, edited by Abner Cohen, pp. 251–80. London:
Tavistock Publications.

Burusratanaphand, Walwipha. 2001. 'Chinese Identities in Thailand.' In
Alternate Identities: The Chinese of Contemporary Thailand, edited
by Tong Chee Kiong and Chan Kwok Bun, pp. 67–83. Singapore:
Times Academic Press.

Buss, Andreas. 1986. 'Max Weber's Heritage and Modern Southeast Asian Thinking on Development.' In *Religion, Values and Development in Southeast Asia*, edited by Bruce Matthews and Judith Nagata. Singapore: Institute of Southeast Asian Studies.

Caplan, Nathan, Marcella H. Choy and John K. Whitmore. 1992. 'Indonesian Refugee Families and Academic Achievement.' *Scientific American*, February: 18–24.

Carstens, Sharon A. 1980. 'Pulai: Memories of a Gold Mining Settlement in Ulu Kelantan.' *Journal of the Malaysian Branch of the Royal Asiatic Society*, LVIII (part 1): 50–67.

Chan, Henry. 2001. 'Ears Attuned to Two Cultures.' In *Cultural Curiosity*, edited by Josephine M.T. Khu, pp. 111–27. Berkeley, CA: University of California Press.

Chan, Kwok Bun, ed. 2000. *Chinese Business Network: State, Economy and Culture*. Singapore: Prentice Hall.

Chan, Kwok Bun, and Tong Chee Kiong. 1998. 'Rethinking Assimilation and Ethnicity: The Chinese in Thailand.' In *The Chinese Diaspora: Selected Essays, vol. 2*, edited by Wang Ling-chi and Wang Gungwu, pp. 1–27. Singapore: Times Academic Press. Reprinted from *International Migration Review*, 27(1): 140–68, 1993.

Chandra Muzaffar. 1987. 'Breaking the Ethnic Trap.' *Aliran Monthly*, 7 (6): 2–3.

Chang, Chung-li. 1955. *The Chinese Gentry: Studies on Their Role in Nineteenth-Century Chinese Society*. Seattle, WA: University of Washington Press.

Chen, Hsiang-shui. 1992. *Chinatown No More: Taiwan Immigrants in Contemporary New York*. Ithaca and London: Cornell University Press.

Chen, Jack. 1981. *The Chinese of America*. San Francisco: Harper & Row.

Chen, Qinan. 1985. 'Fang yu chuantong zhongguo jiating zhidu' (Fang and Traditional Chinese Family System). *Hanxue Yanjiu*, 3(1): 127–84.

Chen, Zhiming. *see* Tan (2001).

Cheng, Lim-Keak. 1985. *Social Change and Chinese in Singapore*. Singapore: Singapore University Press.

Chew, Daniel. 1990. *Chinese Pioneers on the Sarawak Frontier 1841–1941*. Singapore: Oxford University Press.

Chia, Oai-peng. 1987. 'Trust and Credit among Chinese Businessmen in Kelantan.' *Southeast Asia Business*, (University of Michigan) 14 (Summer): 31.

————. 1990. The Chinese in Kuala Krai: A Study of Commerce and Social Life in a Malaysian Town. Ph.D. thesis, University of Malaya.

Choi, C.Y. 1975. *Chinese Migration and Settlement in Australia*. Sydney: Sydney University Press.

Chu, Richard T. 2002. 'Rethinking the Chinese Mestizos of the Philippines.' In *Beyond China: Migrating Identities*, edited by Shen Yuanfang and Penny Edwards, pp. 44–74. Canberra: Centre for the Study of the Chinese Southern Diaspora, The Australian National University.

Chua, Beng-Huat. 1995. Communitarian Ideology and Democracy in Singapore. London: Routledge.

Chun, Allen J. 1989. 'Pariah Capitalism and the Overseas Chinese of Southeast Asia: Problems in the Definition of the Problem.' *Ethnic and Racial Studies*, 12 (2): 233–56.

————. 2000. Diasporas of Mind, Or Why There Ain't No Black Atlantic in Cultural China. Working paper series, Department of Comparative American Cultures, Pullman, WA: Washington State University.

Cihai. 1979. *Cihai*. Shanghai: Shanghai Cishu Chubanshe.

Clammer, John R. 1980. *Straits Chinese Society: Studies in the Sociology of the Baba Communities of Malaysia and Singapore*. Singapore: Singapore University Press.

Cobas, José A. 1987. 'Ethnic Enclaves and Middleman Minorities: Alternative Strategies of Immigrant Adaptation?' *Sociological Perspective*, 30 (2): 143–61.

Comber, Leon. 1983. *13 May 1969: An Historical Survey of Sino-Malay Relations*. Kuala Lumpur: Heinemann Asia.

Coppel, Charles A. 1976. 'Patterns of Chinese Political Activity in Indonesia.' In *The Chinese in Indonesia: Five Essays*, edited by J.A. C. Mackie, pp. 19–76. Melbourne: Thomas Nelson, Ltd. in association with The Australian Institute of International Affairs.

————. 1983. *Indonesian Chinese in Crisis*. Kuala Lumpur: Oxford University Press.

Coppel, Charles A. and Leo Suryadinata. 1978. 'The Use of the Terms "Tjina" and "Tionghoa" in Indonesia: An Historical Survey.' In *The Chinese Minority in Indonesia: 7 papers*, edited by Leo Suryadinata, pp. 113–28. Singapore: Chopmen Enterprises.

Coughlin, Richard J. 1960. *Double Identity: The Chinese in Modern Thailand*. Hong Kong: Hong Kong University Press.

Cox, Oliver Cromwell. 1948. *Caste, Class and Race: A Study in Social Dynamics*. New York: Doubleday & Company, Inc. Modern Reader Paperback Edition, 1970.

Crissman, Lawrence W., George Beattie and James Selby. 1998. 'The Chinese in Brisbane: Segmentation and Integration.' In *The Overseas Chinese: Ethnicity in National Context*, edited by Francis L.K. Hsu and Hendrick Serrie, pp. 87–114. Lanham, MD: University Press of America, Inc.

Cui, Guiqiang. 1990. '*Xinjiapo huaren shetuan yu zhengzhi—huigu yu qianzhan*' [Chinese Associations and Politics in Singapore: Retrospect and Prospect]. Paper presented at the International Conference on Overseas Chinese Communities towards the 21st century, organized by South Seas Society, Singapore, 6–8 November 1990.

Cushman, J.W. 1986. 'The Khaw Group: Chinese Business in Early Twentieth-Century Penang.' *Journal of Southeast Asian Studies*, 17 (1): 58–79.

Dahrendorf, Ralf. 1959. *Class and Class Conflict in Industrial Society*, translated and revised by the author from German. Stanford, CA: Stanford University Press. The original work was published in 1957.

de Azua, Mario Federico Real. 1981. 'Chinese Coolies in Peru: The Chincha Islands.' In *Asiatic Migrations in Latin America*, edited by Luz M. Martinez Montiel, pp. 37–52. Mexico: El Colegio de Mexico.

DeGlopper, Donald R. 1972. 'Doing Business in Lukang.' In *Economic Organization in Chinese Society*, edited by W.E. Willmott, pp. 297–326. Stanford, CA: Stanford University Press.

de Josselin de Jong, J.P.B. 1983. 'The Malay Archipelago as a Field of Ethnological Study.' In *Structural Anthropology in the Netherlands*, edited by P.E. de Josselin de Jong, pp. 166–82. Dordrecht, Holland: Foris Publications. Original Dutch version published in 1935.

de Josselin de Jong, P.E. 1984a. 'A Field of Anthropological Study in Transformation.' In *Unity in Diversity: Indonesia as a Field of Anthropological Study*, edited by P.E. de Josselin de Jong, pp. 1–10. Dordrecht, Holland: Foris Publications.

———, ed. 1984b. *Unity and Diversity: Indonesia as a Field of Anthropological Study*. Dordrecht, Holland: Foris Publications.

Department of Statistics. 1995. *General Report of the Population Census*, Vol. 1. Population and Housing Census of Malaysia 1991. Kuala Lumpur: Department of Statistics, Malaysia.

———. 2001. *Population Distribution and Basic Demographic Characteristics*. Kuala Lumpur: Department of Statistics, Malaysia.

Diamond, Norma. 1969. *K'un Shen: A Taiwanese Village*. New York: Holt, Rinehart and Winston.

Diaz-Trechuelo, Maria Lourdes. 1969. 'The Economic Background.' In *The Chinese in the Philippines 1770–1898, vol. 2*, edited by Alfonso Felix, Jr., pp. 18–44. Manila: Solidaridad Publishing House.

Earl, G. W. 1837. *The Eastern Seas or Voyages and Adventures in the Indian Archipelago*. London: Wm. H. Allen and Co. Reprinted with an introduction by C.M. Turnbull. Singapore: Oxford University Press.

East Asia Analytical Unit. 1995. *Overseas Chinese Business Networks in Asia*. Canberra: East Asia Unit, Department of Foreign Affairs and Trade.

Eberhard, Wolfram. 1962. *Social Mobility in Traditional China*. Leiden: E.J. Brill.

Elvin, Mark. 1973. *The Pattern of the Chinese Past*. London: Eyre Methuen.

Faure, David. 1989. 'The Lineage as A Culture Invention.' *Modern China*, 15 (1): 4–36.

Fei, Hsiao-Tung. 1939. *Peasant Life in China: A Field Study of Country Life in the Yangtze Valley*. London: Kegan Paul, Trench, Trubner & Co., Ltd.

———. 1985. *Xiangtu Zhongguo* [Earthbound China]. Beijing: Sanlian Shudian. First published in 1947.

Fong, Ng Bickleen. 1959. *The Chinese in New Zealand: A Study in Assimilation.* Hong Kong: Hong Kong University Press.

Fong, Timothy P. 1998. 'Monterey Park and Emerging Racial Relations in California.' In *The Chinese Diaspora: Selected Essays, vol. 2*, edited by Wang Ling-chi and Wang Gungwu, pp. 167–80. Singapore: Times Academic Press.

Fraginals, Manuel Moreno. 1981. 'Extent and Significance of Chinese Immigration to Cuba, 19th Century.' In *Asiatic Migrations in Latin America*, edited by Luz M. Martinez Montiel. Mexico: El Colegio de Mexico.

Freedman, Maurice. 1958. *Lineage Organization in Southern China.* London: Oxford University Press.

——— . 1959. 'The Handling of Money: A Note on the Background to the Economic Sophistication of Overseas Chinese.' *Man*, April (89): 64–5.

——— . 1962. 'Chinese Kinship and Marriage in Singapore.' *Journal of Southeast Asian History*, 3: 65–73.

——— . 1965. *Lineage Organization in Southeastern China.* Paperback edition with corrections. London: Athlone Press. First edition, 1958.

——— . 1966. *Chinese Lineage and Society: Fukien and Kwangtung.* London: Athlone Press.

Fried, Morton H. 1953. *Fabric of Chinese Society: A Study of the Social Life of a Chinese Country Seat.* New York: Praeger.

——— . 1958. 'The Chinese in the British Caribbean.' In *Colloquium on Overseas Chinese*, edited by Morton H. Fried, pp. 49–58. New York: International Secretariat, Institute of Pacific Relations.

Furnivall, J.S. 1948. *Colonial Policy and Practice: A Comparative Study of Burma and Netherlands India.* Cambridge: Cambridge University Press.

Gagliano, Felix V. 1970. *Communal Violence in Malaysia 1969: The Political Aftermath.* Papers in International Studies, Southeast Asia, 13, Ohio Center for International Studies Southeast Asia Program, Athens, Ohio.

Gamble, Sidney D. 1954. *Ting Hsien: A North Chinese Rural Community.* New York: Institute of Pacific Relations.

Geertz, Clifford. 1973. *The Interpretation of Cultures*. New York: Basic Books, Inc., Publishers.

Giddens, A. 1984. *The Constitution of Society*. Berkeley, CA: University of California Press.

Giese, Diana. 1997. *Astronauts, Lost Souls and Dragons: Voices of Today's Chinese Australians in Conversion with Diana Giese*. St. Lucia, Queensland: University of Queensland Press.

Glick, Clarence E. 1980. *Sojourners and Settlers: Chinese Migrants in Hawaii*. Honolulu: Hawaii Chinese Center and the University Press of Hawaii.

Godley, Michael R. and Charles A. Coppel. 1990a. 'The Indonesian Chinese in Hong Kong: A Preliminary Report on a Minority Community in Transition.' *Issues and Studies* (Taipei), 26 (7): 94–108.

———. 1990b. 'The Pied Piper and the Prodigal Children: A Report on the Indonesian-Chinese Students who went to Mao's China.' *Archipel*, 39: 179–98.

Goh, Cheng Teik. 1971. *The May Thirteenth Incident and Democracy in Malaysia*. Kuala Lumpur: Oxford University Press.

———. 1977. 'The Chinese in Southeast Asia: From Hua-ch'iao to Hua-i.' In *Masalah-Masalah Internasional Masakini* (7) [Contemporary International Problems (7)], edited by Lie Tek Tjeng and C.P.F. Luhulima, pp.19–23. Jakarta: Lembaga Research Kebudayaan Nasional.

Golberg, Michael A. 1985. *The Chinese Connection: Getting Plugged in to Pacific Rim Real Estate, Trade and Capital Markets*. Vancouver, BC: The University of British Columbia.

Gomez, Edmund Terence and Hsin-Huang Michael Hsiao. 2001. 'Introduction: Chinese Business Research in Southeast Asia.' In *Chinese Business in Southeast Asia: Contesting Cultural Explanations, Researching Entrepreneurship*, edited by Edmund Terence Gomez and Hsin-Huang Michael Hsiao, pp. 1–37. Richmond: Curzon.

Guldin, Gregory Eliyu. 1994. *The Saga of Anthropology in China: From Malinowski to Moscow to Mao*. Armonk, NY: M.E. Sharpe.

Gwee, Thian Hock. 1993. *Mas Sepuluh: Baba Conversational Gems.* Singapore: Armour Publishing Pte. Ltd.

Hall, Laura. 1998. 'The Arrival and Settlement of the Chinese in 19th Century British Guiana.' In *The Chinese Diaspora: Selected Essays, vol. 2*, edited by Wang Ling-chi and Wang Gungwu, pp. 86–111. Singapore: Times Academic Press.

Hamilton, Gary. 1978. 'Pariah Capitalism: A Paradox of Power and Dependence.' *Ethnic Groups*, 2 (1): 1–15.

Hilton, Mike. 1979. 'The Split Labor Market and Chinese Immigration, 1848–1882.' *The Journal of Ethnic Studies*, 6(4): 99–108.

Ho, Eng Seng. 1985. Baba Identity in Penang. Unpublished academic project paper. 127 pp.

Ho, Khai Leong. 2002. 'Bureaucratic Participation and Political Mobilization: Comparing Pre- and Post-1970 Malaysian Chinese Political Participation.' In *Ethnic Chinese in Singapore and Malaysia: A Dialogue Between Tradition and Modernity*, edited by Leo Suryadinata, pp. 137–54. Singapore: Times Academic Press.

Hose, Charles. 1897a. 'Baram: Monthly Report—February.' *Sarawak Gazette*, 27 (375): 74–5.

——— . 1897b. 'Baram: Monthly Report—May and June.' *Sarawak Gazette* 27 (379): 147–8.

Hsieh, Jiann. 1978. 'The Chinese Community in Singapore: The Internal Structure and Its Basic Constituents.' In *Studies in Asian Sociology*, edited by Peter S.J. Chen and Hans-Dieters Evers. Singapore: Chopmen Enterprise.

Hsu, Francis L.K. 1949. *Under the Ancestors' Shadow: Chinese Culture and Personality*. London: Routledge & Kegan Paul Limited.

Huang, Shaolun. 1991. 'Zhongguo wenhua yu xianggang de xiandaihua' [Chinese Culture and Modernization in Hong Kong]. In *Zhongguo zongjiao lunli yu xiandaihua* [Religious Ethics of China and Modernization], edited by Huang Shaolun, pp. 172–99. Hong Kong: Shangwu Yinshuguan.

Hu-DeHart, Evelyn. 1998. 'Race Construction and Race Relations: Chinese and Blacks in 19th Century Cuba.' In *The Chinese Diaspora: Selected*

Essays, vol. 2, edited by Wang Ling-chi and Wang Gungwu, pp. 78–85. Singapore: Times Academic Press.

Ip, Manying. 1990. 'From Sojourners to Citizens: Metamorphosis of the New Zealand Chinese since World War II.' *Asian Culture* (Singapore), 14(April): 195–203.

——— . 1996. *Dragons on the Long White Cloud: The Making of Chinese New Zealanders.* North Shore City, New Zealand: Tandem Press.

Jackson, James C. 1968. *Planters and Speculators: Chinese and European Agricultural Enterprise in Malaya*, 1786–1921. Kuala Lumpur: University of Malaya Press.

Jacques, E.W. 1931. 'A Chinese Loan Society.' *Man*, 31 (216): 225–6.

Jacques, Leo M. 1981. 'Chinese Merchants in Sonora, 1900–1931.' In *Asiatic Migrations in Latin America*, edited by Luz M. Martinez Montiel, pp. 13–20. Mexico: El Colegio de Mexico.

Jesudason, James V. 1989. *Ethnicity and the Economy: The State, Chinese Business, and Multinationals in Malaysia.* Singapore: Oxford University Press.

Jesus Merino, O.P. 1969. 'General Considerations Regarding the Chinese Mestizo.' In *The Chinese in the Philippines 1770–1898, vol.2*, edited by Alfonso Felix Jr., pp. 45–66. Manila: Solidaridad Publishing House.

Johnson, Howard. 1987. 'The Chinese in Trinidad in the Late Nineteenth Century.' *Ethnic and Racial Studies*, 10(1): 82–95.

Khoo, Kay Kim. 1981. 'Sino-Malay Relations in Peninsular Malaysia Before 1942.' In *Ethnic Chinese in Southeast Asia*, edited by C.F. Yong. Special issue of Journal of Southeast Asian Studies, 12(l): 93–117.

——— . 1988. 'Chinese Economic Activities in Malaya: A Historical Perspective.' In *Economic Performance in Malaysia*, edited by Manning Nash, pp. 179–223. New York: Professors World Peace Academy.

Khu, Josephine M.T., ed. 2001. *Cultural Curiosity: Thirteen Stories about the Search for Chinese Roots.* Berkeley, CA: University of California Press.

Kiernan, Ben. 1986. 'Kampuchea's Ethnic Chinese under Pol Pot: A Case of Systematic Social Discrimination.' *Journal of Contemporary Asia*, 16 (1): 18–29.

King, Ambrose Yeo-chi. 1991. 'Kuan-hsi and Network Building: A Sociological Interpretation.' *Daedalus*, Special issue: The Living Tree: The Changing Meaning of Being Chinese Today, 120 (2): 63–84.

Kulp II, Daniel Harrison. 1925. *Country Life in South China: The Sociology of Familism, Phoenix Village, Kwangtung, China*, vol. 1. New York: Bureau of Publications, Teachers' College, Columbia University, pp. 189–96.

Kwong, Alice Jo. 1958. 'The Chinese in Peru.' In *Colloquium on Overseas Chinese*, edited by Morton H. Fried, pp. 41–8. New York: International Secretariat Institute of Pacific Relations.

Kyodo. 2001. 'Suppression of Chinese Culture Ends.' *South China Morning Post*, 19 January, p. 9.

Lai, Him Mark. 1998. 'Organizations among Chinese in America since the Second World War.' In *The Chinese Diaspora: Selected Essays*, vol. 1, edited by Wang Ling-chi and Wang Gungwu, pp. 228–67. Singapore: Times Academic Press.

Lai, Violet L. 1985. *He was a Ram: Wong Aloiau of Hawaii*. Honolulu, HI: University of Hawaii Press, published for the Hawaii Chinese History Center and the Wong Aloiau Association.

Lee, Raymond L.M. 1990. 'The State, Religious Nationalism, and Ethnic Rationalization in Malaysia.' *Ethnic and Racial Studies*, 13 (4): 482–502.

Lee, Sharon. 1992. 'Sharon Lee.' In *Jin Guo: Voices of Chinese Canadian Women*, edited by Momoye Sugiman, pp. 91–8. Toronto, ON: Women's Press.

Lee, Sheng-yi. 1978. 'Business Elites in Singapore.' In *Studies in ASEAN Sociology: Urban Society and Social Change*, edited by Peter S.J. Chen and Hans-Dieter Evers. Singapore: Chopmen Enterprises.

———. 1990. 'The Role of Overseas Chinese Enterprises in Singapore. Hong Kong and Taiwan in the 21st century.' Paper presented at the International Conference on Overseas Chinese Communities towards the 21st century, organized by South Seas Society, Singapore, 6–8 November 1990.

Lee, Siow Mong. 1986. *Spectrum of Chinese Culture*. Petaling Jaya, Malaysia: Pelanduk Publications.

Lee, Wen Ho, and Helen Zia. 2001. *My Country Versus Me: The First-hand Account by the Los Alamos Scientist Who Was Falsely Accused of Being A Spy.* New York: Hyperion.

Li, Guoliang. 1991. 'Zhanhou dongnanya huaren rentong yanjiu de gongshi yu fenqi' [Studies on the Identity of Ethnic Chinese in Postwar Southeast Asia: Consensus and Dissension]. Paper presented at the International Conference on Changing Ethnic Identities and Relations in Southeast Asia: The Case of the Chinese Minority. Organized by the China Studies Programme, De La Salle University and Kaisa Para Sa Kaunlaran, Inc., 8–10 November 1991, Manila. In *The Ethnic Chinese*, edited by Teresita Ang See and Go Bon Juan, pp. 243–49. Manila: Kaisa Para Sa Kaunlaran, Inc.

Li, Minghuan. 1998. 'Transnational Links among the Chinese in Europe: A Study on European-wide Chinese Voluntary Associations.' In *The Chinese in Europe*, edited by Gregor Benton and Frank N. Pieke, pp. 21–41. Basingstoke, UK: Macmillan Press.

Li, Peter. 1998. *Chinese in Canada.* 2nd edition. Toronto: Oxford University Press.

Li, Yih-yuan. 1970. *An Immigrant Town: Life in an Overseas Chinese Community in Southern Malaya.* [In Chinese]. Mgh series B No. 1. Taipei: Institute of Ethnology, Academica Sinica.

Li, Zong. 1998. 'Chinese Immigration to Vancouver and New Racism in Multicultural Canada.' In *Ethnic Chinese at the Turn of the Centuries*, edited by Zhuang Guotu, pp. 443–63. Fuzhou: Fujian Renmin Chubanshe.

Liang, Liji. 1996. *Hubungan Empayar Melaka-Dinasti Ming Abad Ke-15* (Imperial Relations Between Melaka and Ming Dynasty in the 15th Century). Bangi, Malaysia: UKM Press.

Lie, Tek-Tjeng. 1970. 'The Chinese Problem in Indonesia following the September 30 Movement: A Personal View.' *Internationale Spectator*, June, 1145–54.

Lim, Boon Keng. 1917. 'The Chinese in Malaya.' In *Present Days' Impressions of the Far East and Prominent and Progressive Chinese at Home and Abroad; Their History, People, Commerce, Industries and Resources of China, Hong Kong, Indo-China, Malaya and Netherlands India*, edited by W. Feldwick, pp. 875–82. London: Globe Encyclopedia Co.

Lim, How-seng. 1990. 'Familism and Enterprise: The Business World of a Chinese Rubber Magnate in Singapore, Tan Lark Sye.' *Asian Culture*, 14, [in Chinese]: 132–49.

Lim, Joo-hock. 1967. 'Chinese Female Immigration into the Straits Settlements 1860-1901.' *Journal of the South Seas Society*, 22: 58–110.

Lim, Linda Y.C. 1983. 'Chinese Economic Activity in Southeast Asia: An Introductory Review.' In *The Chinese in Southeast Asia. Ethnicity and Economic Activity*, vol. 1, edited by Linda Y.C. Lim and L.A. Peter Gosling, pp. 1–29. Singapore: Maruzen Asia.

Lim, Mah-hui. 1980. 'Ethnic and Class Relations in Malaysia.' *Journal of Contemporary Asia*, 10 (1–2): 130–54.

———. 1983. 'The Ownership and Control of Large Corporations in Malaysia: The Role of Chinese Businessmen.' In *Chinese in Southeast Asia, Vol. 1: Ethnicity and Economic Activity*, edited by Linda YC. Lim and L.A. Peter Gosling, pp. 275–313. Singapore: Maruzen Asia.

———. 1985. 'Affirmative Action, Ethnicity and Integration: The Case of Malaysia.' *Ethnic and Racial Studies*, 8 (2): 250–76.

Limlingan, Victor Simpao. 1986. *The Overseas Chinese in Asean: Business Strategies and Management Practices*. Manila: Vita Development Corporation.

Ling, Huping. 1998. *Surviving on the Gold Mountain: A History of Chinese American Women and Their Lives*. Albany, NY: State University of New York Press.

Liu, Hong. 1997. 'Old Linkages, New Networks: The Globalization of Overseas Chinese Voluntary Associations and Its Implications.' *The China Quarterly*, 155: 582–609.

———. 1999. 'Organized Chinese Transnationalism and the Institutionalization of Business Networks: The Singapore Chinese Chamber of Commerce and Industry as a Case Analysis.' *Tonan Ajia Kenkyu* (Southeast Asian Studies), 37 (3): 391–416.

Liu, Zhiwei. 1997. 'Lineage on the Sands: The Case of Shawan.' In *Down* to *Earth: The Territorial Bond in South China,* edited by David Faure and Helen Siu, pp. 21–43. Stanford, CA: Stanford University Press.

Ly, Phuong. 2003. 'A Chinese American Awakening: Immigrants Help to Reenergize US Christianity.' *Washington Post,* 11 January, p. A01.

Mabbett, Hung. 1976. 'Behind These Doors, A Rare Glimpse of Old Malacca.' *The Straits Times Annual 1976,* pp. 81–5.

Mackie, J.A.C. 1976. 'Anti-Chinese Outbreaks in Indonesia, 1959–68.' In *The Chinese in Indonesia: Five Essays,* edited by J.A.C. Mackie, pp. 77–138. Melbourne: Nelson, in association with the Australian Institute of International Affairs.

Mackie, Jamie. 1991. 'Towkays and Tycoons: The Chinese in Indonesian Economic Life in the 1920s and 1980s.' *Indonesia,* A special issue on 'The Role of the Indonesian Chinese in Shaping Modern Indonesian Life.'

Mahathir bin Mohamad. 1970. *The Malay Dilemma.* The 1981 edition was published by Federal Publications Sdn. Bhd.

Makabe, Tomoko. 1981. 'The Theory of the Split Labor Market: A Comparison of the Japanese Experience in Brazil and Canada.' *Social Forces,* 59 (3): 786–809.

Malaysia Plan. 1976. *Third Malaysia Plan 1976–1980.* Kuala Lumpur: The Government Press.

Mauss, Marcel. 1967. *The Gift: Forms and Functions of Exchange in Archaic Societies.* New York: W.W. Norton & Company, Inc.

McKeown, Adam. 2001. *Chinese Migrant Networks and Cultural Change: Peru, Chicago, Hawaii,* 1900–1936. Chicago: The University of Chicago Press.

McTaggart, W.D. 1971. *The May 1969 Disturbances in Malaysia: Impact of a Conflict on Developmental Pattern.* San Diego, CA: Association for Asian Studies.

Menkhoff, Thomas. 1990. 'Trust and Chinese Economic Behavior in Singapore.' Paper presented at the International Conference on Overseas Chinese Communities towards the 21st century, organized by the South Seas Society, Singapore, 6–8 November 1990.

Miles, Robert. 1980. 'Class, Race and Ethnicity: A Critique of Cox's Theory.' *Ethnic and Racial Studies*, 3 (2): 169–87.

Minchin, Geo. 1870. 'Marriage Customs of Chinese Residents in the Straits of Malacca.' *Notes and Queries on China and Japan* (Hong Kong), 4 (August): 81–6.

Mya Than. 1997. 'The Ethnic Chinese in Myanmar and Their Identity.' In *Ethnic Chinese As Southeast Asians*, edited by Leo Suryadinata, pp. 115–46. Singapore: Institute of Southeast Asian Studies.

Newbold, T.J. 1839. *Political and Statistical Account of the British Settlements in the Straits of Malacca viz. Pinang, Malacca, and Singapore, with a History of the Malayan States on the Peninsula of Malacca.* Vol. 1. London: John Murray.

Ng, Kwee Choo. 1968. *The Chinese in London.* London: Oxford University Press, published for the Institute of Race Relations.

Ng, Wing Chung. 1998. 'Collective Ritual and the Resilience of Traditional Organizations: A Case Study of Vancouver since the Second World War.' In *The Chinese Diaspora: Selected Essays*, vol. 1, edited by Wang Ling-chi and Wang Gungwu, pp. 195–227. Singapore: Times Academic Press.

———. 1999. *The Chinese in Vancouver, 1945–80: The Pursuit of Identity and Power.* Vancouver: The University of British Columbia Press.

NOC. 1969. *The May 13 Tragedy: A Report.* Kuala Lumpur: Majlis Gerakan Negara.

Oetomo, Dede. 1984. The Chinese of Pasuruan: A Study of Language and Identity in a Minority Community in Transition. PhD thesis, Cornell University.

———. 1988. 'Multilingualism and Chinese Identities in Indonesia.' In *Changing Identities of the Southeast Asian Chinese since World War II*, edited by Jennifer Cushman and Wang Gungwu, pp. 97–106. Hong Kong: Hong Kong University Press.

Omohundro, John T. 1981. *Chinese Merchant Families in Iloilo: Commerce and Kin in a Central Philippine City.* Manila: Ateneo de Manila University Press, and Athens, OH: The Ohio University Press.

Ong, Aihwa. 1993. 'On the Edge of Empires: Flexible Citizenship among Chinese in Diaspora.' *positions*, 1(3): 745–78.

————. 1999. *Flexible Citizenship: The Cultural Logics of Trans-nationality*. Durham, NC: Duke University Press.

Ong, Aihwa, and Donald Nonini, eds. 1997. *Ungrounded Empires: The Cultural Politics of Modern Chinese Transnationalism*. New York and London: Routledge.

Ooi, Diana. 1967. A Study of the English-speaking Chinese of Penang 1900–1941. MA thesis, University of Malaya.

Oxfeld, Ellen. 1993. *Blood, Sweat and Mahjong: Family and Enterprise in an Overseas Chinese Community*. Ithaca, NY: Cornell University Press.

Padilla, Amado M. 1980. 'The Role of Cultural Awareness and Ethnic Loyalty in Acculturation.' In *Acculturation Theory: Models and Some New Findings*, edited by Amado M. Padilla, pp. 47–84. Washington DC: American Association for the Advancement of Science.

Pakir, Anne Geok-In Sim. 1986. A Linguistic Investigation of Baba Malay. PhD thesis, University of Hawaii.

Park, Robert Ezra. 1950. *Race and Culture*. New York: The Free Press.

Pe-Pua, Rogelia, Colleen Mitchell, Stephen Castles and Robyn Iredale. 1998. 'Astronaut families and Parachute Children: Hong Kong Immigrants in Australia.' In *The Last Half Century of Chinese Overseas*, edited by Elizabeth Sinn, pp. 279–99. Hong Kong: Hong Kong University Press.

Porter, Gareth. 1980. 'Vietnam's Ethnic Chinese and the Sino-Vietnamese Conflict.' *Bulletin of Concerned Asian Scholars*, 12(4): 55–60.

Portes, Alejandr and Leif Jensen. 1987. 'What's an Ethnic Enclave? The Case for Conceptual Clarity.' *American Sociological Review*, 52 (December): 768–71.

Rabushka, Alvin. 1974. *A Theory of Racial Harmony*. Studies in International Affairs, No.11. Columbia (South Carolina): University of South Carolina Press, for the Institute of International Studies, Durham, NC: University of South Carolina.

Redding, S. Gordon. 1993. *The Spirit of Chinese Capitalism*. Berlin and New York: Walter de Gruyter.

Rodrigo, Milan L. 1998. 'Chinese in Sri Lanka: A Forgotten Minority.' In *The Chinese Diaspora: Selected Essays*, vol. 2, edited by Wang Ling-chi and Wang Gungwu, pp. 231–41. Singapore: Times Academic Press.

Ruan, Chang Rui. 1971. 'Acculturation of the Chinese in Takangk'ou with the Ami.' *Bulletin of the Institute of Ethnology, Academia Sinica*, No. 31 [in Chinese): 47–64.

Rudolph, Jurgen. 1998. *Reconstructing Identities: A Social History of the Babas in Singapore.* Aldershot, England: Ashgate.

Ryan, Edward Joseph. 1961. The Value System of a Chinese Community in Java. PhD thesis, Harvard University.

Salmon, Claudine. 1981. *Literature in Malay by the Chinese of Indonesia: A Provisional Annotated Bibliography.* Paris: Editions de la Maison des Sciences de l'Homme.

Sanders, Jimy M. and Victor Nee. 1987a. 'Limits of Ethnic Solidarity in the Enclave Economy.' *American Sociological Review*, 52 (December): 745–63.

———. 1987b. 'On Testing the Enclave-Economy Hypothesis.' *American Sociological Review*, 52 (December): 771–3.

Sanusi Osman. 1983. 'Ethnicity and National Unity in Malaysia.' *Ilmu Masyarakat*, No. 2: 14–21.

Schermerhorn, R.A. 1978. Ch. 12, 'The Chinese: A Unique Nationality Group'. In *Ethnic Plurality in India.* Tucson, AZ: University of Arizona Press.

Schiller, Nina Click, Linda Basch, and Cristina Blanc-Szanton. 1992. 'Transnationalism: A New Analytical Framework for Understanding Migration.' In *Towards a Transnational Perspective on Migration: Race, Class, Ethnicity, and Nationalism Reconsidered*, edited by Schiller, Basch and Blanc-Szanton, pp. 1–24. New York: The New York Academy of Sciences.

See, Chinben. 1992. 'Education and Ethnic Identity among the Chinese in the Philippines.' In *The Chinese Immigrants: Selected Writings of Professor Chinben See*, edited by Teresita Ang See, pp. 119–29. Manila: Kaisa Para Sa Kaunlaran, Inc., and China Studies Program, De La Salle University. Originally published in *Chinese in the Philippines*, edited by Therasa Carino, pp. 32–43. Manila: De La Salle University, 1985.

See, Teresita Ang. 1997. *Chinese in the Philippines: Problems and Prospects*, vol. 2. Manila: Kaisa Para Sa Kaunlarn, Inc.

See, Teresita Ang and Go Bon Juan. 1990. 'Religious Syncretism among the Chinese in the Philippines.' In *The Preservation and Adaptation of Tradition: Studies of Chinese Religious Expressions in Southeast Asia*, edited by Tan Chee-Beng, pp. 53–65. *Contributions to Southeast Asian Ethnography*, No. 9.

Selvan, T.S. 1990. *Singapore the Ultimate Island: Lee Kuan Yew's Untold Story.* Melbourne: Freeway Books.

Serrie, Hendrick and Francis L.K. Hsu. 1998. 'The Overseas Chinese: Common Denominators of a Changing Ethnicity.' In *The Overseas Chinese: Ethnicity in National Context*, edited by Francis L.K. Hsu and Hendrick Serrie, pp. 1–12. Lanham, MD: University Press of America, Inc.

Shang, William. 2001. 'In My Father's Shadow.' In *Cultural Curiosity*, edited by Josephine M.T. Khu, pp. 187–200. Berkeley, CA: University of California Press.

Shaw, Thomas A. 1985. 'To be or Not to be Chinese: Differential Expressions of Chinese Culture and Solidarity in the British West Indies.' In *Caribbean Ethnicity Revisited*, edited by Stephen D. Glazier, pp. 71–185. Special issue of Ethnic Groups, 6 (2 and 3).

Shellabear, W.G. 1913. 'Baba Malay: An Introduction to the Language of the Straits-born Chinese.' *Journal of the Straits Branch of the Royal Asiatic Society*, 65: 49–63.

Shen, Yuanfang. 2001. *Dragon Seed in the Antipodes: Chinese-Australian Autobiographies.* Melbourne: Melbourne University Press.

Sia, Irene. 1993. 'Robert Kuok: Taipan Incorporated.' In *Formation and Restructuring of Business Groups in Malaysia*, edited by Hara Fujio, pp. 55–69. Tokyo: Institute of Developing Economies.

Siah, U Chin. 1848. 'The Chinese in Singapore.' *The Journal of the Indian Archipelago and Eastern Asia*, 2: 283–9.

Silin, Robert H. 1972. 'Marketing and Credit in a Hong Kong Wholesale Market.' In *Economic Organization in Chinese Society*, edited by W. E. Willmott. Stanford, CA: Stanford University Press.

Simoniya, N.A. 1961. *Overseas Chinese in Southeast Asia: A Russian Study*, translated by US Joint Publications Research Service. Data Paper No. 45. Southeast Asia Program, Ithaca, NY: Cornell University.

Singapore Department of Statistics. 2001. *Census of Population 2000: Geographic Distribution and Travel.* Compiled by Leow Bee Geok. Singapore: Dept. of Statistics, Ministry of Trade and Industry.

Siu, Helen F. 1990. 'Where Were the Women: Rethinking Marriage Resistance and Regional Culture in South China.' *Late Imperial China,* 2(2): 32–62.

Skinner, G. William. 1957. *Chinese Society in Thailand: An Analytical History.* Ithaca, NY: Cornell University Press.

———. 1958. *Leadership and Power in the Chinese Community of Thailand.* Ithaca, NY: Cornell University Press.

———. 1960. 'Change and Persistence in Chinese Culture Overseas: A Comparison of Thailand and Java.' *Journal of the South Seas Society,* 16 (1 & 2): 86–100.

———. 1964a. 'The Thailand Chinese: Assimilation in a Changing Society.' *Asia,* 2 (Autumn): 80–92.

———. 1964b. 'Marketing and Social Structure in Rural China—Part 1.' *Journal of Asian Studies,* 24 (1): 3–43.

———. 1965a. 'Marketing and Social Structure in Rural China—Part 2.' *Journal of Asian Studies,* 24 (2): 195–228.

———. 1965b. 'Marketing and Social Structure in Rural China—Part 3.' *Journal of Asian Studies,* 24 (3): 363–99.

———. 1996. 'Creolized Chinese Societies in Southeast Asia.' In *Sojourners and Settlers: Histories of Southeast Asia and the Chinese,* edited by Anthony Reid, pp. 51–93. Australia: Allen & Unwin.

Slimming, John. 1969. *Malaysia: Death of a Democracy.* London: John Murray.

Smith, Arthur H. 1899 (1969). *Village Life in China: A Study in Sociology.* New York: Fleming H. Revell Co. Reprinted by Greenwood Press, Publishers, New York.

Somers Heidhues, Mary F. 1974. *Southeast Asia's Chinese Minority.* Hawthorn, Victoria, Australia: Longman.

Song, Ong Siang. 1923. *One Hundred Years' History of the Chinese in Singapore.* London: John Murray.

Spiro, Melford E. 1955. 'The Acculturation of American Ethnic Groups.' *American Anthropologist,* 57(6), part 1 (December): 1240–52.

Stenson, Michael. 1976. 'Class and Race in West Malaysia.' *Bulletin of Concerned Asian Scholars*, (April–June): 45–54.

Steward, Julian H. 1973. *Theory of Culture Change: The Methodology of Multilinear Evolution.* Urbana, IL: University of Illinois Press.

Stewart, Watt. 1951. *Chinese Bondage in Peru: A History of Chinese Coolies in Peru, 1849–1874.* Durham, NC: Duke University Press.

Strauch, Judith. 1981. *Chinese Village Politics in the Malaysian State.* Cambridge, MA: Harvard University Press.

Sung, B.L. 1967. *The Story of the Chinese in America: Their Struggle for Survival, Acceptance and Full Participation in American Life — From the Gold Rush Days to the Present.* New York: Collier Books.

Supang, Chantaranich. 1997. 'From Siamese-Chinese to Chinese-Thai: Political Conditions and Identity Shifts among the Chinese in Thailand.' In *Ethnic Chinese As Southeast Asians*, edited by Leo Suryadinata, pp. 232–59. Singapore: Institute of Southeast Asian Studies.

Suryadinata, Leo. 1976. 'Indonesian Policies Toward the Chinese Minority under the New Order.' *Asian Survey*, XVI (8): 770–87.

——— . 1981 [1976] *Peranakan Chinese Politics in Java, 1917–1942.* Revised edition. Singapore: Singapore University Press.

——— . 1988. 'Chinese Economic Elites in Indonesia: A Preliminary Study.' In *Changing Identities of the Southeast Asian Chinese Since World War II*, edited by Jennifer Cushman and Wang Gungwu, pp. 261–88. Hong Kong: Hong Kong University Press.

——— . 1998. *Interpreting Indonesian Politics.* Singapore: Times Academic Press.

——— . 1999. 'The Ethnic Chinese Issue and National Integration in Indonesia.' *Trends in Southeast Asia*, No. 2. Singapore: Institute of Southeast Asian Studies.

Tan, Antonio S. 1985. 'Chinese Mestizo and the Formation of the Filipino Nationality.' In *Chinese in the Philippines*, edited by Theresa Carino, pp. 50–63. Manila: De La Salle University Press.

Tan, Chee-Beng. 1979. 'Baba Chinese, Non-Baba Chinese and Malays: A Note on Ethnic Interaction in Malacca.' Southeast Asian Journal of Social Science, 7 (1–2): 20–9.

————. 1980. 'Baba Malay Dialect.' *Journal of the Malaysian Branch of the Royal Asiatic Society*, 53 (Part 1): 150–6.

————. 1982. 'Peranakan Chinese in Northeast Kelantan with Special Reference to Chinese Religion.' *Journal of the Malaysian Branch of the Royal Asiatic Society*, 55 (part 1): 26–52.

————. 1983. 'Acculturation and the Chinese in Melaka: The Expression of Baba Identity Today.' In *The Chinese in Southeast Asia Identity, Culture and Politics*, edited by L.A. Peter Gosling and Linda Y.C. Lim, vol. 2, pp. 56–78. Singapore: Maruzen Asia.

————. 1984. 'Kin Networks and Baba Identity.' In *Ethnicity and Local Politics in Malaysia, Six Case Studies*, edited by Tan Chee-Beng, pp. 84–97. Contributions to Southeast Asian Ethnography, No. 3 (December).

————. 1985. *The Development and Distribution of Dejiao Associations in Malaysia and Singapore: A Study on a Chinese Religious Organization.* Singapore: Institute of Southeast Asian Studies.

————. 1987. 'Ethnic Relations in Malaysia in Historical and Sociological Perspectives.' *Journal of Malaysian Studies (Kajian Malaysia)*, 5 (1): 99–119.

————. 1988a. *The Baba of Melaka: Culture and Identity of a Chinese Peranakan Community in Malaysia.* Petaling Jaya (Malaysia): Pelanduk Publications.

————. 1988b. 'Nation-Building and Being Chinese in a Southeast Asian State: Malaysia.' *In Changing Identities of the Southeast Asian Chinese since World War II*, edited by Jennifer Cushman and Wang Gungwu, pp. 139–64. Hong Kong: Hong Kong University Press.

————. 1988c. 'Structure and Change: Cultural Identity of the Baba of Melaka.' *Bijdragen Tot De Taal-, Land- En Volkenkunde*, 144 (2 and 3): 297–314.

————. 1989. 'People of Chinese Descent and China: Attitudes and Identity.' *Solidarity*, 123 (July–September): 113–20.

————. 1991. 'The Changing Identities of Baba Melaka.' *Asian Culture*, 15: 38–48. Revised and reprinted in Tan Chee-Beng, *Chinese Peranakan Heritage in Malaysia and Singapore*. Kuala Lumpur: Penerbit Fajar Bakti Sdn. Bhd.

————— . 1992. 'International Conference on Changing Ethnic Identities and Relations in Southeast Asia: The Case of the Chinese Minority, 8–10 November 1991, Manila.' *Archipel*, 44: 3–13.

————— . 1993. *Chinese Peranakan Heritage in Malaysia and Singapore.* Kuala Lumpur: Fajar Bakti.

————— . 1994. 'Culture, Ethnicity and Economic Activities: The Case of the People of Chinese Descent with Special Reference to Southeast Asia.' In *The Ethnic Chinese*, edited by Teresita Ang See and Go Bon Juan, pp. 27–59. Manila: Kaisa Para Sa Kaunlaran, Inc.

————— . 1995a. 'The People of Chinese Descent and Ethnic Relations with Special Reference to Some Economic Explanations.' In *Dimensions of Traditions and Development in Malaysia*, edited by Rokiah Talib and Tan Chee-Beng, pp. 383–420. Petaling Jaya (Malaysia): Pelanduk Publications.

————— . 1995b. 'Chinese Associations in Kapit.' *Asian Culture* (Singapore), 19: 29–42.

————— . 1996. 'Food and Ethnicity with Reference to the Chinese in Malaysia.' Paper presented at the International Conference on Changing Diet and Foodways in Chinese Culture, organized by The Department of Anthropology, The Chinese University of Hong Kong, and The Fairbank Center for East Asian Research, Harvard University, 12–14 June 1996, at The Chinese University of Hong Kong. In *Changing Chinese Foodways in Asia*, edited by David Y.H. Wu and Tan Chee-Beng, pp. 125–160. Hong Kong: The Chinese University Press.

————— . 1997a. 'The Northern Chinese of Sabah, Malaysia: Origin and Some Sociocultural Aspects.' *Asian Culture*, 21: 19–37.

————— . 1997b. 'Comments.' In *Ethnic Chinese As Southeast Asians*, edited by Leo Suryadinata, pp. 25–32. Singapore: Institute of Southeast Asian Studies.

————— . 1997c. 'Chinese Identities in Malaysia.' *Southeast Asian Journal of Social Science*, 25(2): 103–116.

————— . 1999. 'Tradition, Cultural Identity and Chinese Communities.' Paper presented at the International Conference on Tradition and Change: Identity, Gender and Culture in South China, 3–6 June

1999, organized by the Department of Anthropology and New Asia College, The Chinese University of Hong Kong.

———— . 2000. 'Li Yih-yuan and the Study of Chinese in Malaysia.' *Bulletin of the Institute of Ethnology, Academia Sinica*, 89 (Spring): 17–31.

———— . 2001. 'Huaren minzuxue wenhuaquan: Shijie huaren shequn de renleixue yanjiu.' In *Ershiyi shiji de zhongguo shehuixue yu renleixue* [Anthropology and Sociology of Twenty-First Century China], edited by Qiao Jian, Li Peiliang, and Ma Rong, pp. 453–471. Gaoxiong, Taiwan: Liwen Wenhua Shiyegufen Youxian Gongsi.

———— . 2002a. *Chinese Minority in A Malay State: The Case of Terengganu in Malaysia.* Singapore: Eastern Universities Press.

———— . 2002b. 'Chinese Migration, Localization and the Production of Baba Culture. In *Expansion of Chinese World, and the Creation of Cultures: Basic Trends in Asia and Pacific*, edited by Yoshihara Kazuo and Suzuki Masataka, pp. 344–76. Tokyo: Kobundo. In Japanese, translated from English by Kawaguchi Mitsuo.

———— . 2002c. 'Hanhua, zuqun xing yu huayi.' In *Haiwai huaren yanjiu lunji* [papers on the Study of Chinese Overseas], edited by Hao Shiyuan, pp. 231–62. Beijing: Zhongguo Shehui Kexue Chubanshe.

Tan, Liok Ee. 1988. 'Chinese Independent Schools in West Malaysia: Varying Responses to Changing Demands.' In *Changing Identities of the Southeast Asian Chinese since World War II*, edited by Jennifer Cushman and Wang Gungwu, pp. 61–74. Hong Kong: Hong Kong University Press.

———— . 1997. *The Politics of Chinese Education in Malaya 1945–1961.* Kuala Lumpur: Oxford University Press.

Tan, Mely G. 1963. *The Chinese of Sukabumi: A Study in Social and Cultural Accomodation.* Ithaca, NY: Cornell University Southeast Asian Program.

———— . 1987. 'The Role of Chinese Minority in Development: The Indonesian Case.' *Southeast Asian Studies*, 25 (3): 63–82.

———— . 2000. 'A Minority Group Embracing the Majority Religion: The

Ethnic Chinese Muslims in Indonesia.' In *Intercultural Relations, Cultural Transformation, and Identity: The Ethnic Chinese*, edited by Teresita Ang See, pp. 441–6. Manila: Kaisa Para Sa Kaunlaran, Inc.

Tan, Sooi Beng. 1988. 'The Phor Tor Festival in Penang: Deities, Ghosts and Chinese Ethnicity.' Working Paper 51, Centre of Southeast Asian Studies, Monash University.

Teo, Kok Seong. 2003. *The Peranakan Chinese of Kelantan: A Study of the Culture, Language and Communication of an Assimilated Group in Malaysia*. London: ASEAN Academic Press.

Teske, Raymond H.C., Jr. and Bardin H. Nelson. 1974. 'Acculturation and Assimilation: A Clarification.' *American Ethnologist*, 1 (2): 351–67.

The, Siauw Giap. 1966. 'Group Conflict in a Plural Society.' *Revue du Sud-est Asiatique*, No.1: 1–31.

———. 1980. 'The Chinese in Indonesia: A Review Article.' *Kabar Seberang* (James Cook University), No.7: 114–30.

———. 1989. 'Socio-economic Role of the Chinese in Indonesia, 1820–1940.' In *Economic Growth in Indonesia, 1820–1940*, edited by Angus Maddison and Ge Prince. Dordrecht, Holland: Foris Publications.

———. 1993. 'Islam and Chinese Assimilation in Indonesia and Malaysia.' In *Chinese Beliefs and Practices in Southeast Asia*, edited by Cheu Hock Tong, pp. 59–100. Petaling Jaya, Malaysia: Pelanduk Publications.

T'ień, Ju-K'ang. 1953. *The Chinese of Sarawak: A Study of Social Structure*, Monographs on Social Anthropology, no. 14. London School of Economics and Political Science, London.

Trocki, Carl A. 1999. *Opium, Empire and the Global Political Economy: A Study of the Asian Opium Trade 1750–1950*. London: Routledge.

Tunku Abdul Rahman. 1969. *May 13 — Before and After*. Kuala Lumpur: Utusan Melayu Press.

Turner, Jonathan H. and Edna Bonacich. 1980. 'Toward a Composite Theory of Middleman Minorities.' *Ethnicity*, 7 (2): 144–58.

UCSTAM. 1984. *Huawen jiaoyu shiliao* (Historical Sources on Chinese

Education). 33rd Anniversary Publication of the United Chinese
School Teachers'Association of Malaysia (UCSTAM). Kuala Lumpur:
United Chinese School Teachers' Association of Malaysia.

Vaughan, J.D. 1879. *The Manners and Customs of the Chinese of the
Straits Settlements.* Singapore. Reprinted by Kuala Lumpur: Oxford
University Press in 1971.

Wang, Gungwu. 1959. *A Short History of the Nanyang Chinese.*
Singapore: Eastern Universities Press Ltd.

———. 1970. 'Chinese Politics in Malaya.' *China Quarterly*, No. 43,
pp. 1–30. Reprinted in Wang Gungwu, *Community and Nation:
Essays on Southeast Asia and the Chinese.* Kuala Lumpur: Heinemann
Education Books (Asia) Ltd, 1981, pp. 173–210.

———. 1977. 'A Note on the Origins of Hua-ch'iao.' In *Masalah-Masalah
Internasional Masakini* (7), edited by Lie Tek Tjeng and C.P.F.
Luhulima, pp. 7–18. Jakarta: Lembaga Research Kebudayaan
Nasional. Also in *Community and Nation: Essays on Southeast Asia
and the Chinese*, by Wang Gungwu, pp. 118–27. Singapore:
Heinemann Educational Books (Asia) Ltd., for Asian Studies
Association of Australia, 1981.

———. 1979. 'China and the Region in Relation to Chinese Minorities.'
Contemporary Southeast Asia (Singapore), 1 (1): 36–50. Reprinted
in Wang Gungwu, *Community and Nations: Essays on Southeast Asia
and the Chinese.* Kuala Lumpur: Heinemann Educational Books
(Asia) Ltd, 1981, pp. 274–85.

———. 1988. 'The Study of Chinese Identities in Southeast Asia.' In
Changing Identities of the Southeast Asian Chinese since World War
II, edited by Jennifer Cushman and Wang Gungwu, pp. 1–21. Hong
Kong: Hong Kong University Press.

———. 1991a. 'Among the Non-Chinese.' In *Daedalus*, Special issue:
The Living Tree: The Changing·Meaning of Being Chinese Today,
120 (2): 135–57.

———. 1991b. *China and the Chinese Overseas.* Singapore: Times
Academic Press.

———. 1998. 'The Status of Overseas Chinese Studies.' In *The Chinese*

Diaspora: Selected Essays, vol. 1, edited by Wang Ling-chi and Wang Gungwu, pp. 1–13. Singapore: Times Academic Press.

Wang, Jianmin. 1997. *Zhongguo minzuxue shi* (History of Chinese Ethnology), vol. 1. Kunming: Yunnan Jiaoyu Chubanshe.

Wang, L. Ling-chi. 1991. 'Roots and Changing Identities of the Chinese in the United States.' Daedalus, 120 (2): 181–206. Reprinted in *The Living Tree: The Changing Meaning of Being Chinese Today*, edited by Tu Wei-Ming, pp. 185–212. Stanford. CA: Stanford University Press, 1991.

Wang, Mingming. 1999. *Shiqu de fanrong: yizuo laocheng de lishi renleixue kaocha* [Lost Prosperity: A Historical Anthropological Study of an Old City]. Hangzhou: Zhejiang Renming Chubanshe.

Ward, Barbara E. 1965. 'Varieties of the Conscious Model: The Fishermen of South China.' In *The Relevance of Models for Social Anthropology*, edited by Michael Banton, pp. 113–37. London: Tavistock Publications Ltd.

———. 1970. 'Temper Trantrums in Kau Sai: Some Speculations upon their Effect.' In *Socialization: The Approach from Social Anthropology*, edited by Philip Mayer, pp. 109–25. London: Tavistock Publications.

———. 1985. *Through Other Eyes: An Anthropologist's View of Hong Kong*. Hong Kong: The Chinese University Press.

Watson, James L. 1975. *Emigration and the Chinese Lineage: The Mans in Hong Kong and London*. Berkeley, CA: University of California Press.

———. 1985. 'Standardizing the Gods: The Promotion of T'ien Hou ("Empress of Heaven") along the South China Coast, 968–1960.' In *Popular Culture in Late Imperial China*, edited by David Johnson, Andrew J. Nathan, and Evelyn S. Rawski, pp. 292–324. Berkeley, CA: University of California Press.

———. 1993. 'Rites or Beliefs? The Construction of a Unified Culture in Late Imperial China.' In *China's Quest for National Identity*, edited by Lowell Dittmer and Samuel S. Kim, pp. 80–103. Ithaca, NY: Cornell University Press.

Weber, Max. 1951. *The Religion of China: Confucianism and Taoism*, translated and edited by Hans H. Gerth, with an introduction by C. K. Yang. New York: The Free Press.

———. 1958. *The Protestant Ethic and the Spirit of Capitalism*, translated by Talcott Parsons. New York: Charles Scribner.

———. 1964. *Max Weber: The Theory of Social and Economic Organization*, translated and edited by A.M. Henderson and Talcott Parsons, with an introduction by Talcott Parsons. New York: Oxford University Press, 1947. First Free Press paperback edition, 1964.

Weidenbaum, Murray, and Samuel Hughes. 1996. *The Bamboo Network: How Expatriate Chinese Entrepreneurs Are Creating a New Economic Superpower in Asia*. New York: Martin Kessler Books.

Weightman, G.H. 1986. 'Changing Patterns of Internal and External Migration among Philippine Chinese.' *Crossroads*, 2 (3): 83–114.

Wertheim, W.F. 1964. 'The Trading Minorities in Southeast Asia.' In *East-West Parallels. Sociological Approaches to Modern Asia*, pp. 39–82. The Hague: W. Van Hoeve.

Wickberg, Edgar. 1964. 'The Chinese Mestizo in Philippine History.' *Journal of Southeast Asian History*, 5 (1): 62–100.

———. 1965. *The Chinese in Philippine Life 1850–1898*. New Haven, CN: Yale University Press.

———. 1988. 'Chinese Organizations and Ethnicity in Southeast Asia and North America since 1945: A Comparative Analysis.' In *Changing Identities of the Southeast Asian Chinese since World War II*, edited by Jennifer Cushman and Wang Gungwu, pp. 303–18. Hong Kong: Hong Kong University Press.

———. 2000. *Overseas Chinese: The State of the Field*. CCR Discussion Paper Series, Centre for Chinese Research, University of British Columbia.

Williams, Lea F. 1960. *Overseas Chinese Nationalism: The Genesis of the Pan-Chinese Movement in Indonesia, 1900–1916*. Glencoe, IL: The Free Press.

Willmott, Donald Earl. 1960. *The Chinese of Semarang: A Changing Minority Community in Indonesia*. Ithaca, NY: Cornell University Press.

Willmott, William E. 1967. *The Chinese in Cambodia.* Vancouver, BC: University of British Columbia Publication Centre.

Win Shein. 1982. 'The Chinese Community in Burma: Problems in Relations Between Different Ethnic Groups.' *East Asian Civilizations*, 1: 176–85.

Wolf, Margery. 1970. 'Child Training and the Chinese Family.' In *Family and Kinship in Chinese Society*, edited by Maurice Freedman, pp. 37–62. Stanford, CA: Stanford University Press.

Wong, Bernard P. 1967. *The Chinese American Community: Ethnicity and Survival Strategies.* Singapore: Chopmen Enterprises.

———. 1978. 'A Comparative Study of the Assimilation of the Chinese in New York City and Lima, Peru.' *Comparative Study in Society and History*, 20 (13): 335–58.

———. 1979. *A Chinese American Community: Ethnicity and Survival Strategies.* Singapore: Chopmen Enterprises.

———. 1998. 'The Chinese in New York City: Kinship and Immigration.' In *The Overseas Chinese: Ethnicity in National Context*, edited by Francis L.K. Hsu and Hendrick Serrie, pp. 143–72. Lanham, MD: University Press of America.

Wong, Eugene F. 1985. 'Asian American Middleman Minority Theory: The Framework of an American Myth.' *The Journal of Ethnic Studies*, 13 (1): 51–88.

Wong, Morrison G. 1982. 'The Cost of Being Chinese, Japanese and Filipino in the United States 1960, 1970, 1976.' *Pacific Sociological Review*, 25 (1): 59–78.

Wu, David Y. H. 1974. 'To Kill Three Birds with One Stone: The Rotating Credit Associations of the Papua New Guinea Chinese.' *American Ethnologist*, 1 (3): 565–84.

———. 1977. 'Ethnicity and Adaptation: Overseas Chinese Entrepreneurship in Papua New Guinea.' *Southeast Asian Journal of Social Science*, 5 (1–2): 85–95.

———. 1982. *The Chinese in Papua New Guinea: 1880–1980.* Hong Kong: The Chinese University Press.

———. 1990. 'Chinese Minority Policy and the Meaning of Minority

Culture: The Example of Bai in Yunnan, China.' *Human Organization*, 49 (1): 1–13.

Wu, Jianxiong. 1988. '*Shijiu shiji qianwang guba de huagong*, 1847–1874' [Chinese Coolies in Cuba in the Nineteenth Century (1847–1874)]. In *Zhongguo Haiyang Fazhanshi Lunwen Ji* [Collected Essays on the History of Chinese Maritime Development], vol. 3, edited by Zhang Yanxian. Taipei.

Wu, Lily. 2001. 'Going Home.' In *Cultural Curiosity*, edited by Josephine M.T. Khu, pp. 201–24. Berkeley, CA: University of California Press.

Wu, Ming Chu. 1995. Culture, Social Organization and Economic Activities of a Chinese Farming Community: A Case Study of Seckinchan, Selangor, Malaysia. Ph.D. thesis, University of Malaya.

Xiao, Qing. 1987. *Zhongguo Gudai Huobi Sixiang Shi*. [History of Monetary Thinking of Ancient China]. Beijing: Renming Chuban She.

Yan, Yunxiang. 1966a. 'The Culture of Guanxi in a North China Village.' *The China Journal*, 35: 1–25.

———. 1966b. *The Flow of Gifts: Reciprocity and Social Networks in a Chinese Village*. Stanford, CA: Stanford University Press.

Yang, Lien-sheng. 1952. *Money and Credit in China: A Short History*. Cambridge, MA: Harvard University Press.

Yang, Mayfair. 1997. 'Mass Media and Traditional Subjectivity in Shanghai: Notes on (Re)Cosmopolitanism in a Chinese Metropolis.' In *Ungrounded Empire: The Cultural Politics of Modern Chinese Transnationalism*, edited by Aihwa Ong and Donald Nonini, pp. 287–319. New York and London: Routledge.

Yang, Songnian. 1986. *Zhanqian xin-ma wenxue suo fanying de huagong shenghuo*. [Life of Chinese Coolies as Reflected in the Chinese Literature in Prewar Singapore and Malaya]. Singapore: Fern Toh Pau, Singapore National Trades Union Congress.

Yeung, Henry Wai-Chung, and Kris Old, eds. 2000. *Globalization of Chinese Business Firms*. London: Macmillan.

Yin, Alexander Chien-chung. 1981. 'Voluntary Associations and Rural-Urban Migration.' In *The Anthropology of Taiwanese Society*, edited by Emily Martin Ahern and Hill Gates, pp. 319–37. Stanford, CA: Stanford University Press.

Yong, C.F., ed. 1981. *Ethnic Chinese in Southeast Asia.* Special issue of *Journal of Southeast Asian Studies*, 12 (1).

Yoshihara, Kunio. 1987. 'The Problem of Continuity in Chinese Businesses in Southeast Asia.' *Southeast Asian Studies*, 25 (3): 112–29.

———. 1988. *The Rise of Ersatz Capitalism in Southeast Asia.* Singapore: Oxford University Press.

———. 1995. 'The Ethnic Chinese and Ersatz Capitalism in Southeast Asia.' In *Southeast Asian Chinese and China: The Politico-Economic Dimension*, edited by Leo Suryadinata, pp. 66-86. Singapore: Times Academic Press.

Yu, Yingshi. 1987. *Zhongguo jinshi zongjiao lunli yu shangren jingshen* [Contemporary Religious Ethics of China and the Spirit of Businessmen]. Taipei: Lianjing Chuban Shiyue Gongsi.

Yuan, Song'an. 1988. *Bilu huaqiao gaikuang* [A Survey of Overseas Chinese in Peru]. Taipei: Cheng Chung Book Col. Ltd.

Zenner, Walter P. 1987. 'Middleman Minorities in the Syrian Mosaic: Trade, Conflict, and Image Management.' *Sociological Perspectives*, 30 (4): 400–21.

Zhou, Min. 1992. *Chinatown: The Socioeconomic Potential of an Urban Enclave.* Phildelphia, PA: Temple University Press.

.

Index